Acclaim for Judith Freeman's

The Long Embrace

"Atmospheric and unusual. . . . A restless hallucination of a book about a woman obsessed by a mystery that she knows she will never solve—and perhaps does not wish to solve."
—*The New York Review of Books*

"Compelling. . . . Ms. Freeman knows [Los Angeles] as well as Marlowe himself. . . . Like Cissy, when she crooks her finger, it's impossible not to follow."
—*The New York Times*

"A novelist's nonfiction triumph, building a dramatic life of a private couple from sharp-eyed descriptions of their homes, a respect for the few shards of evidence—photos, letters, papers—remaining and a careful reading of Chandler's works."
—*Pittsburgh Post-Gazette*

"Crisp, evocative, [and] steeped in Chandler's diffident, romantic style."
—*The Oregonian*

"In *The Long Embrace*, [Freeman] breathes life into the Chandlers' dwelling places, giving East Coasters a feeling not only for the couple but for the city of Los Angeles itself."
—*Howard County Times*

"Ingenious. . . . [Chandler's] work is more complex than the ideas they were supposed to be about, and the fears they express are more troubling than the mystery genre can contain. Ms. Freeman, I think, comes the closest to pinpointing his appeal."
—Allen Barba, *The New York Sun*

JUDITH FREEMAN

The Long Embrace

Judith Freeman is the author of four novels—*The Chinchilla Farm*, *Set for Life*, *A Desert of Pure Feeling*, and *Red Water*—and of *Family Attractions*, a collection of short stories. She lives in Los Angeles.

www.judithfreeman.net

The Long Embrace

The Long Embrace

RAYMOND CHANDLER
And
THE WOMAN HE LOVED

Judith Freeman

VINTAGE BOOKS

NEW YORK

FIRST VINTAGE BOOKS EDITION, NOVEMBER 2008

Copyright © 2007 by Judith Freeman

All rights reserved. Published in the United States by Vintage Books, a division of Random House, Inc., New York, and in Canada by Random House of Canada Limited, Toronto. Originally published in hardcover in the United States by Pantheon Books, a division of Random House, Inc., New York, in 2007.

Vintage and colophon are registered trademarks of Random House, Inc.

Grateful acknowledgment is made to the following for permission to reprint previously published material:

Farrar, Straus and Giroux, LLC and The Random House Group Ltd.: Excerpt from *Chéri* and *The Last of Chéri* by Colette, translated by Roger Senhouse, translation copyright © 1951 and renewed 1982 by Farrar, Straus and Giroux, LLC. Reprinted by permission of Farrar, Straus and Giroux, LLC. Rights in the United Kingdom for *Chéri* are administered by Secker & Warburg, an imprint of The Random House Group Ltd. **Viking Penguin:** Excerpt from *On the Road* by Jack Kerouac, copyright © 1955, 1957 by Jack Kerouac and renewed 1983 by Stella Kerouac and 1985 by Stella Kerouac and Jean Kerouac. Reprinted by permission of Viking Penguin, a division of Penguin Group (USA) Inc. **Brief excerpts are quoted from the following Raymond Chandler works:** *The Big Sleep* (Alfred A. Knopf, 1939); *Farewell, My Lovely* (Alfred A. Knopf, 1940); *The High Window* (Alfred A. Knopf, 1942); *Killer in the Rain* (Houghton Mifflin, 1964); *Lady in the Lake* (Alfred A. Knopf, 1943); *The Little Sister* (Houghton Mifflin, 1949); *The Long Goodbye* (Houghton Mifflin, 1953); *Playback* (Houghton Mifflin, 1958); *The Simple Art of Murder* (Houghton Mifflin, 1950); and *Trouble Is My Business* (Alfred A. Knopf, 1980).

The Library of Congress has cataloged the Pantheon edition as follows:
Freeman, Judith, [date]
The long embrace : Raymond Chandler and the woman he loved /
Judith Freeman.
p. cm.
Includes bibliographical references and index.
1. Chandler, Raymond, 1888–1959—Relations with women.
2. Authors, American—20th century—Biography.   3. Detective and
mystery stories—Authorship.   I. Title.
PS3505.H3224Z65 2007
813'.52—dc22   [B]2007005087

Vintage ISBN: 978-1-4000-9517-9

Author photograph © Anthony Hernandez
Book design by Wesley Gott

www.vintagebooks.com

Printed in the United States of America
10 9 8 7 6 5 4 3 2 1

For my own beloved, A.H.

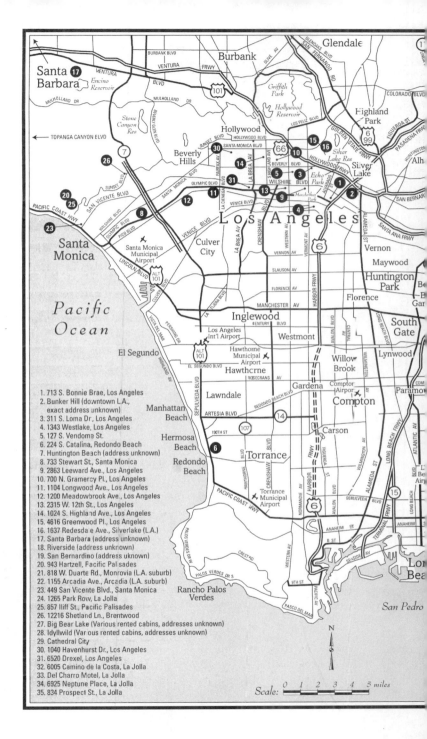

Santa Barbara 🅱

Burbank

Glendale

Griffith Park

Hollywood Reservoir

Highland Park

Hollywood

Beverly Hills

Silver Lake

Los Angeles

Santa Monica

Culver City

Vernon

Maywood

Huntington Park

Pacific Ocean

El Segundo

Inglewood

Westmont

Lawndale

Hawthorne

Willow Brook

Lynwood

South Gate

Manhattan Beach

Hermosa Beach

Redondo Beach

Gardena

Compton

Carson

Torrance

Rancho Palos Verdes

San Pedro

1. 713 S. Bonnie Brae, Los Angeles
2. Bunker Hill (downtown L.A., exact address unknown)
3. 311 S. Loma Dr, Los Angeles
4. 1343 Westlake, Los Angeles
5. 127 S. Vendome St.
6. 224 S. Catalina, Redondo Beach
7. Huntington Beach (address unknown)
8. 733 Stewart St., Santa Monica
9. 2863 Leeward Ave., Los Angeles
10. 700 N. Gramercy Pl., Los Angeles
11. 1104 Longwood Ave., Los Angeles
12. 1200 Meadowbrook Ave., Los Angeles
13. 2315 W. 12th St., Los Angeles
14. 1024 S. Highland Ave., Los Angeles
15. 4616 Greenwood Pl., Los Angeles
16. 1637 Redesda e Ave., Silverlake (L.A.)
17. Santa Barbara (address unknown)
18. Riverside (address unknown)
19. San Bernardino (address uknown)
20. 943 Hartzell, Pacific Palisades
21. 818 W. Duarte Rd., Monrovia (L.A. suburb)
22. 1155 Arcadia Ave., Arcadia (L.A. suburb)
23. 449 San Vicente Blvd., Santa Monica
24. 1265 Park Row, La Jolla
25. 857 Iliff St., Pacific Palisades
26. 12216 Shetland Ln., Brentwood
27. Big Bear Lake (Various rented cabins, addresses unknown)
28. Idyllwild (Various rented cabins, addresses unknown)
29. Cathedral City
30. 1040 Havenhurst Dr., Los Angeles
31. 6520 Drexel, Los Angeles
32. 6005 Camino de la Costa, La Jolla
33. Del Charro Motel, La Jolla
34. 6925 Neptune Place, La Jolla
35. 834 Prospect St., La Jolla

Scale: 0 1 2 3 4 5 miles

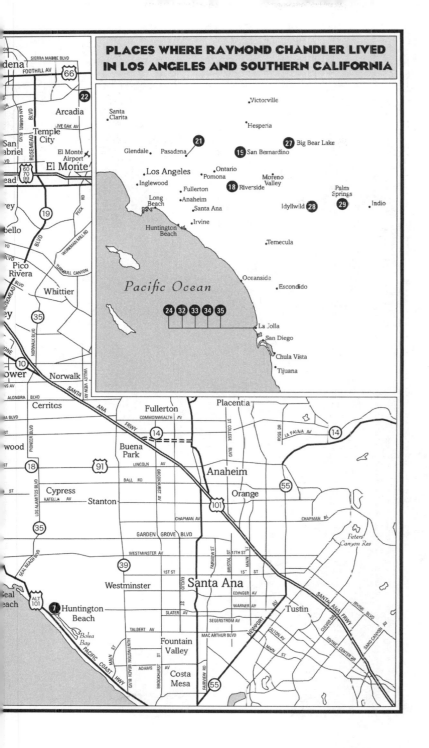

PLACES WHERE RAYMOND CHANDLER LIVED IN LOS ANGELES AND SOUTHERN CALIFORNIA

The Long Embrace

One

n March of 1986 I began reading the collected letters of Raymond Chandler. I was at the time living in an apartment on Carondelet Street in an older part of Los Angeles where Chandler himself had once lived. My neighbors were mostly elderly people who had lived in my building for many years and with whom I had very little contact, except for one old woman who occupied the apartment above me. I had once kicked her little dog when it attempted to bite me as I came up the front steps, and for this she took to tormenting me whenever she could. She would rise early and shuffle past my bedroom window in her heavy leather slippers, speaking baby talk to her small dog or singing loudly, making as much noise as possible in order to interrupt my sleep. She broke flowers off their stems, left bits of paper scattered in my garden. Sometimes when my husband and I returned home, she would be waiting for us and lean out her window and call out in a high, shrill voice, "It's the intelligentsia—the intelligentsia has returned!" She divided the word *intelligentsia* into separate syllables, flinging each one down at us as we hurried to open our door. Only in L.A., I thought, could someone make this word sound like a term of such utter derision.

I had read most of Chandler's novels and early stories by the time I picked up the volume of his letters. In truth, I had become obsessed with Raymond Chandler. Chandler once said that great writing, whatever else it does, nags at the minds of subsequent writers who find it sometimes difficult to explain just why they are so haunted by a particular work or author. I could not deny that I had become haunted by Chandler, nor could I really explain exactly why.

As I continued to go through the letters, I also started to read a biography of Chandler, and the facts of his life began to captivate me. I was especially interested in his relationship with his wife, Cissy, who was much older than he: Chandler was thirty-five when he married Cissy Pascal, in 1924. Cissy was fifty-three, although she listed her age on their marriage certificate as forty-three. It wasn't until much later that Chandler learned he had married a woman not eight years older, as he had thought, but eighteen. Some people believe he never learned her true age, and they could be right. In any case, only slowly, over the course of a number of years, did he figure out that his wife was indeed much older than she claimed, though he may never have known exactly how old she was.

Cissy was exceptionally beautiful and witty and sophisticated, "irresistible," as Chandler once put it, "without even knowing it or caring much about it." At the time she married Chandler, she was said to have the figure and sexual presence of a woman twenty years younger. She was a sensuous woman with a beautiful body, about which she felt no shame. So comfortable was she in her skin that, as Chandler once revealed, she even liked to do her housework naked. But inevitably age took its toll, and by the time Chandler published his first novel, at the age of fifty-one, Cissy was almost seventy and suffering from a lung condition that increasingly confined her to bed. She went from being a wife who offered a lot of sexual enticement to her much younger husband to being a wife who was infirm and required his constant care, whom he nursed assiduously through the abominable anarchy of old age. Still he was completely devoted to her and would later describe his marriage as "almost perfect." When Cissy died in 1954, a few months after his sixth novel, *The Long Goodbye*, was published, Chandler began drinking heavily, attempted suicide, and descended into a grim state of acute alcoholism. He lived less than five years without her—five very difficult and in many ways wretched years. "My only problem," he wrote to a friend during this period, "is that I have no home, and no one to care for if I did have one." In reading his letters, I came to see that what Cissy had done for Chandler was to enable him to live in what Kafka called "the existent moment." Without her he was, literally, dead.

The more I read about Chandler, the more interested in Cissy I became. I felt I knew this woman somehow, or that I could know her and possibly bring her to life if I were to try, even though very little was known about her. She left almost nothing behind at the time of her death, no writings or letters. No biographer of Chandler had ever been able to uncover much information on Cissy. The main problem was that Chandler himself ordered their letters to each other destroyed shortly before his death, even though he had planned to include them in a collection of his letters that was then being discussed and had even written to his English publisher saying, "Some of the letters to my wife are pretty hot, but I don't want to edit anything." In the end, he changed his mind. It was as if he decided that if he must die he would take any memory of her with him, forever keeping her to himself.

For much of Cissy's life—or at least the years she spent married to Chandler—she was a rather reclusive woman, an "enigma," as Chandler scholars are fond of saying. In her later years few people actually met her or were able to provide any recollections of her. Nevertheless, it seemed to me that there were enough references to her in Chandler's letters and, in a more coded way, in his fiction, to begin to compile a portrait of her if only I could connect all the dots. And in this portrait of Cissy, in this attempt to bring her to life, I felt, lay some essence of Chandler himself, the key to his work and his personality. For I had come to believe that it was the domicile—the sanctuary he shared with Cissy and from which the world at large was excluded—that largely formed his views and helped mold the personality of the character he was famous for creating, the private eye Philip Marlowe, with whom he shared a very particular kind of loneliness as well as a sense of sexual anxiety and a code of honor. Cissy was the muse who would inform the central myth of his fiction—that of the white knight whose task it was to rescue those in peril. Actually, two women would, in distinct and yet sometimes similar ways, play this role in his life—his wife, Cissy, and his mother, Flossie (or Florence). Both women, Chandler felt, were in need of rescue and shared certain characteristics—they were almost the same age, for instance, and their names had a faintly similar ring. Yet they were also very different in personality.

Throughout that spring of 1986, I continued reading Chandler's letters with an increasingly focused interest, making notes in a little notebook whenever I found any mention of Cissy—passages such as these, for instance:

> My wife hates snow and would never live where it is snowy. Also as a former redhead she has very sensitive skin and mosquitoes would be enough to drive her into tantrums . . .

> My wife desires no publicity, is pretty drastic about it. She doesn't paint or write. She does play a Steinway grand when she gets time.

> My wife won't fly or let me fly . . .

> I make no secret of my age but printing it on the jacket of a book seems to me bad psychology. I don't think it's any of the public's business. My wife is very emphatic on this point, and I have never known her to be wrong in a matter of taste.

My wife, my wife, my wife. Rarely, if ever, does he refer to her as Cissy—just *my wife,* as if it was their relationship that was paramount. She seemed to me an almost sanctified or totemic figure, a woman on a pedestal (which is where Chandler liked to keep his real-life women, as opposed to his fictional females, many of whom ended up as the villains). As enigmatic or elusive as she may now appear, the actual Cissy had been, as equally, a person who managed to combine a sense of old-fashioned manners with the outlook of a libertine. She was an interesting amalgam of worldly bohemian and refined lady who took tea with her husband every afternoon, accompanied him on long drives up the California coast, made love to him in her overdecorated French boudoir, and listened with him to the same classical music program every evening for nearly thirty years. In those thirty years they were almost never apart. They lived in claustrophobic proximity, with no children and few friends to distract them from their hermetically sealed life.

In time, however, instead of searching for any mention of Cissy in Chandler's letters, I began slowly to discover something else, something that, at least for a while, interested me almost as much as she did. I began to notice how often the addresses at the top of the letters changed, and I started making a list of these addresses, all the places in and around L.A. where the Chandlers had ever lived. Over the course of their marriage the couple had lived in more than thirty different apartments and houses (perhaps, I thought, this is part of the reason Chandler wrote so well about L.A., because he knew it from so many different angles). Sometimes they moved two or three times a year, always leasing furnished places. These moves took them all over the city and its outlying suburbs, from downtown to Santa Monica, Hollywood, the Westlake area, Pacific Palisades, Brentwood, the mid-Wilshire district, Silverlake, Arcadia, Monrovia, San Bernardino, Riverside, and Big Bear Lake, and Idyllwild in the mountains above L.A., and the desert towns of Palm Springs and Cathedral City, until finally he and Cissy bought a house in the charming coastal village of La Jolla, an hour and a half south of L.A., where they settled down for Cissy's few remaining years. The question I kept asking myself was, Why had they moved so often?

It was a question that began to absorb me. I decided to track down every address where Chandler had ever lived in L.A. and photograph what I found. It would be like detective work, I thought. I knew what I was looking for: I was searching for any trace of their lives, anything that would help me understand

Raymond and Cissy Chandler—anything, in other words, that might feed my obsession with a writer whose work I so admired and the wife who had begun to fascinate me. I would be looking for a dead writer, and his mysterious spouse, in a city I knew very well and whose unique distillation of qualities had been first described by Chandler, who at once captured the essence of Los Angeles and transformed it into myth. His work was forever wedded to the city, just as the city would always bear the stigma (if one can call it that) of his rather dark and violent vision. As a friend said to me when we were discussing Chandler, *Funny how L.A. made him the writer he was and in return he gave the city a lasting image.*

It was this mirror world of author and metropolis that began to fascinate me.

Often, as the weeks passed, during which time I was engrossed in rereading Chandler's letters, I would break off my reading and head out into the city to explore one or another locale he had mentioned. I remember one afternoon going to the old Union Station, the railroad depot in the oldest part of downtown L.A., located near Olvera Street, the touristy area of little Mexican restaurants and shops where the original Pueblo of Los Angeles was located and where one could still visit the old adobe hacienda owned by the first Spanish land-grant family who settled here. As far as I could tell, Union Station looked pretty much as it had when Chandler described it in *Playback*, his final novel, except that it no longer handled the rail traffic that it once had when it was first built in the mid-1930s. The interior was still resplendent, with Spanish tiles and graceful vaulted archways, and the palms and jacarandas growing in front of the station looked as if they had been there from the beginning. The only difference seemed to be that now many fewer trains arrived and departed each day, and the huge vaulted waiting room appeared almost eerily empty, although here and there a person could be seen sitting in one of the padded high-back wooden seats, quietly reading a book or gazing around the room, eyeing the occasional fellow passenger with lingering interest.

Not many people in America traveled by train anymore, especially on the West Coast and the station had a somewhat haunted feeling. A great portion of the lobby had been cordoned off by a metal grating and was no longer used, the section with the long row of windows where tickets were once sold. I assumed people now bought their tickets over the Internet or by telephone. Looking through the grating at the cordoned-off area, I thought how ghostly and still it seemed in there, and I imagined how it must once have teemed with travelers, embarking on and disembarking from the great railway trains such as the Sunset Limited, the California Zephyr, and the Santa Fe Super Chief, the glittering, streamlined transcontinental train that used to link L.A. with the rest of America, bringing the stars and those longing for Hollywood fame as well as ordinary Americans to the new city of dreams before airlines took the business away.

It was the Super Chief that brought Eleanor King to L.A. Eleanor, the heroine of *Playback*—an "unhappy girl, if I ever saw one," as Philip Marlowe says. I had brought along a copy of *Play-*

back and I sat down in the lobby of the cavernous train station and opened it and read the description of her as she arrives in the station and enters the lobby where I was then sitting:

> She wasn't carrying anything but a paperback which she dumped in the first trash can she came to. She sat down and looked at the floor . . . After a while she got up and went to the book rack. She left without picking anything out, glanced at the big clock on the wall and shut herself up in a telephone booth. She talked to someone after putting a handful of silver into the slot. Her expression didn't change at all. She hung up and went to the magazine rack, picked up a *New Yorker*, looked at her watch again, and sat down to read.
>
> She was wearing a midnight blue tailor-made suit with a white blouse showing at the neck and a big sapphire-blue lapel pin which would probably have matched her earrings, if I could see her ears. Her hair was a dusky red. . . . her dark blue ribbon hat had a short veil hanging from it. She was wearing gloves.

I read this last paragraph over again, because aside from my interest in Cissy and in collecting a list of all the places where Chandler had ever lived, I had also begun noting passages in Chandler's fiction where he described the clothing his characters wore. These descriptions of the men's clothes and the women's clothes were rendered in careful, often exquisite detail, with sometimes very humorous asides. What people wore mattered very much to Chandler, and in his books he evoked a style of dressing that seemed to have largely disappeared. Who wore gloves anymore? Or hats—let alone hats with veils? When I read his descriptions of clothing I felt I entered another world, a world that held out an attraction to me. In this world people dressed in stylish outfits: they drank cocktails and smoked cigarettes, sometimes fastened to long, slim holders, and it didn't seem there was very much that a little repartee and a decent martini couldn't fix.

I had heard that there was a little café and bar—a nice, newer place in Union Station—and I found it and sat down in the bar and ordered a drink. I asked the waiter to bring me a gimlet—one of Chandler's favorite drinks—made of half gin and half Rose's lime juice, which he claimed beat a martini hollow. It came in a small carafe sitting in a little silver tub of ice with a chilled martini glass to pour it into. I sipped the drink slowly, intrigued by the intense taste.

I wondered if Chandler and Cissy had passed through this station very often. Years ago, when I first moved to L.A., I had taken trains from here. Once I boarded the Coast Starlight to visit my brother in San Francisco. The train ran up the California coast, through the towns of Ventura and Santa Barbara and San Luis Obispo. I remember the trip as being very beautiful, with the views of the sparkling Pacific and unpopulated stretches of golden hills and coastline where the tracks ran and which one would never glimpse from a car. Another time I took the Desert Wind, which ran north across the Mojave Desert, past Las Vegas— I remember sharing a table in the dining car with a thin, garrulous man who explained, over a hasty dinner, his formula for winning at blackjack and who got off the train in Vegas with a gambler's glittering eagerness already showing in his eyes, while I traveled on to Salt Lake City, passing through the hauntingly beautiful red rock country of Utah, the state where I was born. And twice I took the Santa Fe Super Chief to Flagstaff, Arizona, in order to meet my parents there, overnight trips during one of which I remember reading an entire Ursula K. Le Guin novel as we hurtled through the night, an experience that increased the sense of timelessness and dislocation that often accompanies train travel.

Those trips had all happened long ago, and in my mind, as I sat there in the bar, sipping my drink, which had a rather oily-looking chartreuse color and tasted strangely both sweet and acidic, they seemed almost to have occurred in the same era as *Playback,* as if Eleanor King and I had both passed through Union Station at about the same time, although of course she was an imaginary character and I was not. Still it was all bygone. That sense of bygone was a sort of nostalgia, a catchall feeling that allowed me to imagine the world Chandler had once known, as well as my own past. It had been over twenty years since I had taken the Coast Starlight, and the Desert Wind, and the Santa Fe Super Chief.

The bar seemed suddenly very quiet. I realized I was the only patron left in the place at that time in the afternoon. The lunch crowd had gone. The cocktail and dinner crowd had yet to arrive. I felt the bartender glance over at me occasionally and I wondered what he thought. A woman alone, drinking hard liquor at three in the afternoon. I felt I was becoming a bit strange to myself, and I knew it had something to do with the way my interest in Chandler and Cissy was beginning to take over my own life. I knew my obsession could quite possibly be the beginning of a new book, but what sort of book? I was a novelist, not a biographer, and what sort of story did I imagine I might make out of the lives of Raymond and Cissy Chandler?

I took out my notebook and turned back to an entry I had made weeks earlier while reading *Footsteps: Adventures of a Romantic Biographer,* by Richard Holmes, an exploration of the lives of four writers—Robert Louis Stevenson, Mary Wollstonecraft, Percy Shelley, and Gerard de Nerval: *Perhaps I could follow in their footsteps,* I had written, *like Holmes following Stevenson, pursue the physical trail of their path through the past. I might never catch them. But maybe, if I'm lucky, I might catch an occasional glimpse of these fleeting figures.*

I closed my notebook, called for my bill and paid it, and left the bar. I felt an excitement turning inside me. I had realized two things while sitting in the bar:

I did not want to write a biography of Chandler and his wife.

But I did want to write a book about them. I wanted to track them down, to pursue their physical trail, and although I did not yet understand all the reasons why I wanted to do this, I thought maybe some of those reasons would become clear as I went along.

Many years passed, however, and my resolve and excitement came to nothing. I got caught up in other projects, and the longing I had felt that day in the bar at Union Station seemed to dissolve. And yet somewhere in the back of my mind the Chandlers continued to exert a force on my imagination, and I often found myself thinking of them, of their oddly affecting relationship, and their strangely peripatetic lives, Cissy's mysterious allure, Chandler's inconsolable grief at her death, and the strangely enduring bond that had held them together for so many years.

And then one morning I awoke in a different mood. I felt ready to begin the book I had imagined writing many years earlier. The excitement I had originally felt at the thought of writing about Raymond Chandler and his wife seemed as fresh as if the idea had just occurred to me. I was not looking to create a fictional relationship, and yet I did want to be free to imagine their lives. I wanted to know them so intimately that it would amount to a kind of haunting. It never occurred to me that there was anything strange in this wish. It seemed simply to be the desire of the writer whose longings rarely, if ever, conform to easy explanation. If there was a pattern to be found in my obsession—some sort of logical connection to my own life—I knew I might be the last to discover it, and that should I ever do so, it could likely be years after my search was completed.

$\mathcal{T}wo$

The first place where Raymond Chandler had lived in L.A., 613 South Bonnie Brae, was only a few blocks from my own apartment on Carondelet Street, near Alvarado and Third, and this made it seem even more appropriate as a starting point. I would start where Chandler had begun, in the old neighborhoods near downtown. I found the leather notebook in which I had made my initial notes many years earlier and put it in my bag, and then I quietly left my apartment, hoping to escape the notice of my neighbor.

Toward the end of his life, Chandler came to feel that L.A. had become a grotesque and impossible place to live. It was a "jittering city," sometimes dull, sometimes brilliant, but always depressing to him. By then, he had lost it as a locale, both as a place to live and to set his fiction; he had also lost the affection he'd once had for the place. He disliked what the city had become. I looked at the dusty, dead shallow-planted palms that rose out of little squares of dirt cut out of the sidewalks running down Alvarado Street. This was a hard neighborhood—the area around MacArthur Park—and it only looked harder on a dreary and gray winter day. Sometimes I wondered if the prevalent grayness was smog, or fog—what the weather forecasters liked to call the marine layer—or perhaps some deadly combination of the two, a damp, particulate soup of pollution. Not that it much mattered. It was dirty. It was gray. It was L.A.—a poor neighborhood on an overcast day.

Still I was fond of the city. I thought of Los Angeles as the place where America existed in its most completely realized incarnation. (Wallace Stegner once referred to California as "America only more so.") Perhaps this is why people despise it so. It was raw with longing and need, an unbridled exercise in exploitation and hype, a city with only the barest historical context, centerless, as people are so fond of saying, and dominated, like no other city in the world, by the cult of personality and the body—a shape-shifting city you could make into anything you wanted. L.A. was to America what America was to the rest of the world, a place viewed with an extraordinary mixture of envy and contempt.

In his later years, Chandler commented that he felt L.A. had completely changed in the years since he'd arrived. Even the weather was different. "Los Angeles was hot and dry when I first went there," he said, "with tropical rains in the winter and sunshine at least nine-tenths of the year. Now it is humid, hot, sticky, and when the smog comes down into the bowl between the mountains which is Los Angeles, it is damned near intolerable."

He first arrived in the city in 1913, a well-dressed and elegant young man, twenty-four years old. Though he had spent most of his youth in England, he was actually born in Chicago in 1888. He once said that if he were ever to write a nonfiction book, it would probably turn out to be the autobiography of a split personality. He was a man of opposites: a staid accountant and a purveyor of crime stories. A man of two continents, two centuries, two languages. Drank himself out of a job as an accountant. In his forties taught himself to write. He was both social and antisocial, kind and acerbic, friendly and aloof. A man who held to his English public school manners while writing about the sordid world of L.A. Above all, two contradictory tendencies struggled in him: an inclination to reject the world in favor of solitude and a deep longing to escape the often overwhelming sense of loneliness that plagued him for much of his life.

His father was American, his mother Irish, both from Quaker

backgrounds. He was conceived in Laramie, Wyoming, then a raw frontier town. His father worked as an engineer for the railroad; he was an alcoholic and a womanizer who abandoned the family when Chandler was only seven. At the time, Chandler and his mother were living in a residence hotel in Plattsmouth, Nebraska. He never saw his father again.

His mother returned to Ireland and cast herself on the mercy of her dour and disapproving relatives, moving in with Chandler's grandmother and aunts. Later they moved to London, where his uncle Ernest owned property, and he gave Chandler and his mother a flat to live in, though they often had to change residences to accommodate other renters. Uncle Ernest agreed to pay for his education at a very good private school, Dulwich College, where Chandler excelled in the classics. It was from all accounts a lonely childhood. His mother never remarried. And Chandler always seemed to understand that once he left school he would be forever responsible for her.

After his graduation from Dulwich, in 1906, he spent a year

abroad, studying languages in France and Germany. His uncle pushed him to become a civil servant, and upon his return from the continent he found work as an accountant with the admiralty, a job he hated and quit after a few months. He tried his hand at writing, producing some unremarkable poems and essays, and then, in 1912, he decided to leave England and come to America. Why? As Chandler himself put it, "America seemed to call to me in some mysterious way."

On the boat that brought him to America, he met the Warren Lloyd family from Los Angeles, who were returning from a year abroad. The Lloyds were wealthy and cultivated, just the sort of people Chandler liked. Warren Lloyd was a graduate of Yale, his wife, Alma, a singer and sculptor. They were traveling with their two children, Estelle and Edward. Warren was trained as a lawyer, but he also had an interest in the occult and the new field of psychology: he was a devotee of Madame Blavatsky and had recently published a book called *Psychology Normal and Abnormal*. The Lloyds encouraged Chandler to come to Los Angeles, where they promised to help him find work and introduce him to society. Had he not met the Lloyds, it is unlikely Chandler would ever have ended up in L.A., but as it was, after months of working his way across the country, he arrived in the city and took the Lloyds up on their offer of help.

L.A. was a brand-new metropolis when Chandler arrived, attracting people from all over the country but particularly from the Midwest with claims of a climate so healthful it could cure any ailment. It was the first city in America to be packaged and sold like a commodity, marketed to the people of the United States just like automobiles or cigarettes or toothpaste through the cleverest of advertising campaigns. Referred to as a tropical paradise for Americans, it was said to be a place so sublime it was billed as "the American Italy" or "Italy closer to home." An Italy, in other words, without a troublesome foreign language. No strange money, either, or unfamiliar food, but rather an incredibly alluring new metropolis, a place where the rank growth of fruit and flowers and

the strange golden light and gentle climate ("Sleep under a blanket all summer! Wear only a sweater in the winter!") created a sense of paradise on earth.

Into this paradise came Raymond Chandler. Los Angeles really *was* a kind of Eden when he arrived, just waiting for the one item to make its allure total and complete and usher in what J. B. Priestley once described as our "brand-new busy world." When Henry Ford began mass-producing that item, and when the railroads finally connected L.A. with the rest of the country, there was no stopping the influx of people who swarmed to Southern California to take advantage of its perfect climate and myth of easy living.

I drove down Alvarado, heading south past MacArthur Park with its two halves divided by Wilshire Boulevard. I was thinking about how few parks were ever made in Los Angeles, how the city fathers hadn't felt that kind of common public space was necessary, certainly not after the automobile arrived. The automobile made parks (what one urban planner had called the lungs of a city) obsolete—made walking and common public space quite unnecessary. With a car, the whole glorious space of Southern California, with its ocean and beaches and deserts and mountains, became one vast personalized recreational area. But MacArthur Park—then called Westlake Park—was established before the automobile took complete hold of L.A., when the electric trams provided excellent public transportation for the city's citizens and the borders of the metropolis had not yet been extended to include single streets that were sixty miles long.

I was trying to imagine how this park must have looked to Chandler when he moved into this neighborhood compared to how it looked now. In recent years it had become a sadly degenerate public space, a tattered and shabby expanse of bare dirt and worn grass and neglected trees, with a boarded-up little boathouse overlooking a small polluted lake, where out-of-work men and newly arrived immigrants slept rough beneath the rattling palms. Not long ago I had walked through the park and stopped to read a sign posted near a tunnel running beneath Wilshire Boulevard:

Welcome to MacArthur Park

There is a "No Tolerance" policy in MacArthur Park and the Alvarado Corridor. If you choose to conduct criminal activity, you will be caught and prosecuted. The following is outlawed: illegal possession of hypodermic needles, possession of shopping carts, open containers, possession of controlled substances, including cocaine base, marijuana, methamphetamines, or narcotics paraphernalia; no loitering for narcotics, no graffiti, littering, prostitution, or uncertified highway carriers of persons; no throwing substances at vehicles, no sitting, lying or sleeping on public sidewalks, no panhandling, gambling or dicing or being present at gambling, no violating curfew, no indecent exposure in park, removing recyclable material; no swimming in lake, no diving, camping, or lodging; dogs must be on leash, no bicycles, no skating, no skateboards, no open fires, no littering, no amplified sound.

The sign gave you a sense of the place. What would prompt authorities to outlaw the possession of shopping carts? What were uncertified highway carriers of persons?

The truth was you could buy anything around here, and pretty much do anything you wanted, because the police had more or less given up on MacArthur Park. The park was often the first stop on the immigrant path to assimilation. Only poor people lived in this neighborhood now, and who cared about them?

The fetid little lake in the southern portion of the park gave off a rank smell, and the fountain in the middle ejected a limp plume of spray that drifted away as it descended. I remembered how once, years ago, when the lake had been drained for cleaning, I took a walk around its perimeter and observed the years of junk that had built up on the bottom—grocery carts and baby strollers, clothing, shoes and bottles and cans, layers and layers of trash, amid which I half expected to see a body or two. It had become a violent place, this park. At one point the Rampart Police Division had established a permanent substation in the old boathouse to deal with the crime, but, overwhelmed and facing budget cuts, the police simply disappeared after a while, and the park went back to being the province of pushers and thugs. The homeless once again arranged themselves in bedraggled lumps on broken benches, and anxious-looking young men stood at the curbs surrounding the park, flipping elaborate hand signals at passing motorists, advertising the availability of everything from crack to crank, weed and prostitutes, fake IDs—whatever you needed or wanted. I used to walk my dog in the park when I first moved to the neighborhood twenty years earlier, but I rarely walked there anymore. It wasn't so much that it didn't feel safe, at least in the daylight hours. It just felt depressed and neglected. And filthy. I found it hard to enjoy a dirty park where everywhere you looked you saw a decaying world.

When Chandler moved to this area, MacArthur Park was the western edge of the city where major development more or less stopped: Hollywood was nothing more than a cluster of little houses and Beverly Hills a country village—but Westlake Park, as MacArthur Park was then known, was a thriving upper middle-class urban neighborhood populated by wealthy families who had built nice big houses with money made in real estate, oil, and the movie business. The leading men of the city lived here—men like Warren Lloyd. MacArthur Park was new and green and graceful, a place to stroll on Sundays and show off your kids and your well-dressed wife. You could rent a canoe and paddle around the lake and get an ice cream cone from the refreshment stand. The boat-house was a grand affair; the trees were lush and beautiful, and there were graceful walking paths and cactus gardens. The park had not yet been desecrated by city planners who decided to route a major thoroughfare—Wilshire Boulevard—right through the middle of the park and cut it in two. L.A. had just become the first city in America to be illuminated by electric lights, and the interurban system of all-electric trams—the "Red Cars"—pro-vided excellent public transportation. The First Los Angeles Aque-duct had been completed in 1913, the year Chandler arrived, and the water from distant rivers and lakes had been successfully diverted—stolen, really, under the most devious circumstances—for the new metropolis, presented to its citizens at the opening ceremony by the waterway's chief architect, William Mulholland, a man of few words, who pointed to the gushing water and said, "There it is . . . take it."

There it is, take it. A mantra. A capitalist credo for the sensibility that had created this city.

There it is. Take it.

Now the red cars were gone and that "brand-new busy world" ushered in by the automobile was in full flower. Now the city's public transportation—a system of lumbering and polluting buses—was used mostly by the elderly, the workers, and the poor. In L.A., that's how you knew you were *really* poor, if you couldn't even afford a car. MacArthur Park had become one great outdoor homeless and immigrant encampment, a sad and shabby place. The big houses in the neighborhood had all been torn down, or boarded up, or divided into dilapidated apartments owned by indifferent landlords. It was all different now. As Chandler noted, even the weather seemed to have changed.

I wondered what I'd find at 613 South Bonnie Brae, whether the large house the Lloyds had once occupied (and where Chandler lived when he first arrived) would still be standing. As I turned onto the street, I noted the atmosphere of poverty and decay—the yellowed lawns in front of little houses with peeling paint, the apartments with bars on the windows, the buckled sidewalks and trash blown up against fences and trees. I had a hard time even locating the address: there didn't seem to be any 613 South Bonnie Brae, and then I realized that on the lot where the Lloyds' house had once stood there were now three little businesses—Cuscatlan Latino market, Clarita's Unisex Beauty Salon, and a little storefront evangelical church, Centro Misionero Belhem y El Amor de Cristo, a white wooden building with a red bleeding heart painted above the door. It was now possible to get a Coke and a haircut, and pray, all on the same spot where Chandler had started out in L.A.

I pulled up to the curb and parked across from the market and watched the owner come out and stand on the sidewalk and light a cigarette. He looked up and down the street and then his eyes fixed on me as he continued to smoke, very slowly and deliberately. Some boys were kicking a soccer ball around in the street. It was hard to imagine what this street had looked like in 1912. Everything seemed to have changed. Yet down the way I could see one large house, a lone three-story Victorian with turrets covered in scallops and ornate woodwork, and a deep wraparound porch with carved pillars. Once this street had been lined with grand houses, similar to the house I could still see—a house that must once have been very beautiful but now looked like a decaying relic, ruined grandeur. Had the Lloyds' house looked anything like that?

For a while after he arrived in L.A., Chandler lived with Warren and Alma Lloyd and their two children. Fourteen-year-old Estelle had a crush on Chandler. Later there would even be talk of Estelle perhaps marrying him, when he'd returned from World War I and Estelle had become a young lady. For now she was simply part of a vibrant household, presided over by artistic parents who attracted like-minded people to their weekly Friday night musical and literary soirees, a bohemian set that Warren Lloyd had dubbed The Optimists, of which Chandler soon became a part.

The Optimists. I could not imagine a more inappropriate label for Chandler. It seemed equivalent to calling Philip Marlowe sunny. But maybe the term wasn't so inappropriate for the young Chandler, the pre-Marlowe Chandler, the handsome, elegant, and well-dressed young man with the public school accent and polished manners who fit so easily into life on Bonnie Brae and the Lloyds' Friday night parties.

It was at one of these soirees that Chandler met Cissy and Julian Pascal. Julian Pascal was a pianist and composer, born in the West Indies as Goodridge Bowen. He had taught music in London and then moved to New York, where he met Cissy Hurlburt, whom he had married in 1907. Like so many people, Julian Pascal had been drawn to L.A. for its climate—his health was poor and he was hoping for a cure—and also by the burgeoning music life in the city. When the Pascals first moved to L.A., Cissy seems to have had theatrical aspirations, which she soon gave up for the role of housewife: she also played the piano—not as well as her husband but well enough to have for a while considered a career as a pianist. Both Julian and Cissy entertained at the Lloyds' musical evenings. The men often played chess early in the evening. There were poetry recitations, and sometimes they read aloud the poetry that Warren and Alma and Chandler had collaborated on. Often Warren presided over sessions at the Ouija board where, with guests gathered around him, he would consult the spirits.

The man who owned the Cuscatlan market finished his cigarette and went back inside. For a while there was nothing but the sound of the wind in the palms and the kids playing in the street.

I took out my notebook and looked at some notes I had made under the heading of "Chandler, Personality. Excerpts from letters."

My wife tells me I have a beautiful character. Have you a little liar in your home? I am one of those people who have to be known exactly the right amount to be liked. I am standoffish with strangers, a form of shyness which whiskey cured when I was still able to take it in the requisite quantities. I am terribly blunt, having been raised in that English tradition which permits a gentleman to be almost infinitely rude if he keeps his voice down.

I'm strictly the background type, and my character is an unbecoming mixture of outer diffidence and inward arrogance.

At times I am extremely caustic and pugnacious; at other times very sentimental. I am not a good mixer because I am very easily bored, and to me the average never seems good enough, in people or anything else . . . I am not only literate but intellectual, much as I dislike the term.

I was looking for the voice of the young Chandler . . . but I didn't find it there in those passages. The letters in which I might have discovered that voice had all been destroyed—if they ever existed at all. This was the older Chandler, the world-weary, introspective, nothing-to-lose-by-being-honest Chandler. And yet it was just this bluntness, this honesty and ability to look at things squarely that was part of what had drawn me to him in the first place. Chandler, who existed largely apart from the world, had not cultivated the desire to be liked and instead found it better to be frank.

Honesty had become a critical part of Marlowe's character as well: "Are you honest?" a woman asks him at one point. "Painfully," he answers. "I heard you leveled with customers," says another client. "That's why I stay poor," Marlowe replies.

It may also have been why Chandler stayed rather friendless for much of his life. I wondered if his bluntness had been there from the beginning. I suspected it had. Yet in the early photographs of him, taken when he was in his twenties, he's usually smiling and his boyish good looks lend him an air of appealing lightness. In a photograph taken in southern Germany in 1907, during the year of his grand tour, five years before he arrived in L.A., his gaze is direct and almost disarmingly natural. He looks not at the camera but at some distant point to the left: he sits in a chair and holds an open book in his hands, and his mouth is drawn into the most subtle and winning little smile, like a little masculine replica of the Mona Lisa.

A few people dressed in white and all clutching bibles approached the church across the way, and one older woman took a key out of her purse and unlocked the door. They all went inside, leaving the door open. I could see into the stark, bleak-looking little room where metal folding chairs were lined up on either side of an aisle. Churches like this one had sprung up all over L.A. in recent years, especially in the poorer neighborhoods. I was always noticing them now, so many little churches occupying small storefronts where previously there had been a donut shop or a café or a vacuum store—some failed business of one sort or another that had been replaced by the business of God. Everywhere I looked I saw these little churches, on every street. There was the Abundant Mission Church and Iglesia Cristiana Jesucristo Rey and Light Mission Center and Praise Christian Fellowship and Foursquare Gospel Church and the World People Church, Our Lady of Loretto and the Salon Del Reino de Los Testigos de Jehova and many, many more—I had made a list of dozens of such places in my neighborhood alone—which catered to different races, from Filipino to Korean and many Latino groups. For a newly arrived family from El Salvador or Guatemala or Mexico these little churches were like a life raft in a stormy sea of change, places where you could worship with your own kind, in a language you understood, and with the bible in his hand maybe the husband wouldn't succumb to drink, and the kids could avoid drugs, and the wife could feel hope, and nobody would have to feel alone. That's how I sometimes thought of it, anyway, when I thought of it at all.

As I sat looking into the interior of Centro Misionero Belham y El

Amor de Cristo, it occurred to me that Chandler had understood this city in a way no other writer had, how it was a place of extremes and addictions, cults and corruption, hedonism and a strangely virulent puritanism. "I was the first to write about Southern California in a realistic way," he once said. "Now half the writers in the country piddle about in the smog. To write about a place you have to love it or hate it or do both by turns, which is usually the way you love a woman. But a sense of vacuity and boredom—that's fatal." Los Angeles, he said, was just a tired old whore to him now.

Reina de la Ciudad de Los Angeles: Queen of the City of the Angels, a tired old whore. In the sun-drenched streets of the New American Paradise, Marlowe found his own heart of darkness.

The church across the way seemed emblematic to me of something that had always been a part of L.A., something Ray must have seen firsthand from the moment he arrived, and that is what a fertile ground L.A. was for the many forms of religious fervor that took root here—what Edmund Wilson, in a 1930s essay on L.A., called "all the little god boxes." When Ray arrived in 1913, L.A. was overrun with militant moralists and reform-minded preachers and health-nut gurus, body-worshippers, yogis, cultists of all stripes, but it was also exquisitely corrupt, with gambling and prostitution and graft and greed rampant everywhere, a city where every kind of chiseling flourished. By the time Aimee Semple McPherson established her Angelus Temple in 1919 and began drawing worshippers by the thousands to watch her preach, dressed in her flamboyant costumes (Mayan princess, Greek goddess, vestal virgin), the reformers and preachers and moralists could hardly keep pace with the con artists. It had always been a two-tiered city, Los Angeles, pretty on the outside, rotten underneath, a place where the cops and politicians were as crooked as the crooks, and nobody would come to understand this better than Raymond Chandler.

But it must have been beautiful when he first arrived. It must have seduced him, as it would so many others.

Not long after Ray arrived, Warren Lloyd found him a job working for the Los Angeles Creamery as an accountant. The offices were on South Olive Street in downtown L.A. Chandler sent for his mother, Florence, who came from London to live with him. That must have been the plan: He would go to America and get settled and then she would come to live with him and they would get an apartment and set up house together, just the two of them, as they had done so often in the past. It did not mean an end to his friendship with the Lloyds or his attendance at the Friday night soirees with The Optimists. Florence fit easily into this circle, made up, as it was, of people of varying ages, and soon she was taking part in the musical evenings and poetry readings and the sessions at the Ouija board, with Warren and Alma and Estelle and Edward, and Cissy and Julian, to whom she took a special liking because not only was Julian close to her own age but he had once lived in London.

Sometimes Ray and Warren would go to the movies together. The big picture palaces were just opening then—like the ornate Million Dollar Theatre on North Broadway and the Rialto and Grauman's Chinese Theatre. They liked melodramas, in part because Warren often liked to conduct a little experiment with the audience, as part of his fascination with human psychology. He and Ray would sit on opposite sides of the theater and, at a certain point in the movie, always during a particularly serious or sad moment, one of them would begin laughing and then, from the other side of the theater, the other would join in. The object was to see how many people in the audience they could get to laugh with them at an inappropriate moment. Often they were successful. The point must have been to prove how sheeplike people can be. How they could be led into ignoring their own sensibilities in favor of some kind of groupthink. Just the opposite of how a man like Philip Marlowe would behave. The loner, suspicious of humanity and its motives. Always holding himself apart, outside the mainstream, marching to his own tune.

I sat in my car at the curb a little longer. Whatever sort of life Ray had led here briefly on Bonnie Brae was long gone, effectively erased by time. The people were dead, the houses destroyed, even the language of the neighborhood had changed. Gone, too, Ouija boards, Madame Blavatsky, and evenings where people entertained one another with songs and poems. Still I could imagine what it had been like at the Lloyds'. The alcohol-infused evenings, the sense of cultured, intelligent guests, a feeling of bonhomie, a young and attractive crowd. A little chess. Music, with Julian at the piano, Alma singing. Dancing later in the evening. Cissy—beautiful and high-spirited, reputed to be very witty and amusing, and theatrical in both manner and dress—effortlessly holding everyone's attention. She had style. She had class. She spoke in a kind of upper-class faux-English accent, perhaps picked up from her husband. She was newly arrived from New York, enigmatic about her past but leaving no doubt that it was colorful. Her charm was natural, her appeal immediate. She won people over easily, without visible effort. Years later Ray would tell a story about her, how once, when they were in a car and she was driving, she was stopped by a policeman and in the middle of speaking with him, she accidentally ran over the policeman's foot, and then frustrated, she put the car in reverse and ran over his foot again, and yet the policeman was so utterly charmed by her that all he did was smile and let her off without a ticket.

How appealing she must have been to Chandler, right from the beginning. A woman with a resourcefulness and intelligence to match his. And a cynical attitude toward convention. None of the vulnerability and sadness of his mother—the fragility of an abandoned woman. In her life, it was Cissy who'd done the abandoning, not the other way around. By the time she met Chandler, she was on her second husband.

Later he wrote of her,

When she was younger, she used to have sudden and very short-lived tempers, in which she would throw pillows at me. I just laughed. I liked her spirit. She was a terrific fighter. If an awkward or unpleasant scene faced her, and at times we all face that, she would march right in, and never hesitate a moment to think it over. And she always won, not because she deliberately put on the charm at the tactical moment, but because she was irresistible without even knowing or caring about it.

Sexy and experienced, witty and confident, she was everything a young man could want in an older woman. He was sexually repressed and shy, inexperienced with women. Little wonder he found her irresistible.

Cissy was born in Perry, Ohio, in 1870, as Pearl Eugenia Hurlburt, but she left Ohio at around the age of twenty and moved to New York City. She settled in Harlem sometime in the early 1890s and immediately changed her name to Cecilia, shortened to Cissy. She set about reinventing herself, giving herself a new name, dumping the provincial Pearl for the more modern and snappy-sounding Cissy. In Harlem, she rented an apartment on Lenox Avenue, and she began studying piano. To make money she also became an artist's model—part of a bohemian high-life set that used opium. Soon she was posing nude for artists and photogra-

phers (Ray later owned some of these nude photographs of her—what ever happened to them? I wondered). She was even said to have been the model for a large nude painting of a beautiful blonde that hung for many years in the bar of either the St. Regis Hotel or the Plaza in New York City.

Living in turn-of-the-century Harlem, she was far away from the parents back home in Ohio. She had a sister, Lavinia, who would later come to live in L.A. and with whom she seems to have been close. But in New York she was rather blissfully free of family and her midwestern past (Ohio, as someone once said, was a place made for leaving). During her time in Harlem she had married a salesman with the rather fleabitten name of Leon Brown Porcher. What did he sell—life insurance? kitchenwares? ladies' undergarments? Seven years later she divorced Porcher and married Julian Pascal, alias Goodridge Bowen, classical pianist and composer, formerly of the West Indies and London, a move that would seem to have increased her social standing, and then later she would leave the older neurasthenic Julian for the much younger Raymond Chandler, and what this told me was she was a woman who seemed to have no difficulty making up her mind about what she wanted in life and going for it, no matter the amount of change involved. If it caused some temporary difficul-

ties—she would still *march right in,* as Ray had put it, to get what she wanted, and *she always won,* because she was *irresistible.* Her appeal for Chandler, their attraction to one another, didn't happen overnight. It built over a period of five or six years, and it had begun here, on Bonnie Brae, when they both belonged to The Optimists, and she was still married to Julian, and Ray lived with his mother.

Once his mother had arrived from England, Ray rented an apartment for the two of them near Angel's Flight, in the Bunker Hill area of downtown L.A. I didn't have an exact address—I just knew they had lived somewhere near the top of the little funicular that used to serve the area and take people up and down the steep hill. It was an area Chandler had described in one of his early stories, "The King in Yellow," and which he used again, in much greater detail, in *The High Window:*

> Bunker Hill is old town, lost town, shabby town, crook town. Once, very long ago, it was the choice residential district of the city, and there are still standing a few of the jigsaw Gothic mansions with wide porches and walls covered with round-end shingles and full corner bay windows with spindle turrets. They are all rooming houses now, their parquetry floors are scratched and worn through the once glossy finish and the wide sweeping staircases are dark with time and with cheap varnish laid on over generations of dirt. In the tall rooms haggard landladies bicker with shifty tenants. On the wide cool front porches, reaching their cracked shoes into the sun, and staring at nothing, sit the old men with faces like lost battles.
>
> In and around the old houses there are flyblown restaurants and Italian fruit stands and cheap apartment houses and little candy stores where you can buy even nastier things than their candy. And there are ratty hotels where nobody except people named Smith and Jones sign the register and where the night clerk is half watchdog and half pander.

Out of the apartment houses come women who should be young but have faces like stale beer; men with pulled-down hats and quick eyes that look the street over behind the cupped hand that shields the match flame; worn intellectuals with cigarette coughs and no money in the bank; fly cops with granite faces and unwavering eyes; cokies and coke peddlers; people who look like nothing in particular and know it, and once in a while even men that actually go to work. But they come out early, when the wide cracked sidewalks are empty and still have dew on them.

It's an acute portrait of a neighborhood, of downtown L.A. during a certain period of decay, which has lasted now for many years, and when it was written, in the 1930s, it was an accurate description. It reflects one of the things Chandler did for the mystery novel, which was to imbue it with extraordinary detail and create an atmosphere so thick and rich that the landscape really comes alive—and it includes also his trademark of style, the brilliant similes, so evident here in this passage: *Old men with faces like lost battles. Women who should be young but have faces like stale beer. People who look like nothing in particular and know it.*

When I arrived at Bunker Hill, I noticed the funicular was still there, though it was the only feature of the landscape that seemed not to have changed, and even it was rusted and no longer in use following an accident a few years earlier that resulted in the death of a tourist.

Tourist. I had read somewhere that the word was invented in L.A. to describe the throngs of Middle Americans who flocked to Southern California in the winter months for the domestic equivalent of the European Grand Tour, some of whom wrote laudatory accounts of their sojourns, such as the one published in Nebraska in 1912 called *Uncle Jim and Aunt Jemimy in Southern California.* Chandler had also lived in Nebraska and thus could be thought of as having certain midwestern roots himself, though certainly not as deep as the Uncle Jims and Aunt Jemimys, the so-called hog-and-hominy crowd who flocked here by the tens of thousands.

The Midwest would turn up in more than one of his stories and novels, however, as if he knew that the exotic taproot of Southern California extended a thousand miles or more to the plainer heartland of America, like a gardenia growing out of a spud.

When I moved to L.A. in the late 1970s, my first impression of the place was that it was one big garden, flowered and perfumed, full of luscious blooms—trees studded with huge creamy magnolia blossoms and pink and yellow frangipani, jacaranda trees with their clouds of exquisite flowers lining entire streets and creating extraordinary canopies of lavender. Everywhere there were bushes loaded with yellow and red hibiscus, and camellias and gardenias, and the almost sickening odor of night-blooming jasmine hung on the air—everywhere this almost funereal smell and garish beauty. It all seemed so untamed to me, as if these plants didn't actually belong to anyone but were part of some natural and rampant floral disorder, a special endowment, like a native birthright instead of being transplants from the Old World and the South Seas. Having moved to L.A. from the rather monochromatic world of the Great Basin, I couldn't quite fathom such a lurid landscape or understand why anyone would actually go out and buy flowers at a florist shop when there were so many everywhere for the picking. But I quickly realized that once you picked these exotic flowers, they almost immediately began to lose their beauty: they drooped and wilted, they shriveled, darkened, and soon died—the camellias and magnolias that turned an ugly rusty color, lantana that dropped yellow dust and smelled like cat piss, frangipani that simply withered, flowers that seemed to perish more rapidly than other cut blossoms. I learned you couldn't take this beauty inside: it was if it was meant to be admired from afar—say from the window of a passing car.

The other thing I realized about L.A. was how everyone created their own little private paradise within this greater garden, a refuge that, if you were lucky, you didn't have to leave too often. I remember meeting a well-known screenwriter at a party a few months after I settled in and how, when someone asked how she was doing, she answered she'd had a terrific week because she hadn't had to leave her house for five straight days.

The flowers didn't want to come inside, the people didn't want to go out. L.A. had its own measures. Rhythms. Quirks. Everything was always moving . . . or else it became very, *very* still.

When Ray and his mother lived on Bunker Hill, the big houses he described in *The High Window* had already been broken up into apartments. Perhaps they had a haggard landlady like the one he described, and Ray went off to work each morning, to his job at the Los Angeles Creamery on South Olive Street and balanced the ice cream accounts for which he was responsible, while Florence walked down the hill to Central Market, the great collection of food stalls that is still there between Broadway and Hill, and did the marketing and then went home and cooked dinner and they ate together, just mother and son, as they had done Ray's whole life. She was not an old woman then, Florence. She couldn't have been more than fifty—just a few years older than Cissy—a woman who might still have made a match for herself, freeing her son to move on and lead his own life. But she never did that. She never

remarried. Later Chandler said he wished that she had. His mother was a beautiful woman, he said, and she might have married: there had been a few suitors, but he felt she had been too concerned for him. After his father's disappearance she never wanted to take a chance on another man, a stepfather who might end up disappointing him again.

There's a picture of Florence from this time. In this photo there is about her an air of melancholy, or disappointment, a rather nakedly sad look most evident in her eyes and the set of her mouth. She's not unattractive, but neither is she beautiful. It's interesting to compare this picture with one of Cissy, showing her at a very young age. Cissy is exquisitely lovely. Her face is shown in three-quarter profile and she wears a white dress, pulled off her shoulders and revealing a graceful neck and the sort of skin, as Chandler once wrote, that an old rake dreams of. Her features are classically perfect—a beautiful mouth, fine nose, large soft eyes with shapely brows. Her hair is a mass of soft curls, a style she would maintain throughout her life. She's movie-star beautiful. And yet the pose is anything but glamorous. She looks incredibly soft and gentle, very natural and lovely.

⌐The two women were in fact of opposite temperament—one a victim who never overcame her husband's abandonment, the other a survivor who never minded abandoning a situation if her own welfare demanded it. And yet in later photographs showing both women at about the same age, what is striking is how much they resemble each other in a certain way.⌐

There was no place for me to park near Bunker Hill, and nothing of the neighborhood where Chandler had lived left to see. I realized at that moment, and not for the last time, what a city of architectural disposability L.A. really was, how quickly one thing was turned into another, buildings torn down, replaced by something else. The rather short history of the city was constantly being erased, like a throwaway metropolis, ensconced in happy amnesia. The house on Bonnie Brae was gone. Ditto the dilapidated old mansions on Bunker Hill. As I turned onto Third Street and headed west I wondered what I'd find at 311 S. Loma Drive, the place where Ray and his mother had moved next.

This was no longer an attractive area of the city, these neighborhoods close to downtown. Though once an area of beautiful houses, the hard-core urban center had been increasingly neglected over many decades, shunned by those with money in favor of the ever-expanding suburbs and beach communities. And yet one could still find pockets of beauty and gracefulness. I knew that on the corner of Loma Drive and Third Street, very near the address I had for Chandler and his mother, there stood a magnificent old YWCA building, the Mary Andrews Clark Memorial Home, which had a stately feeling and pretty shaded gardens, a place that in recent years had been turned into low-income housing. Once, when I was looking for inexpensive office space, I'd investigated the possibility of renting a room there only to discover it was run like a lockdown facility where everyone had to sign in at a security desk, and the bathrooms were shared with other residents, many of whom were recovering addicts or on parole. I decided to pass on the place.

Ray had rented a bungalow court apartment a half a block from the Mary Andrews Clark Memorial Home; the home, built in 1912, would have been just a few years old when he and his mother moved to the neighborhood and was filled with young ladies who'd come to the city for adventure or to seek their fortune. The Chandlers' apartment would also have been within easy walking distance of the trolley lines that served downtown.

I wasn't surprised, somehow, to find that the bungalow court apartments at 311 S. Loma had also been destroyed. A huge new low-income housing project, called Casa Loma, occupied the whole block. I parked the car anyway and got out and walked down the street. Casa Loma was covered with scaffolding, and workmen were repairing cracks in the stucco. Even though the place didn't look more than a few years old, it appeared very cheaply made, as if it were already falling apart. I noticed an old bungalow court complex across the street—the Loma Garden Apartments—now cordoned off with chain-link fencing, and I wandered over and looked into the courtyard. This was the sort of bungalow court complex where Ray and his mother would have lived, of the same vintage as the one that had been torn down across the way. The bungalow court was a style of apartment housing unique to Southern California: separate little units, often of vaguely Spanish design. There were, however, also Tudor bungalow courts, and mini–French château bungalow courts, and thatched-roofed English cottage bungalows, and Seven Dwarfs bungalows—the idea easily accommodating various styles because this, after all, was L.A., where no architecture was considered inappropriate or outlandish, and set designers who worked in the film business began influencing the architecture of the city, realizing their fantasies on a domestic scale. Bungalow court units were joined by common walkways and little garden areas, which allowed a sense of living not so much in apartments as in separate little houses. The idea was that in L.A. everyone should enjoy the outdoors, have a bit of garden, a little private paradise. But again the neighborhood was so changed that I could not feel, standing there in the late afternoon light with a homeless man diving through a dumpster nearby, anything of Chandler or the life he and his mother might have led here. It had become a run-down neighborhood, infused by a feeling of decay and an air of dispirited poverty.

I got in my car and drove back to Third Street and turned left, heading west into the fading sun. I felt like making one more stop before going home. I was curious to see the place where Julian and Cissy Pascal had lived. If it was still there. The Pascals had lived close enough that Ray and his mother could easily have visited them by taking a short trolley ride. Maybe they even owned a car by then. It's not known when Ray got his first automobile, but what is known is he developed a lifelong love of cars.

Warren Lloyd had a big convertible, and often he organized driving trips with various members of The Optimists. They'd take dirt roads through the unpopulated regions that lay between downtown and Beverly Hills, sometimes heading over Cahuenga Pass to the San Fernando Valley, which was then still farmland dotted with citrus groves. Sometimes they'd make a day of it and take a picnic—Warren and Alma, Ray and his mother, and Cissy and Julian—or they'd stop at the roadside inn at the base of Cahuenga and order a meal. Clearly Ray took to this aspect of life in Southern California—the world of cars and driving and motion, the possibility of moving oneself (caught in the very word *auto-mobile*) from one place to another with unprecedented ease, under one's own control and powers, unlike the earlier conveyances, the horse-drawn carriages or even trains whose frequency and destination were beyond one's control. It's hard for us now to imagine the freshness of this idea for that first generation of drivers, the excitement the *auto-mobile* must have engendered, and also the sense of freedom and pleasure it imparted to its owner, especially in a climate like Southern California's where in an open car, motoring beside the sea or through the hills and surrounding desert, you could so easily feel yourself an intimate part of the sunny and balmy world that encircled you.

But Chandler must also have sensed how there was an elusive

quality here, something about the climate that cheated the senses by the very evenness of it all—the weather, the lack of pronounced seasons, the people who all walked alike and worked as if in a dream with no awareness of the passage of day, that peculiar lack of time and season, days and nights so alike in warmth and brightness and beauty. One day Chandler would subvert all that brightness, making it dark, and turn L.A. into a city of rain-slicked avenues and dark banked canyons, where a powerful undertow of corruption ate away at everything, a kind of airless underworld composed of, in his own phrase, mean streets. The lovely drives in the sunny convertible with Warren and The Optimists would, in time, become excursions to run-down roadhouses or shacks on half-made roads at the city's edge where drugged and helpless women awaited rescue by Philip Marlowe, and by then even the ocean would have turned ugly, like a fat washerwoman trudging home. But when the city was still new to him, it was immensely alluring, a city of imagination that could be reinvented with each dawning day.

At what point during those first five years that they knew each other, before Ray went off to war, when Cissy was still married to Julian and Ray was still living with his mother, had they realized they were in love and there was no turning back? Cissy made the decision to leave Julian for Ray during the time she lived in the house on Vendome, sometime early in 1919. It was a decision that upset Florence Chandler very much. She did not want Cissy to leave Julian Pascal, and even more, she did not want her to marry her son.

The Pascal house at 127 S. Vendome was still there, a small stucco place painted a rather festive shade of yellow. It was an ordinary-looking house of very modest proportions. Somehow I expected something grander. Almost all the houses on the street were small one-story cottages and bungalow-style dwellings with little lawns or gardens and cluttered yards, the kind of houses that were built by the hundreds of thousands in this city. The street was lined with skinny palms that seemed outrageously tall compared to the squat little houses and afforded no shade at all, just fantasy and drama. There was a sign for some kind of income tax business affixed to the house next to where the Pascals had lived. Vendome looked like any one of a hundred streets in L.A., any one of a thousand. It looked like a kind of nothing neighborhood that you would never notice or think about unless you happened to live there yourself.

In 1917, with war still raging, Ray had made the decision to enlist in the Canadian army, and along with Gordon Pascal, Julian's son (and Cissy's stepson), he joined the Gordon Highlanders and was sent to France to fight. Florence, who by then had become very close to the Pascals, moved into this house on Vendome with Julian and Cissy. With their sons heading off to Europe to fight, it must have seemed natural for them to wait out the war years together. Never mind that one of the sons was no doubt already in love with his pal's stepmother.

I couldn't help wondering if one of the reasons Ray enlisted and went off to Europe to fight was because he found himself in the untenable position of being in love with another man's wife—and not just any man, but a man who had befriended him and whom his mother was very fond of.

Ray and Cissy wrote to each other while he was away, initially perhaps under the guise of exchanging news about Cissy's stepson, Gordon, but over time the letters became more intimate. They could confide feelings to each other in print that they had perhaps been too reticent to express in person, and it was through the exchange of letters that the relationship began to deepen. Chandler saw action in France, as the leader of a platoon that was wiped out by German artillery—he was injured and sent to England to recover and then be discharged. He would never write about his war experiences, nor did he speak about that time except to say that "Once you've had to lead a platoon into direct machine-gun fire, nothing is ever the same again." As a result of his correspondence with Cissy, he seems to have felt more confident in pursuing his interest in her once the war was over.

He did not return immediately to L.A., however, but lingered in Seattle with a friend from the war and then found a job in San Francisco working for an English bank. He did come home for Christmas that year, in 1919, to the Pascal house on Vendome. He found his mother was ill and spending increasingly long periods of time in bed. In a short poem he wrote at this time he spoke of "the secret and silence and perfume . . . in the quiet house of all the dead."

Was the secret he alluded to an affair that he had begun with Cissy before going off to war, or perhaps the feelings they had revealed to one another in letters while he was away? And was the silence that of his mother, who may have already begun to suspect that her son and Cissy were falling in love?

Later Ray would claim that he rescued Cissy from a very unhappy marriage, but it's not clear just how true this is. We have only Ray's word that she was unhappy, and other evidence suggests that she took her time making up her mind as to whether or not to leave her husband and that she agonized over the decision.

He wrote many poems at this time, some of them clearly love poems for Cissy, including one that contains this verse:

> *The touch of lips too dear for mortal kisses*
> *The light of eyes too soft for common days*
> *The breath of jasmine born to faintly lighten*
> *The garden of ethereal estrays.*

One wonders just what sort of ethereal estrays he was speaking of. Perhaps he and Cissy met in the garden of this house when others were sleeping or away. Ray was an immensely handsome young man: in one photograph, taken just after the war, he exudes a kind of suave Fitzgeraldian elegance, and it's not hard to see why Cissy was attracted to him.

In another, more humorous poem, also written for Cissy at this time, he becomes more playful. It begins:

> *I bowed down to your feet with reckless words*
> *Sipping the tea, sipping the goddamned tea,*
> *And no one heard but you, and no one smiled,*
> *They were not there. They died before their deaths.*

One can imagine the scene that inspired the poem—an afternoon gathering in the living room of this little house on Vendome—with Julian and Cissy, and Florence and Ray, all taking tea, a polite exchange, and Ray subversively courting Cissy with his reckless words, which no one hears but her. The others are simply not there. In the eyes of the lovers, they have already begun to die.

There was another line in that poem that caught my attention: *I bowed down to your feet . . .*

I had noticed in Ray's writing an obsession—not so much with women's feet but rather their legs. Ray seems to have had a fetish, perhaps a not uncommon thing for men of his day whose exposure to the female body was so restricted. Legs in sheer stockings, feet in alluring high heels, these are images that recur throughout the novels and stories. One of my favorite such passages comes from *Playback,* and it also reveals Ray's flair for capturing a sense of female fashion:

She was quite a doll. She wore a white belted raincoat, no hat, a well-cherished head of platinum hair, booties to match the raincoat. She had a pair of legs . . . that were not painful to look at. She wore night sheer stockings. I stared at them rather intently, especially when she crossed her legs and held out a cigarette to be lighted.

"Christian Dior," she said, reading my rather open mind. "I never wear anything else. A light, please."

If Ray did have a fetish, it was clearly one that Marlowe had inherited and which reached its literary apogee in a story called "English Summer," which Ray wrote later in his life, in which there is a scene of almost orgasmic intensity between a booted upper-class English woman, sitting astride a horse, and an American man who encounters her on a bridle path and begins fondling her leather-clad leg. The woman turns out to have a voracious sexual appetite, and she takes him home to her castle and seduces him. It made me think of something I had come across in M. G. Lord's book *Forever Barbie: The Unauthorized Biography of a Real Doll,* part of an interview Lord conducted with a woman who published a magazine for men with leg and foot fetishes:

I learned that men get security from legs, because when a little child is scared, he grips his mother's legs. They're always trying to get up under the skirt, holding on to the legs—and the legs represent safety. A loving mother may pick up the child and hold him, but a less loving, harsher mother may just leave the child down there, so the legs are all he gets. When a boy with a stern, withholding mother grows up, he often fastens on a harsher, more demanding woman as his love object.

He may also fasten onto the idea of legs as being the sexiest, most irresistible part of woman.

Whether any of this really fits with Chandler's life, who can say? But it did seem possible, given his history—the fact that as a child he'd been so dependent on his mother, who definitely appears to have had her stern and disapproving side.

What is more important than any specific fixation Chandler might have had on a particular female body part is his clear tendency to fetishize certain things, a crucial element in the nature of his imagination. He had a need to romanticize, to endow objects and particular people and scenes in his books with a special meaning, with an enhanced aura, and his fetishizing of women's legs is just one part of this greater tendency.

Initially, Cissy may have spurned Ray's romantic advances. Another poem written at this time, "Ballad of a Pale Beauty," begins:

> A lady of pure incessant grace
> Whose classic nose disdains the hungry Goth,
> Within whose eyes peace hath a dwelling place,
> You never bowed the knee to Ashtaroth.
> Cold distant star that never singed a moth,
> Calm symphony in unimpassioned gray
> You are not wine, you are not even froth—
> I think I will not marry you today.

There is no question this poem was meant for Cissy, and the lines suggest a coolness on Cissy's part. The poem goes on to detail her resistance to his advances. She flees "the touch that might upset your hair." Her bosom "never pants in disarray," and therefore, he repeats the refrain, "I will not marry you today." She "held love's bow, and might have held his mace," but turned away and "fled from the shocking toll, found it no doubt too big a price to pay." The poem concludes:

> Ah well, I am no beggar with a bowl,
> I think I will not marry you today.
> Princess of dalliance, on whose hidden shoal
> The deep sea vessel rots its bones away
> Love never missed the empty tricks you stole,
> I know I shall not marry you today.

Even Ray called his poems "grade-B Georgian." Still, throughout his life he turned to writing poetry in order to express his feelings, in particular his romantic impulses, and this poem may reflect a frustrating period in his courtship of Cissy—the "Princess of dalliance" who argued, perhaps with good reason, that leaving Julian for Ray was simply "too high a price to pay."

After the 1919 Christmas holidays were over, however, things began to change. Ray returned briefly to San Francisco and got a job with the *Daily Express* newspaper, but he lasted only a week. Perhaps he took the job in frustration, to show Cissy that he would leave if she could not commit to him. It's possible he didn't know what to do about his feelings for Cissy, but in the end he must have realized he needed to return, and together they decided to face the situation squarely.

When he returned, it became apparent to everyone that he and Cissy were in love. Julian Pascal, as would be expected, was very upset. It was decided the situation needed to be discussed by all parties, and a series of meetings was arranged with Cissy and

Julian and Ray, presided over by Warren Lloyd, the self-taught psychologist whose interest in the human psyche had compelled him to write *Psychology Normal and Abnormal* in 1908, at a time when the whole field of psychology was still very young, a book written, as he states in the introduction, "for thinkers and students in the problems of life's riddles." Estelle Lloyd also joined these discussions, helping to sort out the life riddle facing their friends—namely, should Cissy and Julian stay married, or should Cissy leave Julian for Ray?

These meetings were observed by Warren's youngest son, Paul Lloyd, who was fourteen at the time and who later reported eavesdropping on the sessions through an open window while ostensibly playing outside. He remembered how his parents would sit down with Julian and Cissy and Ray to discuss the situation and how this went on over a period of several weeks, and how Cissy would say that she loved Julian but she loved Ray more; what could she be expected to do? Finally Cissy made up her mind. She chose Ray, she did love him more, and it was decided that she should seek a divorce, not the quickie divorce available in Reno— they were all too conventional for that option—but a California divorce, which required a yearlong wait and which would become final in 1920. There was no hurry, anyway. Both Chandler and Cissy understood that it would not be possible for them to marry right away because of his mother.

Florence was not happy with her son, possibly because she felt he had broken up the marriage of two people who had been very kind to her, with whom she had lived for several years. Or perhaps she was simply jealous of Cissy and disapproved of her son's involvement with a woman almost her own age, although it seems that no one knew exactly how old Cissy really was. As Cissy's sister Lavinia once said, Cissy would do anything to disguise her true age.

Chandler could not, or would not, go against his mother. Instead of moving in with Cissy or marrying her when her divorce became final, he rented an apartment for himself and his mother in Redondo Beach, at 224 S. Catalina Street, near the old pier—a building long since destroyed and replaced by condominiums—hoping perhaps that the sea air might improve his mother's health, and he rented another apartment for Cissy in nearby Huntington Beach. With two women now to support, he needed more income. He found a job in the booming oil business, then entering its heyday in Southern California. With the help of Warren Lloyd, he was hired as an accountant for Dabney Oil Syndicate (whose oil wells were mainly in the Signal Hill area, not far from Redondo Beach), and for four years they lived this way—Ray and his mother in one apartment, Cissy in another. About this period we know very little, except that Chandler worked at an office in downtown L.A., on Seventh at Olive Street, sometimes visiting the oil fields in Signal Hill, and that he commuted each day between Redondo Beach and downtown, and became more successful, eventually assuming the title of head accountant. He continued to see Cissy and spend as much time with her as possible, given his own responsibilities, foremost of which was his mother, who had cancer and became increasingly ill until finally she died, after a painful and lengthy struggle with her disease, in January of 1924, having barely reached the age of sixty.

His mother's death freed him finally. He and Cissy were married two weeks later, on February 6, 1924, in a ceremony held in downtown L.A., with Warren Lloyd as a witness. On the marriage certificate, the fifty-three-year-old Cissy knocked a cool decade off her life. And no one was the wiser.

There was really nothing more to see on Vendome Street except the little banana-yellow house with security bars on the windows, a place that suggested none of the drama that had taken place within its walls over eighty years ago when Paul Lloyd had stood at the window, listening to the agonized discussions over Cissy and Ray's future. The afternoon was fading. Long shadows, cast by the skinny palms, fell across the facade of the little house that now looked so quiet and innocuous.

I drove down to Wilshire and turned left, heading toward downtown. The tall glass buildings looked brassy and gold in the setting sun. I figured I'd stop for a drink at the H.M.S. Bounty, an old wood-paneled bar with funky nautical decor that was straight out of Chandler's era. The restaurant adjoined an old hotel called The Gaylord, which opened in 1923 and for many years was one of L.A.'s hot spots. The newly constructed Gaylord rose with a singular verticality from the horizontal expanse of the city fanning out below and afforded a view of the grand display of the Ambassador's manicured gardens across the street.

Cissy and Ray had rented a number of places in this neighborhood, the area around the old Ambassador Hotel. The Ambassador was now abandoned, closed up, and waiting for its next incarnation. The Los Angeles School District had recently taken possession of the property under the law of eminent domain, and it now appeared that the once great hotel, site of the legendary Cocoanut Grove and the place where Robert Kennedy was assassinated by Sirhan Sirhan in a pantry near the kitchen, was about to be turned into an elementary school for Mexican and Korean children. A great behemoth of a hotel, it was now neglected and shabby, surrounded by dying palms and parched birds-of-paradise. But once it had been the jewel of L.A. hotels. The opening-night party, on New Year's Eve in 1921, was described as a kind of coming-out party for Southern California, with three thousand

guests in attendance: as one newspaper reporter put it at the time, "The splendor of the setting for the affair probably has never been equaled on the Pacific Coast."

Years ago, when I first moved to the neighborhood, I used to come to the Ambassador almost every day. There was a swim club I had joined which entitled me to use the hotel's pool and the sauna, and I would ride my bike from Carondelet and stroll through the beautiful gardens to the pool, then swim laps and sunbathe in the company of the hotel's attractive guests before heading home again, feeling that for a brief time I had entered the world of "old" L.A. When my husband and I married, it was also where our wedding guests had stayed. I had always had a fondness for the place. Now it was empty, boarded up, surrounded by a high fence. Its untended garden had become home for dozens of feral cats.

The Ambassador stood directly across the street from the H.M.S. Bounty and the Gaylord Hotel, which had now been converted into apartments. As I pulled up to the curb and shut off the engine, a cat suddenly leapt out of the bushes behind the chainlink fence and with a ferocity that took my breath away pounced on a fat pigeon, sinking its teeth and claws into the wildly struggling bird, and then began dragging it away into the bushes.

It was a strange, violent moment. Blood, feathers, the screech of the bird, the swift attack, the cat who looked larger and wilder than any normal cat, springing so suddenly and viciously on the bird, and then the horrible struggle, the dying pigeon being dragged away. This was a cat not of the domesticated variety that relies on kitty chow and the kindness of humans but rather a hunter who had honed exquisite skills. And here she was, living in the shadow of the crumbling Cocoanut Grove, whose awning now tilted at a precarious angle as if it were about ready to fall over.

There weren't many people in the H.M.S. Bounty. It was still early, just after five o'clock. But the regular bar patrons for which the Bounty was famous had already lined up at the long curving wooden bar and were chatting in small groups and watching the TV sets. I joined them, taking one of the last available stools, and ordered a gimlet. The bartender, a young Asian woman, brought me a martini glass filled to the brim with the faintly neon green liquid.

There is a passage from *The Long Goodbye* about that moment in the day when a bar opens for business—not a restaurant bar, like the H.M.S. Bounty, but a real bar, like those Chandler had known and frequented and written about in his novels:

> I like bars just after they open for the evening. When the air inside is still cool and clean and everything is shiny and the barkeep is giving himself that last look in the mirror to see if his tie is straight and his hair is smooth. I like the neat bottles on the bar back and the lovely shining glasses and the anticipation. I like to watch the man mix the first one of the evening and put it down on a crisp mat and put the little folded napkin beside it. I like to taste it slowly. The first quiet drink of the evening in a quiet bar—that's wonderful.

After a while an older couple came in and sat in one of the booths. I could tell they were regulars from the way the waitress greeted them—perhaps a couple who lived in the neighborhood and had been coming to the Bounty for many years. The waitress herself seemed like a relic from another time, a thin, frail woman with a stiff ash-blond wig whom I had seen many times. Someone told me she had once been a roommate of Jane Russell's. Now she seemed far too old to be doing the hard work of waitressing. And yet she was agile and energetic, with a quietly pleasant manner. She had one of those faces you see sometimes in L.A. on women who you know are old but still look girlish. Not the plastic surgery look of Beverly Hills but something less easily describable. It was the look of a woman who had lived on her own most of her life and had always worked and taken buses everywhere and who had grown slightly eccentric with age, her clothes out of fashion, her manner quaintly out of step, yet one who had not cared to change her look or makeup except to add a wig when her hair began to thin. Somehow she gave off a dignified air, in spite of her menial job, with her established routines, her regular friends, her independence and innate attractiveness: long beyond the age of retirement she had continued to work, because she needed the money and also because it was what she was used to doing, what she still liked to do. These kinds of women always fascinated me.

It wasn't the waitress, however, that caught my attention. It was the man and woman she had just seated at a red leather booth against the wall, an elderly couple who appeared very old-fashioned in both dress and manner, and who had about them an aura of frailty but also of granite-etched longevity: they gave off an air of a binding relationship that now rendered them almost mute with familiarity. Silently they picked up their menus and just as silently laid them down again and gazed beyond each other. They ordered their martinis with sudden smiles—a brief burst of animation—and just as suddenly resumed their quietude, their unreadable expressions. When the drinks came, they clinked their glasses cautiously and looked briefly into each other's eyes, then brought their drinks to their lips simultaneously. There was something about the woman in particular that I found haunting— the dyed blond hair styled in a youthful fluffiness, the frilly clothing, the still-beautiful face now caked with foundation and powder, the carefully applied lipstick and mascara and the trim figure, and, perhaps most striking of all, the sense of a woman unaware of the impression she was making on others. The man with her was well dressed and had a dapper air: he wore a suit and tie and he seemed rather courtly. When he spoke to the waitress he attempted to be amusing and familiar. But as soon as the waitress left, the couple fell silent. They sat quietly, staring beyond each other, as if at a loss for something to say. They sat this way for a long while.

Later in his life, when Ray had become successful enough to indulge his whims, he created a list of rules to which he required strict obedience from all those who would drink or dine with him. The rules were as follows:

1. No one was allowed to buy a drink at his table in any bar.
2. No prices were to appear on menus for his guests.
3. He would not sign a check in front of a guest.
4. If taking a lady out, he would arrange for her menu to be handwritten.

"I suppose this may all sound a bit chi chi," he said, "but dammit I'm entitled to a few tricks."

The man at the table with his wife seemed to have no tricks, except the one of appearing thoroughly interested in the bad nautical painting hanging on the wall behind his wife's head. I couldn't get the idea out of my mind that I had conjured this couple and that somehow they were an incarnation of the Chandlers. Had it really been Ray, he would have been livelier—the best of company, as someone once said, fond of entertaining and telling stories. He would have been talking to Cissy—courting her, as he said he did every day of their married life—instead of sitting silently across from her. And had it really been Cissy, there would have been attempts at conversation—about the decor, or the people in the bar, or the fact that a strange woman in a dark jacket was sitting at the bar staring at them, and why?

I turned back to my drink. From somewhere, perhaps the lobby of the old Gaylord Hotel that adjoined the restaurant, I could hear the faint sound of a song—*I'll be seeing you, in all the old familiar places*—an old song, dated and slightly corny, and yet also rather beautiful and somehow perfect for the moment. All the world felt suddenly nostalgic. I could have been anywhere. In any city. Any bar. Caught in any era, as long as it was a previous one. Both time and place seemed fused to an indefinable moment. And it was all bygone.

After a while, I paid my bill and left, but not before noticing that the elderly couple were still sitting silently across from one another in the booth, not speaking, not even looking at each other, but rather simply staring at their plates and quietly eating their food, like two people lost to the world.

Three

I t was a winter of heavy rains. The storms came early in January
and pounded the city for days, heavy tropical downpours that
turned streets into rivers and intersections into little lakes dotted with stalled cars. This was Los Angeles in one of its extreme
modes, a city plagued by mud slides and floods. Multimillion-
dollar houses began sliding down eroded cliffs, and in narrow
banked canyons, boulders broke loose from the rain-soaked hill-
sides and crashed through bedroom walls, killing people sleeping
in their beds. Everywhere roads were closed, trapping stars in
their Malibu mansions. People huddled under umbrellas, dashed
from doorway to car, slogged and sloshed through water, wondering, when would it all end?

But the rain did not end, not in January anyway. It went on into
February, then March, with only an occasional brief respite. The
rain began to break records. It was the third wettest season in history. Then the second. By mid-March it looked to be the rainiest
winter on record. The weather had begun to feel biblical.

As the rain continued I stayed indoors and read. I watched films
based on Chandler's work or inspired by his stories. I rented *The
Big Sleep*, with Humphrey Bogart and a very young Lauren Bacall
playing the icy Mrs. Regan—her second big role after *To Have and
Have Not*. Chandler hadn't much cared for Bacall's performance.
She was the sort of actress, he said, who should have stayed a
carhop. But he loved Martha Vickers as the nymphy Carmen

Sternwood, Vivian's thumb-sucking younger sister who's caught up in a blackmailing scheme.

I watched *Murder, My Sweet,* an adaptation of *Farewell My Lovely* (the novel was filmed no less than three different times), starring Dick Powell and Claire Trevor, and thought Powell made a terrific Philip Marlowe. He had such a simple, honest face and the kind of tough yet ordinary decency that fit with the character: the scene where he's all doped up and just coming to his senses is one of the best in the movie. Claire Trevor, as Velma, made an incredible femme fatale with her helmet of lacquered platinum hair and sultry sense of evil. As a Chandler movie, they don't get much better.

I watched Robert Mitchum and Charlotte Rampling in another, sexy adaptation of the same book, and fell in love with the scene where Rampling is slowly crossing her long, long legs and Mitchum spends what seems like two full minutes staring at them before he speaks. Mitchum filled the screen with his great brooding presence, and physically he seemed a lot more like Marlowe than Bogart's smaller, tough-guy version, although I loved Bogart's performance, too, the way he delivered the wisecracks and the understated drollery he brought to the role.

I watched Robert Altman's 1973 adaptation of *The Long Goodbye,* with Elliott Gould as Philip Marlowe—not really Chandler, and not Marlowe either, but still good. Sterling Hayden, as Roger Wade, delivers an amazing performance as an alcoholic writer on his last legs, and Nina Van Pallandt, as his wife, is surprisingly good as the seductress who betrays her husband.

I watched *Lady in the Lake,* the 1947 adaptation of Chandler's novel, with Robert Montgomery as Marlowe, a film in which the camera becomes subjective and assumes the first-person perspective, as if the whole movie is shot through Marlowe's eyes so that you see Marlowe only when he enters a room and faces a mirror. It's a gimmicky idea—one that Chandler himself first came up with—and it doesn't work. But what bothered me most about the film was that Montgomery's Marlowe is a misogynist, a snarling hater of women. It just wasn't a Marlowe I wanted to see. And

Audrey Totter's wide-eyed histrionic performance as the cunning and manipulative Adrienne Fromsett is so embarrassingly bad it feels campy.

I rented a movie called *A Pure Formality*, shot in France and directed by Giuseppe Tornatore, with Roman Polanski in a brilliant performance as a police inspector in a small French town who is interrogating a novelist, played by Gérard Depardieu. It rains throughout the entire movie, a steady hard rain visible through a window. The entire story takes place in the interrogation room, where buckets have been strategically placed to catch the leaks from the ceiling: in atmosphere and tone, the film owed everything to Chandler and the rainy season in L.A.

And then I watched *Chinatown*, the most brilliant movie of them all, and the one that caught the true corruption and moral bankruptcy of L.A., based on the scandalous Owens Valley water swindle of the early twentieth century, and in a short documentary that followed the film, both the director, Roman Polanski, and the screenwriter, Robert Towne, credited Chandler as their inspiration. "I think the story of a private eye in L.A. has to be told very subjectively," Polanski said. "It is all seen and told by the character that is played by Jack Nicholson. If he faints, it's a blackout: when he opens his eyes, he sees Faye Dunaway. It's very much like Raymond Chandler's novels." Towne said that Chandler was more of an inspiration in terms of his feeling for the city than anyone else. He added that he'd gotten the idea for *Chinatown* after reading an article about Chandler and L.A.

The rain didn't shut the city down, it just made it hard to go anywhere, so I gave up trying. I stayed home and read Chandler's early stories. I came across many scenes where it was raining. I especially liked this passage from a story called "Killer in the Rain":

The rain splashed knee-high off the sidewalks, filled the gutters, and big cops in slickers that shone like gun barrels had a lot of fun carrying little girls in silk stockings and cute little rubber boots across bad places, with a lot of squeezing.

L.A. cops, however, weren't behaving quite so nicely in this season of rain. A thirteen-year-old boy was shot for simply stealing a car—a black boy, of course, unarmed and killed as he sat in the car and attempted to give himself up. He made the mistake of putting the car in reverse and bumping the cop car—thirteen-year-olds make pretty lousy drivers after all—and for this he was killed.

It had been only a few years since a massive scandal rocked the Rampart Police Division, the department that served my neighborhood, which was reported to have the highest crime rate in the city. A group of bad cops from the narcotics squad was revealed to have committed murder and extortion. They had planted evidence on gang kids, then shot them; they had terrorized the local Latino population, stolen money from old ladies and young girls, pilfered drugs confiscated in busts, threatened ordinary people who'd done nothing wrong. It was a story Chandler would have loved. A big mean goon of a cop named Rafael Perez, leader of the pack of rotten narcs, a guy who liked to hang out with rappers and live the high life, was finally sent away for a while, and the scandal died down. Nobody really believed it was the end of police corruption, however. There was no end to such corruption in L.A.

I spent a good part of the rainy months huddled in the Special Collections Department of the Charles E. Young Research Library at UCLA, going through the Raymond Chandler archive, all twelve boxes, with approximately two dozen files to each box. It was too wet to be out on the streets, tracking down his residences, so I stayed indoors, working quietly at a long wooden table in a room lined with beautiful old volumes. I immersed myself in Ray's world. I pored over old manuscripts and original letters, typed on blue paper and signed with a simple "Ray." I made notes, and more notes. I felt I could hear his voice as clearly as my own:

12/11/48 TO CHARLES MORTON, EDITOR OF THE *ATLANTIC MONTHLY:*

I am a very happy man I haven't a brain in my head, an idea on my mind, or a longing in my soul, except for a convertible.

A friend of mine said to me rudely, you're too old for a convertible. What kind of filthy talk is that? I'm just at the age to be a well-groomed roué.

4/17/50 TO HIS AGENT, CARL BRANDT:

I had a rather depressing experience the other night. I reread an old story of mine called "Finger Man," published in 1934. I don't think I'd change a word of it and I don't think I've learned a damned thing since I wrote it.

6/17/49 TO HAMISH HAMILTON, HIS ENGLISH PUBLISHER:

I am very uneasy in mind. I seem to have lost ambition and have no ideas anymore . . . I read these profound discussions . . . about art, what it is, literature, what it is, and the good life . . . and what is the definitive position of Rilke or Kafka . . . and it all seems so meaningless to me. Who cares?

9/15/49 TO DALE WARREN, PUBLICITY DIRECTOR OF HOUGHTON MIFFLIN:

The news from here is rotten. Nervous, tired, discouraged, sick of the chauffeur-and-Cadillac atmosphere, bored to hell with the endless struggle to get help, disgusted with my lack of prescience in not seeing that this kind of life is unsuited to my temperament.

10/5/51 TO HAMISH HAMILTON:

I am worn down by worry over my wife . . . Cissy can do very little, she has lost a lot of ground in the last two years . . . She has a constant cough which can only be kept down by drugs, and the drugs destroy her vitality.

I came across the letters in no particular order. Some were written while he still lived in L.A., others after he'd moved to La Jolla. The mood in the letters shifted rapidly. In one letter he was feeling happy and optimistic; in another I could feel an icy edge of despair. The despair was connected to Cissy's declining health. And also the fact that in La Jolla he found himself marooned among the idle rich, for whom he'd never had any respect. When he left L.A., he lost his locale, the gritty, seedy world that had given his stories their edge and vitality. He may have come to despise L.A., that most soulless of cities, "the biggest hick town in all the hick land," as one writer put it, the city Ray once said had as much personality as a paper cup, but he still needed it in order to write. La Jolla was dead ground for him, creatively speaking. And it wasn't as if he didn't know what the problem was. "I know what is the matter with my writing or not writing," he wrote to a friend. "I've lost any affinity for my background. . . . Los Angeles is no longer my city and La Jolla is nothing but a climate and a lot of meaningless chi-chi. I know I sound like a bitter and disappointed man. I guess I am at that."

I continued to look for traces of Cissy in the letters. Most of the references involved the state of her health, which was never very good. I came across numerous references to drugs—Cissy taking this or that drug, to ease her pain, to relax her, to help her sleep— and I began to wonder, could Cissy over a period of years have developed an addiction to mood-altering or painkilling drugs? I had nothing more than a suspicion, born of the numerous references to drugs in Ray's letters and a sense that maybe her earlier use of opium might at least have predisposed her to abuse.

Increasingly I felt her life with Chandler had not been easy, especially in the early years. During the 1920s, Chandler was a successful oil company executive, making a very good salary but also beginning his lifelong affair with alcohol. It is unlikely he'd done any serious drinking before he went away to war, but his time in the service changed all that:

When I was a young man in the RAF I would get so plastered that I had to crawl to bed on my hands and knees and at 7:30 the next morning I would be as blithe as a sparrow and howling for my breakfast. It is not in some ways the most desirable gift.

No, not really a desirable gift at all, even though he became legendary for never suffering from hangovers, no matter how much he'd drunk the night before. His alcoholism would become the monkey on his back, would eventually bring him down and cause his marriage to founder, alienate his coworkers and friends, and end up getting him fired from Dabney Oil. But for a while there it helped him feel cocky and smart and sure. He was a shy man, and like many shy people, he found that alcohol made him bolder and more confident.

When Cissy and Ray got married, they could afford to live very well, but they didn't. He seems to have been suspicious of wasting money, afraid he'd never have enough. Shortly after the wedding, Ray left the beach community where he'd been living with his mother and moved back to the city center. Cissy had already rented half of a modest double house at 2863 Leeward Avenue in a rather characterless neighborhood, not far from Bonnie Brae and Westlake Park. Like a man looking for sure footing, he settled with Cissy in the area of the city where he'd started out.

Leeward Avenue was near enough to my apartment that I could walk there, and one day, when there was a break in the rain, I decided to do just that. I headed down Rampart Boulevard to Wilshire and turned right. The old Bryson Apartments, a ten-story white stucco building, stood on the corner of Wilshire and Rampart. The Bryson was the sort of place Chandler might have used in a novel: it was of the right period and in a neighborhood where he set many scenes in his stories. It seemed to me he had once described the Bryson and the carved lions that guarded the entrance to the building in a passage in *The Lady in the Lake,* but later when I went looking for such a scene I discovered he had actually been writing about the Bryson Tower, a more upscale sort of place a few miles away on Sunset Place.

Nevertheless, the lions were still there, at the older Bryson, their paws and manes a little eroded and discolored from the weather and years of corrosive smog. An air of faded grandeur clung to the premises. The neighborhood had gotten tough—too tough to attract upscale tenants anymore. It was hard to know who lived at the Bryson now. A metal security gate protected the entrance. You needed a key to get in. I wanted to have a look in the lobby so I loitered out front for a while and then easily slipped inside when a resident unlocked the gate. The lobby was cool and quiet—and dead. A worn oriental carpet covered the floor. It felt like the waiting room of a funeral parlor. Still it was sort of touching to see how a little vestige of the past had been preserved in the form of a scarred-up old baby grand piano standing in one corner of the lobby, surrounded by a few worn plush chairs, as if to suggest the tenants gathered here in the evenings for cocktails and a little Cole Porter. I noticed a security camera on the ceiling and felt sure my entrance and little tour of the lobby were being recorded. I thought about how many of Chandler's stories and novels featured a house detective whose job it was to protect the premises, which could be either a hotel or an apartment building. House detectives used to be as common as crooks in L.A. Now security came in the form of the omniscient eye of a video camera and the unseen humans to whom the images were transmitted— when such humans actually existed.

One of Chandler's early stories, "I'll Be Waiting," is about a house detective named Tony who works at the Windemere Hotel, and a young woman, Miss Cressy—a name with a distinct echo of Cissy. Miss Cressy is staying at the Windemere for a while. Most of the action takes place in the lobby of the hotel—and the radio room that adjoins it—where Miss Cressy hangs out, listening to the radio until the wee hours of the morning. The lobby of the Bryson reminded me very much of the description of the Windemere's lobby in "I'll Be Waiting." It was of the same vintage, had the same feel, and I could almost imagine Miss Cressy lounging in one of the worn chairs and taunting Tony with lines like, "Got the eye on me, haven't you, flat foot? . . . What did I do wrong?"

Miss Cressy hasn't done anything wrong. Tony is simply attracted to her—like Cissy, she's a beautiful redhead with pale skin. He spies on her when he finds her sleeping in the radio room late at night. "He just watched her, his mouth a little open. There was a quiet fascination in his limpid eyes, as if he was looking at an altar. The girl slept on, motionless, in that curled-up looseness achieved by some women and all cats."

Miss Cressy lives in the tower apartment, and Tony studies her sleeping form as if looking at an altar. Tony and Miss Cressy end up spending hours in the radio room, listening to music together, and it wasn't hard to imagine that the dialogue in the story might have been taken from real life—I felt it, in any case, in certain lines. "Make me some of that Mozart," Miss Cressy says to Tony at one point, meaning turn the dial to the classical station. "It's too late," Tony sighs. "You can't get it now." At another point Miss Cressy says to Tony, "I wish you'd talk to that radio. It sounds like a pretzel being bent." And when the music finally ends, she says to him, "Make me a story. I'm bored."

Was this the way Cissy and Ray talked to each other? There is no way to know, but I felt that it wasn't far off the mark. You can hear the tone of Marlowe's wisecracking in Ray's letters. Cissy, who was reputed to be funny and witty, must have played along with Ray's humor and encouraged it (he credits her in his journals with coming up with similes for him, including the line "as rare as a fat postman"). Repartee, the capacity for witty conversation, is now for the most part a lost art, but someone like Chandler, who put a high value on wit, no doubt savored such conversations with his wife. I felt I could hear their voices in an exchange between Miss Cressy and Tony over Benny Goodman.

"You like Goodman?" Tony asked.

"This jitterbug music gives me the backdrop of a beer flat," the girl replied. "I like something with roses in it."

That's what Ray liked . . . music with roses in it, something romantic, the music, say, of Mozart, one of Chandler's favorite composers. "I think Mozart was the greatest man that ever lived," Tony says at one point, "and Toscanini is his prophet." Even Miss Cressy's outfit seems like something Cissy might have owned—lounging pajamas made of heavy ribbed silk and embroidered with black lotus buds.

There was one line in the story, however, that more than any other brought Cissy to mind. In an effort to frighten or caution Miss Cressy, Tony tells her that the woman who previously occupied the tower apartment where she is staying had jumped off the balcony one night, a suicide. But the news doesn't faze Miss Cressy, who replies coolly, "Redheads don't jump, Tony. They hang on—and wither."

Ray wrote that line in 1939, when he was fifty-one and Cissy was almost seventy. By then he knew that Cissy was older than she had claimed. He could see the future, and it was a future with an ailing, aging wife whose energy was already beginning to wither.

I left the Bryson and walked down Wilshire to Lafayette Park and turned south on Hoover until I came to Leeward and crossed to Magnolia Avenue. There were no magnolias on Magnolia. They seemed to have all been cut down. There was no double house either on the corner of Leeward and Magnolia where the Chandlers had once lived. It was gone, as gone as any charm the neighborhood might once have had. A little row of cheap stucco apartments had replaced it. The stucco had the sort of finish that reminded me of thick swirls of frosting on a cheap cake. Whoever lived there wasn't shy about hanging out their undies in public. They had filled an outside clothesline with massive white bras and big-sized ladies' cotton underpants. The garments wiggled in the breeze, less obscene than simply desultory, hanging there beneath the lowering skies. It was hard to imagine them ever drying in this weather.

I wondered what Cissy had done with her time while they lived here on Leeward, during the first year of their marriage. She never held a job while with Ray. Her interests seem to have been reading and music, but it's doubtful she had access to a piano at this time. After her divorce from Julian, Cissy had put most of her furniture in storage, perhaps thinking she and Ray would buy a

place and she would get her belongings out later, but for over twenty years they continued to rent furnished apartments as they moved from place to place, and the furniture stayed in storage. I supposed she had kept house, vacuuming and dusting while sometimes naked (I wondered, what was *that* about? I still didn't get it). Chandler later claimed she was a very good cook, something he was proud of, and certainly shopping and the preparation of meals took up a lot of her day. In other words, she made a home, which was just what Ray needed.

There was no question in my mind that sex was very much a part of their relationship in spite of their difference in age, or maybe in fact *because* of it. Chandler had little sexual experience, if any, himself. His coddled childhood, the absence of a father or any significant male figure in his early life, the years spent in an all-female household presided over by his grandmother—"my stupid and arrogant grandmother," as he put it—and his education at an all-boys school known for its strict moral code had, as John Houseman once said, left a "sexually devastating" mark on him. He once said he had never masturbated as a young man because he had been told that if you did that and then later you met the woman of your dreams you would be disappointed, and he did not want to be disappointed. This alone is a telling idea—imagining that coitus could end up being less pleasurable than so-called self-abuse. He also reported that the most disturbing thing about the months he spent studying in Paris was having to walk past all the prostitutes when he came home at night. These were dirty, nasty things—masturbation and prostitution—and one gets the feeling that in his mind they were commensurate with evil and may have kept him a virgin. It would fall to Cissy—the older, twice-married woman—to ease the stranglehold of repression.

How effectively she was able to do this of course no one knows, but there is the reference Ray once made to their letters as being "pretty hot" (and Cissy being "highly sexed"). Cissy kept a stagily erotic pink boudoir, filled with Hollywood-style French furniture and a pink ruffled bedspread, and she tried to emphasize her femininity and youthfulness by dressing in what we would now call age-inappropriate clothes. Did she enjoy sex with her young husband? Why not? Was he romantic with her? Absolutely. Very early on she gave him the nickname "Raymio." Throughout his life Ray was an intensely romantic man, and when it came to women he knew the importance of both the small and the large gesture in making them feel not only desired but valued.

Cissy was a very good dancer and so was Ray (he maintained a life-long love of ballroom dancing). In their early years together they went out dancing often. It's not hard to imagine them as making a very elegant couple on the dance floor. Ray's favorite dance was the waltz, nice and slow and very romantic, with lots of bodily contact. It was the era of the supper club, a now almost extinct establishment but then in its glory days. The supper club wedded together the idea of dining with dancing. Tables were placed around a dance floor, so the diners could see the dancers, and vice versa, and thus the evening could be passed in eating and drinking and dancing, all interspersed, in a romantic atmosphere where watching other people was part of the pleasure and entertainment. There was no shortage of such places in L.A. in the 1920s, the most famous of which was the Cocoanut Grove in the Ambassador Hotel, just a few blocks from Leeward Avenue where the Chandlers lived in the mid-1920s. The Cocoanut Grove was aptly named: guests entered through ornate Moroccan-style doors, embellished with gold leaf and glass etched with palm trees, and were met by the maître d', who escorted them down the wide plush grand staircase—perfect for making the dramatic entrances favored by actresses and actors—to their reserved tables. Overhead, soaring about the room, were coconut trees made of papier-mâché, salvaged from the set of Valentino's *The Sheik*. Stuffed monkeys hung from the palms, their amber eyes electrified and winking at the revelers. Above, on the fake blue sky, stars twinkled, and at one end of the room, a waterfall splashed against a lurid Hawaiian landscape. It was the sort of backdrop, stagy and ornate, against which the Chandlers, both of whom were highly clothes conscious and dressed for effect, would have made an attractive and dramatic couple.

. . .

Toward the end of his life Ray wrote a column for the *San Diego Tribune* on the subject of sex. He was filling in for his young friend Neil Morgan, a San Diego journalist who regularly wrote the column. It was a strange subject for Chandler to address in such a breezy format, and the piece he wrote is filled with intriguing revelations about his feelings on the subject.

He begins by stating that the column he is writing is going to be about sex, but advises his readers not to "scream yet—I may be able to handle it.

> After all, what ever sex is, would I be writing about it or would you be reading about it if we didn't have it? Roughly, as it has been explained to me confidentially, there is a slight biological difference between men and women. After thirty years of a perfect marriage, I suppose I should understand this—but somehow *I never thought about it in those terms.*

The italics are mine, but the statement is purely his, and it's an intriguing one. When I first read it, I thought, what does *that* mean? Obviously he's having one off on us, setting up the piece with humor, but he turns more serious suddenly and implies that he never really thought of his "almost perfect" marriage in terms of sex.

> If you love a woman as completely and forever, as I did, you somehow don't think of it in that way. You think only of the wonder and the glory; and when you watch your wife die by half-inches, you still think of the wonder and the glory—not at all of what they call sex.
>
> Sex to us Americans has become a thing we can't be honest about. We approach it as we approached liquor during the prohibition period. We seem to be out to prove something which doesn't have to be proved at all; it already exists. Sometimes it works, sometimes it doesn't. We don't even try to find out why, because we are too stupid to admit or understand

67

that the relations of the sexes are always very delicate even with the nicest sort of people.

Interestingly, he makes no reference to the fact that the first honest effort to understand sexual behavior in America had, in fact, already been made by Dr. Alfred Kinsey, who had recently published his seminal study of sexual behavior among American males. It's as if Chandler were unaware of this work, but we know that he wasn't. Helga Greene, his British literary agent and friend toward the end of his life, reported that Chandler used to read the Kinsey report accompanied by "chortles of laughter." In any case, he continues his essay by laying out his idea of marriage:

Marriage is a perpetual courtship. In mine, and this is perhaps too personal, I always felt that I had to win my wife every day as though we were meeting for the first time. Perhaps this was an eccentricity, even an arrogance on my part—but that's how it was and that was how we loved.

He ends the piece by saying,

You can make all sorts of jokes about sex, mostly lewd (I've made them myself), but at the bottom of his heart every decent man feels that his approach to the woman he loves is an approach to a shrine. If that feeling is lost, as it seems to have been lost (in this country at the moment) all of us are lost with it. The glory has departed. All that is left is to die in the mud—a pretty end to a great nation.

That was written in 1957, two years before Chandler's death. The whole piece seemed sort of cracked to me when I first read it. It felt as if it had been written, as it most likely was, by a man in his cups. Ray was drinking heavily during this period. On the other hand, I didn't doubt that he believed every word that he said. The question was, what did it mean?

I thought it meant that sex troubled and confused him, that it was problematic, even between the "nicest" people. It seemed to me that the sense of "glory and wonder" was more important to him than the sex, at least when it came to his wife. There was no use demeaning the goddess, especially as she grew older, by subjecting her to sex. (A mistress, yes, but not a wife.) Otherwise you just end up feeling "mired in the mud."

It reminded me of something else I had come across while going through Chandler's papers at UCLA, something he had written to James Sandoe, a librarian and reviewer of crime fiction with whom he had corresponded for over a dozen years without ever actually meeting him. To Sandoe he had written, "I find it impossible to respect a woman who lives with a man. She can sleep with him all she blame pleases and with whomever else she pleases and in whatever place she pleases, but the tawdry imitation of domesticity gets me down."

The tawdry imitation of domesticity. It wasn't sex that cheapened a woman. It was playing house when she wasn't married.

When Ray and Cissy arrived at 2863 Leeward Avenue, Ray had already been working for Dabney Oil Syndicate for several years. He had a good salary. A new Chrysler Roadster for his personal use and a Hupmobile for driving down to the oil fields in Signal Hill, near Long Beach. He had a beautiful and intelligent wife. He dressed in immaculately tailored clothes and had the manners of an English gentleman, with the accent to match. Cissy was soignee, a sophisticate with an enigmatic past. She even pronounced her new name "CHOND-lah," giving it a nice little upper-class tweak. Together they gave off a cultured and civilized air, admittedly somewhat at odds with their choice of modest dwellings. They must have seemed more than a little exotic to the midwestern transplants who surrounded them in the neighborhoods where they chose to live—but that would only have strengthened their sense of bonding, the us-against-the-world feeling that kept them close. It also heightened the role of their rituals—the regular afternoon tea that would later become a feature of their life and the hours they spent together every evening listening to the *Gas Company Evening Concert* of classical music. Chandler would always take pride in Cissy's ability to play the piano, even though it must have been difficult for her to stay in practice during their peripatetic years, having no easy access to her instrument. One senses that for him it was the mark of a cultured woman and an indication of impeccable taste that Cissy was so talented, and the music they loved to listen to would provide a lifelong bond. After she died, he would gravitate to women who could also play the piano.

From the early 1920s on through the early '30s, Chandler worked downtown in the Bank of Italy building on the corner of Seventh and Olive Streets, where Dabney Oil had its offices. I wanted to see that building, or whatever, if anything, was left of it, so I walked up to Wilshire Boulevard and waited for the bus. There seemed no point in walking all the way back to my apartment just to get my car. Besides, I liked taking buses in L.A. Most people in my immediate circle of friends preferred to stick to their automobiles— those "baroque extensions of the ego," as Tom Wolfe once called them. I often took the bus to the main library downtown, where I liked to work. It gave me the feeling, even temporarily, that I was actually a part of a real city. What was missing in L.A., as James Cain once pointed out, with its emphasis on cars and speed and movement, was the "perpetual invitation to explore, to linger, and enjoy the beckoning jumble of a city like Paris or New York." For me, taking a bus was like accepting that invitation.

The fog had come after the rain, and as I stood on Wilshire Boulevard, waiting for the bus, I felt a rippling vapor moving across the landscape. The mist seemed to become clotted in the trees and clung to the crowns of palms, obscuring their fronds so that they looked like gigantic crenulated stumps sticking up in the air. Mornings were composed of a dusty gray light, diffused and yet bright, the sun like a pale yellow lightbulb shining through the steam of a shower. It was not a gloomy light but still rather unsettling, the way the mist clung to everything. It felt damp and gruellike, as if meant to dissipate at any moment, revealing the old familiar contours of L.A. But instead the fog hung around, glowing with a faintly golden aura, as if lit by some grave solar event.

The bus appeared suddenly out of the fog. I got on and paid my money and began looking for a seat. A homeless man was sprawled across one of the long bench seats that face each other at the front of the bus, the place where I usually sat. He was lying on his side, taking up the whole seat, his head propped up on his hand and holding forth loudly, talking to another man who sat nearby facing forward. I sat next to this man and began listening to their conversation.

"Say you're in a store, you know, just an ordinary convenience store," the homeless man said, "and the owner thinks you're stealing something and he chases you outside and he threatens you and says he's going to call the police if you ever come back. And say you go back and the police come and you haven't done anything but the owner makes them think you have. And then the cops take you outside and push you around. Is that right? I mean, is that right?"

"That is not right," the man next to me said, "but, you know, there are assholes everywhere. What are you going to do?"

"Say you go to another store," the homeless man said, "and the owner of that store says you can't come in or he'll call the cops and instead he just throws you out. What do you do about that?"

"You don't do nothin'. Because there's nothin' you can do. You hope somebody treats him that way someday. He'll get his, don't worry. It always happens that way."

"Say you're sleeping outside a building, just curled up against a wall somewhere. You know, not hurting anybody, not doing anything, just sleeping on the ground, trying to get some rest. And a security guard comes and wakes you up and tells you to leave because you're on private property, and then he sprays you with Mace. And say he calls the cops and when the cops come they blame you because the security guard tells them that you threw something at him and that's why he had to spray you with Mace. I mean, is that right? Is that right?"

"It ain't right, but he probably has the law on his side because you were on private property."

"But say you were leaving. Say you were already leaving the property when he hit you with the Mace. Is that right?"

"That is not right, but I would say there is nothing you can do. It's not like the cops are out there to protect you. They don't care about *you*. They're there to protect property. Everybody knows that property in this society is more important than people."

The conversation went on, with the homeless man providing the hypotheticals, and the man who sat next to me—who was certainly disheveled and a bit odd but probably not homeless himself—responding to him very thoughtfully and carefully. I was struck by the reasonable way they proceeded to discuss what were really all the unreasonable situations the homeless man had found himself in. And in each story, the police seemed to play a role, never, of course, taking the part of the homeless man. Were his stories true, or fabricated, or like most stories a bit of both? For some reason I thought of the title of an old book I had come across in the library, *Our Lawless Police*, written in 1931 by a man named Ernest Hopkins, an attempt to examine why police lawlessness was so prevalent in L.A., and with it a tradition of brutality. The criminology of violence, the denial of individual rights, and the infliction of cruel punishments as well as overtly racist police behavior had a long history in this city. And of course this is what Marlowe understood—that the little man could never count on the institutions of society to protect him—and it was this realm in which he operated as a private investigator, in that borderland, that liminal space between the law and the needy.

There is about Marlowe himself a little of the spirit of the man who wins and yet never really wins, because the forces he opposes never really go away. He's a moralist who finds it difficult to conceal his contempt for the diseased world in which he must live. This was a little like the homeless man. He, too, seemed to be not so much contemptuous but rather astonished by the barrage of discrimination and ill-treatment he had to continually suffer.

By the time I reached my stop downtown, their talk had turned to dogs, how you could tell which ones you could trust and which ones you couldn't. "Rottweilers are the worst, man," the homeless man said. "Never trust a rottweiler."

Visitors to L.A. are often surprised to learn that the city even has a downtown. Tourists go to Disneyland or Universal Studios; they head for Santa Monica and the beaches; they stop in Beverly Hills, check out Rodeo Drive, sign up for a bus tour of the stars' homes, or take a walk along Hollywood Boulevard and visit Grauman's Chinese Theatre or maybe nip into a naughty underwear store. For years the downtown district of Los Angeles has been in decline, ignored by tourists and locals alike. The big department stores closed in the '70s and '80s and relocated to malls in other parts of the city, then more businesses left, and soon block after block of buildings were empty. Big buildings. Old buildings. Sometimes very beautiful buildings. All abandoned, left to molder and decay, to collect grime and graffiti. Often in the windows of these abandoned buildings one could see signs advertising the availability of the premises as locations for filming movies or television series.

Even as early as the '30s and '40s people (or at least affluent white people) were deserting the downtown core for more desirable locations. The abandonment of the city center had begun in Chandler's time. The grand old houses on Bunker Hill had become a slum, neglected and despised, an area for derelicts and bums who watched as the neighborhood slid further and further downhill until a plan for redevelopment was hatched, and the great mansions and rooming houses and Victorian apartment buildings were completely razed, making room for the modern steel and glass office buildings that replaced them, erasing all sense of the city's early history. By the 1980s, many of the great movie palaces had closed or been turned into indoor flea markets, and some of the downtown areas had become so Latino that to walk down

Broadway, for instance, felt more like walking down a main thoroughfare in Mexico City than one in L.A.

But recently downtown had begun experiencing a renaissance. It had become cool. It wasn't only the artists now, those urban pioneers who are always willing to go in search of cheap rents and loft space, who were interested in the area. Developers had begun buying up the old buildings, remodeling them, and turning them into lofts and condominiums. For years, downtown had the reputation as a tough place, especially at night when the workers went home to other parts of the city, leaving the streets to the wanderers, the dispossessed, and the homeless—in other words, those who had no choice but to deal with the grime and the crime and the dark. Now it was different. People were beginning to move downtown to live in these newly refurbished buildings—couples whose children were grown and who wanted a different life in a "new" urban world; workers who wished to live closer to their jobs; and the young and hip who liked the coolness of it all. It wasn't happening fast, this transformation of downtown, but it

was definitely happening. And for one who had always liked exploring the city and been intrigued by an older and grittier L.A., it was something I liked to see. A city coming back to life.

The Bank of Italy building, at 649 South Olive Street, where Chandler had worked in the offices of Dabney Oil Syndicate, from 1923 until 1932, was still there. Closed up. Abandoned. Showing signs of age and neglect. But still there. It was a handsome building, too. Ten stories, a neoclassical rusticated base made of granite block and tan brick, with eight fluted columns across the front, rising up three floors—monumental and beautiful columns capped with ornate crowns. A plaque on the corner informed me that the building had been erected in 1923—the year before Ray and Cissy were married. It was a brand-new building when Dabney moved its offices to the premises and Ray came here to work.

I stood on Seventh Street, where the entrance to the building was located, and stared at the three sets of cast bronze double doors that once led to the lobby. The doors were beautifully made, cast in a pattern of floral rosettes each set within a square. They were surrounded by an ornate stucco frieze that showed the figures on U.S. coins—Lincoln's head from the Lincoln penny, the buffalo and Indian head that had once adorned the nickel, George Washington, the Statue of Liberty, etc.—all enfolded in a delicate pattern of scrolls and fleur-de-lis and forming an attractive border. Above each set of doors was a cream-and-brown marble lintel capped by a brass bald eagle meant to hold a flag, and across the front of the building, in large letters, was written GIANNINI PLACE. The building had somehow escaped vandalism. The beautiful doors and the friezes of coins had not been defaced by graffiti. They were worn and neglected and locked against the world, these doors that Raymond Chandler had passed through every working day for the nine years he spent here, but they had not been damaged.

I peered through a filthy ground-floor window into the abandoned lobby, but there was nothing to see except a vast and empty space. The ceiling seemed to rise to a vertiginous height, and floating there, in beams of light, a profusion of dust motes glittered like gold dust. The motes were illuminated by a broad square beam—light as hard-edged as a golden board, and yet thin and insubstantial, a board of nothingness, without true form or weight. The longer I stared upward at the high ceiling and the beam of light, with my head tipped painfully back, the more I felt as if the old lobby were growing taller and larger, and I began to feel dizzy and turned away.

Across the street, just opposite the Bank of Italy, a large old brick building with graceful lines and rounded corners was being remodeled. Workers were installing attractive new windows. It gave me hope that the Bank of Italy building, too, might one day be reclaimed.

It's been said that the story of the development of L.A. is the story of three things—oil, real estate, and the movies. By working in the oil business and the movies, and by changing residences so often, Chandler would become an expert on all three.

When he began working at the Bank of Italy building, L.A. was billed as "the newest city in the world." Ray would have looked down from his window at what one early arrival, Carey McWilliams, called "the aimless, restless movement of the armies of people with nothing to do who were going nowhere in particular." Because L.A. drew so many retired people and invalids from the very beginning—people who didn't necessarily have to work—it has always been marked by a certain languorousness, an idleness in the population—*armies of people with nothing to do, going nowhere in particular.*

Hundreds of thousands of people moved to L.A. in the 1920s, the largest internal migration in the history of the country and the first migration of the automobile age, made possible by the new all-weather highways that had begun to span America. What the gold rush had been to northern California, the real estate oil motion picture boom was to Southern California—a bonanza affair, with millions of dollars pouring into L.A., undermining the social structure of the community, warping and twisting its sensibilities. L.A. was full of bizarre attractions, like the bird recital at the California School of Artistic Whistling, or the animal show at the Gay Lion's Farm Ranch, which featured Mrs. Gay, bedecked in a fur stole, stretched underneath a lion who straddled her.

The movie business attracted the odd and freakish types—dwarfs and pygmies, one-eyed sailors, show people, misfits and pimps, gamblers and con men and racketeers, bunko artists and wannabes of all types, including hundreds of handsome young men and beautiful women who imagined themselves making their debuts on the big screen. It was a great melting pot of miscreants and millionaires, a place of tremendous longing and vulnerability, and it's not surprising that the 1920s was a decade of major scams and scandals. Ray saw all this firsthand, and in time, this sense of exquisite corruption and unbridled excess would find its way into his fiction. *Noir*, though the word had not yet been coined, was really born in the twenties as the flip side of the dream, the fantasy of the promised Eden, the underside of the nightmare, the funhouse mirror reflecting the internal corruption.

By the midtwenties, there were more than four hundred oil wells producing 700,000 barrels a day in the Los Angeles Basin. Many of these oil wells were in residential areas. There were oil

wells in people's backyards, derricks in their gardens and lining ordinary streets, towering over neighborhoods and pumping crude night and day, like the derricks that can be seen from Sternwood mansion in *The Big Sleep*.

> The Sternwoods, having moved up the hills, could no longer smell the stale sump of the oil, but they could still look out of their windows and see what had made them rich. If they wanted to. I don't suppose they wanted to.

The market for oil was enormous thanks to a rapidly escalating automobile industry (Henry Ford alone sold 15 million cars in America between 1907 and 1926). The brand-new busy world had arrived. Los Angeles was rich with oil: two of L.A.'s fields were producing 20 percent of the world's supply. And Raymond Chandler was at the center of the action. He wrote later,

> I was an executive in the oil business once, a director of eight companies and a president of three, although actually I was simply an overpaid employé. They were small companies, but very rich. I had the best office staff in Los Angeles and I paid them higher salaries than they could have gotten anywhere else, and they knew it. My office door was never closed, everyone called me by my Christian name, and there was never any dissension, because I made it my business to make sure there was no cause for it. Once in a while, not often, I had to fire someone—not someone I had picked myself, but someone who had been imposed on me by the big man—and that I hated terribly, because one never knows what hardship it may mean to the individual. I had a talent for picking out the capabilities of people.

The big man Chandler refers to, the man who founded the company and presided over it, was Joseph Dabney, a friend of Warren Lloyd's, though eventually the Lloyds would have a falling-out with Dabney and take him to court for having cheated them out of money; Chandler would testify against his former employer on behalf of the Lloyds. Later Chandler would say that he had wasted ten years of his life working as the factotum of a corrupt millionaire, but at the time he was employed by Dabney, he seems to have taken some pleasure, or at least pride, in his job.

I noticed that near the Bank of Italy stood Clifton's Cafeteria, once an institution in L.A. I walked down Seventh Street and stood in front of the ornate metal grillwork covering the front of the old café, which, until it closed a few years back, was one of the oldest restaurants in the city. The building was now empty, but the big sign was still there, painted on the side of the brick building:

Clifton's Silver Spoon
CAFETERIA · SOUPEASY · PASTRY SHOP
Best in the West
For more than half a century

Clifton's had been opened in 1931 by Clifford Clinton, a former missionary in China who operated his cafeteria—one of the first of its kind—on a principle of Christian charity. Its slogans were "Pay what you wish" and "Dine free unless delighted." (Later Clinton would become a reformer and take on a corrupt city hall and police department and be harassed and denigrated for his efforts.) Ray must have eaten lunch at Clifton's Cafeteria when it first opened, since it was close to his office, even though by and large the experience of eating out in restaurants was not one he cherished. Not even a drink or two, he said, could prepare one for the substandard food. Highbrow or low, it didn't matter: American food was the problem. "We consider the better than average American eatery not fit to eat in," Chandler complained once to a friend in a letter. And the less than average—the drive-ins and drugstore counters and hot dog and hamburger stands that were springing up all over L.A., dispensing what would become that ubiquitous feature of the American dining experience, *fast* food—left him even colder.

What I had come to realize in the process of reading about L.A. during its formative years was how the idea of fast food not only sprang up here but took on pervasive cultural connotations. This was in part due to the idleness and loneliness of the population, and the creation of "state societies" meant to counteract that loneliness.

The notion of the state societies was born in the mind of a man named Col. C. H. Haskins, who realized that the transplants from the Midwest who arrived in California in the first decades of the century suffered from intense feelings of alienation and dislocation. What they needed was a means of connecting with people from "home." And so societies were formed by state—the Iowa State Society, the Kansas State Society, the Colorado State Society, etc.—in order to draw people from a certain state together for picnics or meals of one sort or another. The societies soon began meeting in new low-cost cafeterias, like Clifton's. It was loneliness—that sense of deep alienation from one's true home and community—that drove people to begin to eat out en masse.

What Chandler understood, and what he wrote about so well in his novels, was the fact that a new kind of American loneliness was born in L.A., in people who found themselves marooned in paradise, lonely amidst abundance and incredible wealth, lonely in a seemingly incurable fashion, lonely in spite of the crowds and opportunities, because suddenly they had been cut off from their past, from all that was familiar and had given meaning and shape to their lives, a widespread feeling that took hold in large numbers of people. This was the loneliness Marlowe would come to embody—a haunting sense of detachment from any sense of origin, family, or roots. There was no cure for this new brand of loneliness—the aching, really terrible loneliness apparent on the faces of people in the streets and parks, the boardinghouses and hotels, and the cafeterias where the "lonely societies" met. These clubs were formed to ease that longing for home, a home that was elsewhere. In cafeterias like Clifton's, fast food, cheap food, food you selected yourself and put on a tray and pushed along a metal railing, became inextricably wed not to mere nourishment but to the possibility of escaping a haunting emptiness for a while. The popularity of the cafeteria in L.A. was primarily due to the loneliness of the people. It was a friendlier type of eating place than a normal restaurant. And then there was the possibility of meeting someone—anyone, someone as lonely as you were—in the ultra-plebeian atmosphere of a cafeteria.

This was the true lure of fast food, and perhaps it helps explain why it has assumed such an important place in American culture. Fast food is about estrangement and existential ennui, about loneliness, and boredom, and absence, and an arresting of traditional patterns of family life and social context. Who cares if the meal is inferior? If it gets you out in the world. If it gives you something to do. And the chance of meeting other people. Chandler seemed to have understood this very early on, how the empty and manic nature of our eating habits was being formed by the increasing speed with which life was lived, and was fueled by a restless and lonely populace who could afford to eat out. He also saw how the urge for quick and easy profits drove it all. Here is Marlowe, in a passage from *The Little Sister:*

I ate dinner at a place near Thousand Oaks. Bad but quick. Feed 'em and throw 'em out. Lots of business. We can't bother with you sitting over your second cup of coffee, mister. You're using money space. See those people over there behind the rope? They want to eat. Anyway they think they have to. God knows why they want to eat here. They could do better out of a can. They're just restless. Like you. They have to get the car out and go somewhere. Sucker-bait for the racketeers that have taken over the restaurants.

They're restless, like you. They have to get the car out and go somewhere.

Ray saw the restlessness and boredom firsthand. He saw the Iowans with their fat pig buttons and hog-and-hominy slogans gathering here at Clifton's, right near his office. And most of all, he saw the loneliness that brought them all together and how that loneliness was destined to become part of our new rootless society, how it would not simply go away, no matter how affluent our society became. The Big Lie—the cardinal deception of American civilization—was that prosperity and consumption brought personal contentment and deliverance from the past. Chandler came to understand that money and privilege and possessions were traps, and that the past was, in fact, inescapable.

It had begun to rain again, a light, precautionary rain, like a mist blowing off falling water. I caught the westbound bus on Wilshire Boulevard and headed home. The bus was crowded for a Saturday afternoon. Chinese, Japanese, Latino, African American, Filipino—and all combinations of the above—surrounded me. All of us transplants to this region, like the trees and the flowers. L.A. has been called The Great Tent—land of all faiths and all faults. And all races as well. One of the most polyglot, racially mixed cities in the world.

I thought about the first residents of this land, the only true natives—the Serrano, Luiseño and Gabrielino, the Juaneno and Cahuilla and Yanan peoples, none of whom referred to themselves by these names but were assigned them according to the Franciscan missions that had absorbed them, and almost none of whom made it into the twentieth century.

Los Angeles had sprung up on the site of what had once been the Indian village of Yang-na.

Among the Southern California Indians, warfare had been virtually unknown, and slavery was not practiced. The Native religion had no evil spirits until the idea of the devil was introduced by the Catholic padres. When the Spaniards came and established the missions, the Indians had been forced to accept Christianity. They were herded into well-guarded mission compounds. They became slaves. Women were raped, and the native population was soon ravaged by venereal disease, which infected even the newborn children, three-fourths of whom died within their first two years. The Indian women began aborting their babies rather than carrying them to full term, a practice that enraged the priests. Any woman who miscarried was punished by having her head shaved. Then she was flogged for fifteen days, placed in iron manacles for three months, and required to appear every Sunday in church and stand through the service holding a hideously painted wooden child in her arms. The Indian population of Southern California was decimated by the priests and their mission system. Many tribes became extinct. What remained were only the words of their languages, words that became attached to the land as place-names: Azusa, Cahuenga, Cucamonga, Jurupa, Lompoc, Ojai, Yucaipa—and yes, Malibu, home of the stars.

I got off the bus at the corner of Wilshire and Alvarado, at the edge of MacArthur Park. A huge crowd had gathered in the park, and I thought I'd find out why. The pathway through the park was lined with flags and banners, announcing a meeting of Los Grupos de Sicoterapia de la Linea del Dr. Ayala. Most of the banners were in Spanish, but I came across one in English: "The Psychotherapy Groups of Dr. Ayala is a community of men, women, and adolescents, pursuing the restructuralization of personality, stopping and preventing the ingestion of alcohol and drugs, seeking to work with the mind, trying to establish better basis for the future of humankind, therefore reach a true community in exercise of nature with lofty interpersonal relations. Thanks, Dr. Ayala!"

Food tables had been set up and there was the smell of barbecue on the air. The crowd was largely composed of men of all ages who stood about on the grass, untroubled by the light rain—hundreds of men, young and old. A great tent had been set up near a stage. Suddenly the music began, lively horns and drums, the kind of music that produces excitement, and the men began streaming toward the stage, whipped up by the sound of the music. Beneath the big tent, men stood and waved their arms in the air, they lifted their hands and clapped and called out, "Dr. Ayala! Dr. Ayala," their voices rising into one concerted chant: *Dr. Ayala! Dr. Ayala!* It was part religious revival, part theater, part rock-concert frenzy, complete with stern-looking black-shirted guards with cell phones who were patrolling the perimeter of the gathering and who eyed me suspiciously because I did not have the white tag hanging around my neck, identifying me as a member of Los Grupos del Dr. Ayala. And then Dr. Ayala appeared, a small, elderly man who bore a slight resemblance to Gandhi. He was brown-skinned and balding and dressed in a light suit: he walked beneath a white canopy that was held by his assistants and which protected him from the rain, and slowly, as if part of a royal procession, he made his way among his admirers, and the shouts and the clapping grew louder and louder. The crowd erupted at the sight of their leader making his way into their midst, and there was more whistling and shouting and clapping and calls of "Dr. Ayala! Dr. Ayala. Gracias, Dr. Ayala! Gracias, Dr. Ayala!"

I was transfixed by the spectacle, by the mass frenzy, the adulation, the sight of so many men, all Latino, and all, apparently, committed to stopping drugs and alcohol and seeking to work with the mind, "restructuralizing" their personality in order to establish better relationships and a better future world. And why not? This was L.A. This was the place to make your life over, to start again, to find salvation, if not through Dr. Ayala, through someone else.

There had never been a shortage in L.A. of people ready to save your soul, to cure your ills, redeem your mind, and generally change your sorry ways. The strange thing was, the men around me looked vigorous and healthy. They looked sharp. They looked clear and strong, standing in the middle of MacArthur Park, L.A.'s drug wonderland.

As I turned to leave, a rather dour-looking woman stopped me; she did not have Dr. Ayala's tag around her neck. She was Mexican and middle-aged and rather poorly dressed and she held the hand of a small shy girl, perhaps her daughter. They had no umbrella to protect them from the rain, only a bible covered in a plastic wrapping, which the woman clutched to her breast. She looked at me very seriously and said, "Excuse me, but I am from the Baptist Church and I want to ask you, if you were to die today, are you sure you would go to heaven?"

I stared at her. I didn't know what to say. I wanted to laugh. I wanted to say, *Hell no.* I wanted to tell her I didn't discuss religion with total strangers. But mostly I just wanted to get away from her.

Instead I mumbled, "Uh, no," feeling oddly embarrassed (or was it disconcerted?) by her question.

"You will *not* go to heaven?"

"I doubt it," I said, and then I laughed, for no real reason, and turned away from her and left her standing there, still holding the hand of her small silent daughter, clutching the bible covered in plastic.

She stared after me as I walked away, shaking her head sadly. By then the rain had begun to come down hard again, the big fat drops bouncing off the pavement like lively little grasshoppers jumping everywhere.

Four

I t haunted me that all Cissy's letters had been burned, and with them the possibility of ever hearing her voice.

As far as I knew, only one thing written in her own hand had survived—a comment she had made in one of Ray's notebooks—and as revealing, as intriguing as this one comment was, it amounted to no more than a passing whisper.

Why had he burned their letters to each other? What was in them he didn't want anyone to see? For many years he had kept her letters tied in a packet with a green ribbon, a lover's gesture if there ever was one, and after she passed away, he took solace in rereading her words: he wrote in a poem that "at least her letters will not die." And yet he had them burned at a trash dump.

Among those letters he destroyed were some written to each other in the late 1920s, the period when their marriage endured its most severe test. During this time they had briefly separated, and it would have been natural for them to write to each other. It was the last time in their lives they would ever spend any time apart—perhaps also the last time they felt the need to write any letters. What might those letters have revealed about Cissy's state of mind and her capacity to endure such an erratic period in Ray's life, the pain she must certainly have suffered, or his own remorse for his bad behavior? There was no way of knowing.

Around this time I made one of those entirely chance discoveries that sometimes occur and which seemed to explain something that had baffled me—namely why Cissy had done her housework naked. In passing, an architect friend had mentioned a book that had just been published on a house in Palm Springs, designed by Richard Neutra and commissioned by a certain Mrs. Miller who asked Neutra to devise a system of blinds for the windows because she often did her housework naked. She was a devotee of a certain kind of exercise system developed by a woman named Bess Mensendieck in the early twentieth century.

Mensendieck was an expatriate American who in the late 1800s went to Paris to study sculpture but instead became alarmed at the poor posture of the live models used in her art classes and decided to study anatomy instead, becoming one of the first accredited female physicians in Europe. She did research into kinesiology and musculature, and eventually created a system whose aim it was to develop, through training in certain exercises, an aesthetic understanding of the human figure and improve the posture of humankind.

The Mensendieck System of Functional Exercises focused on everyday movements, such as walking, sitting, dressing, and undressing—and also routine household work like ironing and vacuuming and dusting. She encouraged women to turn these ordinary household chores into beneficial body-toning and posture-improving exercises. Ironing, for instance, could be done in such a way as to give the arms and upper body a workout. Ditto vacuuming for the legs and buttocks. A series of drawings demonstrated just how to get maximum benefit from such mundane tasks and also improve posture. These exercises could be performed naked, presumably to allow freedom of movement and increase body consciousness. According to Mensendieck, even putting on and taking off a fur coat provided an opportunity for a woman to exercise and encourage proper body alignment.

The Mensendieck method became popular in Europe, especially Germany, where, perhaps not surprisingly, it was embraced by the Weimar Republic. Her first book, *It's Up to You*, was published in Germany. It included partially nude photographs of women in various postures, engaged in ordinary tasks. She returned to the United States in 1905 with the hope of publishing

It's Up to You in an American edition, but she could find no publisher. The Comstock Laws prescribed a year in jail and a $1,000 fine for books containing "unclothed bodies," so she returned to Europe, where her books became very popular. Eventually, however, *It's Up to You* was published in America and her methods for achieving good posture and body toning attracted a sizable following, especially on the West Coast, where such fads had wide appeal.

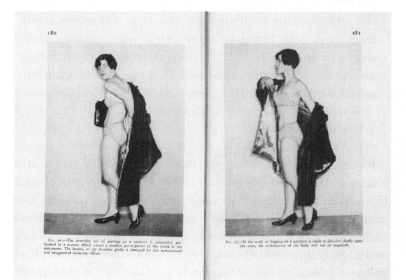

ILL. 76.—The everyday act of putting on a garment is frequently performed in a manner which causes a needless participation of the trunk in the movement. The beauty of the shoulder girdle is damaged by this unwarranted and exaggerated muscular effort.

ILL. 77.—If the work of slipping on a garment is made to devolve chiefly upon the arms, the architecture of the body will not be impaired.

It seemed very likely to me that Cissy had heard of the Mensendieck method, perhaps while she still lived in New York, and become a devotee. In many ways she was a perfect candidate for the method: she was not an inhibited person and had no problem being naked, having already become accustomed to posing nude for male artists. Nudity—especially the use of nude photographs as a blackmail device—would come to play an important role in Chandler's novels, and I think Cissy's history of posing nude, and the nude photographs of her that Ray owned, as well as her early drug use, all found their way into the plots of his fiction, most notably in the character of Carmen Sternwood, the drug-addled nymphomaniac in *The Big Sleep.* Cissy's ability to be naked in a very natural way also figured into other stories, as in this scene between Marlowe and Miss Vermilyea from *Playback:*

> I took hold of her and she came into my arms without a word . . . I put her down on the bed. I peeled her skirt up until I could see the white thighs above her long beautiful nylon-clad legs . . . I went to the door and switched the light off in the room. There was still a glow from the hall. When I turned she was standing by the bed as naked as Aphrodite, fresh from the Aegean. She stood there proudly and without either shame or enticement . . . she pulled the bedcovers back and lay on the bed shamelessly nude. She was just a beautiful naked woman completely unashamed of being what she was.
>
> "Satisfied with my legs?" she asked.
>
> I didn't answer.

It's interesting that there are three references to the idea of shame in this passage—or more correctly, shamelessness, as if this was something worth not just noting but emphasizing. Like Anne Riordan in *Farewell, My Lovely,* a woman Marlowe almost makes love to, Cissy was an uninhibited redhead with a beautiful body. She had presented herself to Ray as a whole woman, physically, emotionally, and intellectually alive and full of that quality he prized above all others—namely vitality—and yet as grateful as he was to have found her, and as much as he continued to court her in order to keep her, cracks began to appear in their marriage sometime in the mid-1920s, just a few years after their wedding.

The reasons for this varied, but Ray's increased drinking was no doubt a major cause of the problem. He'd also begun to suspect that Cissy was much older than she had claimed, a realization brought on in part by the fact that her health began to slowly deteriorate. She was often ill, suffering from bronchitis and pneumonia (no doubt she had been a lifelong smoker), and he began going out in the evening without her. He also began drinking heavily and experiencing his first blackouts—periods during

which he did things and went places he could later remember
nothing about. He had befriended a group of his coworkers from
Dabney Oil, men more or less his own age who were all starting
families with their young wives—Milton Philleo and Orville Evans
and Louis Knight—with whom Ray often formed a tennis four-
some for weekend games. He had a great fondness for sports,
especially tennis, swimming, and diving. He was in his physical
prime; Cissy was not and appears to have taken no exercise at
all, outside her Mensendieck-influenced housework. The tennis
games with his coworkers became weekend rituals for Ray, but
they did not include Cissy, who more and more stayed home and
shunned any socializing, often pleading illness. Certain people
who knew her felt that she did this in order to get her husband's
increasingly waning attention as well as his sympathy, and for a
while it seems to have worked. But increasingly, he began to drift
away.

As his drinking worsened, Ray's behavior became more erratic,
and soon he was disappearing for days at a time without telling
anyone where he was. When he did show up for a tennis game and
the cocktails that always followed (or sometimes preceded) the
games, he could become suddenly depressed and his behavior
might turn offensive. He began alienating his friends, and even
the normally tolerant Milton Philleo, who often accompanied him
on his drinking binges, grew tired of his behavior, particularly
after an offensive incident, reported by Chandler biographer
Frank McShane, in which Ray arrived at the Philleo house to pick
up Milton for a game of tennis, and Milton told him his wife was ill
in bed and he wanted to stay home with her. Not willing to accept
this situation, Ray, who had no doubt been drinking, went into the
bedroom and tried to pull Mrs. Philleo out of bed. Enraged by his
friend's behavior, Philleo ordered Chandler to leave the house, but
when he didn't hear the sound of the front door opening and closing he went to the living room, only to find Ray standing with a
gun pointed at his head. He had mistaken a closet for the front
door and discovered a pistol. Philleo ordered Ray to put the gun
down and leave, which he did without any argument.

It would not be the only time during this period in his life when Ray would threaten suicide. He was unhappy with the state of his life and subject to wild feelings of despair. Alcohol played a big part in his mood swings. But something else was at work as well. He often found himself now in the company of the young wives of his friends and associates, and he must have realized that he was missing the quality of parity in his marriage and the youthful love that they were enjoying.

Did he have a feeling of being cheated, duped when Cissy had lied to him about how old she was, and he now understood he had been deceived? This would not be a happy recognition—in fact, it would have been something of a shock—but that recognition would also have forced him to begin to recognize something about himself. He had married a woman almost his mother's age, yet he had only himself to blame for being so credulous, and he must have realized with equal force that in some way he wanted to be deceived. Whatever it was that allowed him to be duped, he was still enough under its spell (which was Cissy's spell, the aura of the "irresistible" older woman) to stay with his marriage, even as he began to chafe against it. But he couldn't fool himself any longer. He understood she was older—how much? He must have wondered, but I don't think he knew. In effect he was caught in a contest between two human impulses—urges that characterize so many human situations—what we struggle against or what we accept, and at the heart of what he must have discovered about himself during this period in the early years of their marriage was this truth, that he could not see his predicament simply as a conflict of the willing and unwilling but one of deception (hers) and volition (his). This understanding would play itself out in his fiction in extremely complex ways and cause him to create a hero who was effectively beyond the reach of women yet constantly under their spell.

Ray knew that he and Cissy would never have children, and perhaps that idea didn't greatly trouble him. ("I love to hear the patter of little feet," he once said, "running away from me.") Still the fact that his friends and colleagues were starting families could only have pointed up Cissy's more advanced age, a topic about which he'd grown increasingly sensitive. Perhaps it was inevitable their lives began to diverge, with Chandler spending more time away from home, either at work or on evenings out with his friends, as well as the weekends devoted to college football games and tennis. He even took flying lessons for a while. He took pride in his athleticism, and in Southern California, where both the cult

of the body and the cult of the outdoors were being constantly promoted, it was easy to nurture these interests and find in them a source of pleasure. Unfortunately, it was a world that didn't, and perhaps couldn't, include Cissy.

People began shedding both clothes and customs as soon as they arrived in Southern California. The cult of the body, for which L.A. is justly famous, snubs tradition, formality, and dignity—all elements of the society Chandler had left behind in London. Sunbathing, nudity, bare heads, open-necked shirts, the general casualness of attire were all encouraged by the sunny climate. Photographs of Chandler from the early 1920s show him at the beach, lying on a blanket on his side with his upper body propped up against a beach chair. He wears what looks like a woolen bathing costume—trunks and a long, sleeveless tunic—and he's smiling for the camera. He appears not only fit and trim but very happy there on the sand, with a wooden beach house in the distance.

Another early photograph shows him outdoors in a park somewhere, sitting on the grass with his mother. She looks at the camera rather sternly and is wrapped up in a dark coat with a hat pulled down over her forehead, even though the sun is out and shining full force. Ray, who is hatless and dressed in a suit and tie, reclines on his side, smoking a pipe, with his back turned toward his mother.

The picture of him on the beach is a straightforward shot of a man who appears happy and relaxed, enjoying the sun and surf. The picture in the park with his mother has a very different feel to it. For one thing, mother and son are both overdressed for the casual setting, lending the scene a certain stiffness, and there is also in the attitude and position of their bodies a sense of boredom with, or indifference to, each other.

Aside from these pictures of Ray in the 1920s, there are two oth-

ers from this period that fascinate me. I've studied them many times, searching for clues as to Ray's state of mind during this time. One shows him and his colleagues from Dabney Oil—three dozen or so people—who stand outdoors, against a backdrop of the Dabney Oil fields at Signal Hill. They are lined up in front of tin shacks and tall oil derricks, and the women wear corsages or hold sprays of flowers, as if the occasion for the photograph is a celebration of something. Chandler, on the far left, is in the back row along with other men, all of whom wear suits and ties, and the women are lined up in the front row. Joseph Dabney, a short, portly gray-haired man, stands front row center, flanked by young women. There are altogether about a dozen women in the photo, secretaries or office workers. Which one of these women, I wondered, might be the secretary from the office, never named, with whom Chandler had an affair? Is it the girl in the fur-trimmed coat, clutching the white gloves, looking shyly at the camera? Or the one with the fetching hat with the jewel on the brim? The girl in the long necklace who looks a little coy—or perhaps the one next to her in the light dress and open coat who squints against the sun? Maybe it's the young woman standing directly in front of Ray, with the pretty smiling face and the choker of pearls who has the most winningly open look of anyone in the picture. She certainly seems a possible candidate: there's something about her proximity to Ray—and why wouldn't the lovers have opted to stand close to each other? In any case, she's pretty. She's fresh-looking. And she's young. Very like, in other words, the actual person with whom Ray did begin to disappear for weekend trysts. And yet the most likely candidate, I came to believe, is a woman who worked in accounting with him—Emily T. Moore, who stands fifth from the left in the first row, her body slightly eclipsed by the women on either side of her. The evidence for this deduction is admittedly flimsy, but on one copy of this photograph Ray wrote the names of every person portrayed, and in every case the women are simply named with a first and last name—with the exception of Miss Emily T. Moore, whose middle initial is included. Isn't it likely that he would have known his mistress's

middle initial, and not the others? Perhaps. Or it could also simply be a matter of coincidence.

The other photograph shows Chandler at an annual oil industry banquet, held in 1927 at the Biltmore Hotel in downtown L.A. A couple of hundred men are gathered in a huge dining room, some dressed in formal wear, others in dark suits. Chandler is simply a face in the crowd. Nothing distinguishes him from the other oil industry executives except perhaps the heavy black-framed glasses he wears and the look of boredom on his face. It was just this sort of affair, drenched in male bonhomie with the alcohol flowing freely, that could bring out his worst side. According to one colleague, Chandler would often get so drunk at these gatherings that he would make a "nuisance" of himself, growing loud and garrulous and holding forth in a boring fashion in a pathetic attempt to impress the bevy of showgirls who had been hired for entertainment.

. . .

One would never guess from the amount of alcohol consumed in the 1920s that this was the era of Prohibition in America. The amendment banning the manufacture, sale, or transportation of intoxicating liquor had become law in 1919. But of course it proved impossible to enforce. It simply encouraged racketeering. It undermined the whole notion of law. And it contributed to the wild, illicit atmosphere of L.A. Nowhere was that abuse more public than in Hollywood, where scandals involving actors and women, liquor and wild parties, drugs and sex, made regular headlines.

As Ray's drinking worsened, his performance at work and his home life both suffered. The blackouts—the periods of alcohol-induced amnesia—increased. He disappeared for days at a time, sometimes in the company of the secretary from work, for whom he had rented an apartment. He would no longer come home at night. Sometimes he checked into the Mayfair Hotel on West Seventh Street, and from his room on an upper floor he made phone calls to friends in which he threatened to commit suicide by jumping from a window. But the calls came so often, the threats of suicide were so frequent, that soon people no longer took him seriously. Given this kind of behavior, inevitably his friends began to dwindle.

By this time Cissy and Ray had left the house on Leeward Avenue. Already they began to establish the pattern of moving once or twice a year. From Leeward they moved to 700 N. Gramercy Place, on the corner of Melrose Avenue, a three-story apartment building that, as I discovered when I drove over there one day, is still standing, though it had become shabby and grimy with age. Bars now covered the windows, and the entrance was no longer even visible, screened off behind a thick metal grill and locked gate. The place badly needed paint. It was hard to discern any charm the building may once have had, and I found myself thinking again of how sad it was that so many parts of the city had been left to decay while other areas had become so gentrified as to be largely unaffordable for all but a small number of the city's citizens.

From Gramercy the Chandlers moved to Meadowbrook Avenue, not far from Wilshire Boulevard, the street that threaded through many of the neighborhoods where they would live, and from Meadowbrook they moved to West Twelfth Street, and then to Longwood Avenue, all in the mid-Wilshire district. Not much remained of these places. A new mode of living—fast, crude, vivid—had urged constant renovation over the decades. I was discovering how many old well-built apartments had fallen victim to the urge to tear down, and whole sections of Los Angeles, like Bunker Hill, were forever disappearing, leaving almost nothing of their original character behind.

Again, I asked myself, why *had* Chandler moved so often, right from the beginning? Later in life, in a conversation with Somerset Maugham, Chandler attempted to explain why he had led such a peripatetic life, even as he continued to fantasize about where he might move next: "I've always been a gypsy at heart, Mr. Maugham, accustomed to a more nomadic lifestyle. I seem to require an ever-changing scene and new people . . . I'm constantly seeking new places to stimulate me."

This is the romantic version of the story. Ray was not always the best one to illuminate his behavior—his explanations could range from the bluntly truthful to outright dissembling—but in these words one does get a sense of how necessary these ceaseless relocations were to him and how readily he embraced the idea of continual upheaval, how in the irresoluteness of place and the desire for movement he found the stimulus necessary for his imagination. It's a not uncommon urge for many writers to change locales, live in other countries for a while, experience different vistas and cultures, though the remarkable thing about Chandler is what a small geographical patch he ended up continually circling over the course of his three dozen or so moves.

The automobile, and his love of driving, made all these moves possible, enabling him and Cissy to regularly pack up their possessions and haul them off to a different neighborhood in another part of the city—a furnished apartment near the beach, a little house in Hollywood, a cabin in the mountains, or a motel in the desert. He and Cissy could continually explore new landscapes in part because they lived in the place where the automobile took hold with such a virulence, where it became not a luxury but a necessity as the public transportation system was dismantled, consciously and willfully, through corrupt schemes involving public officials and rubber companies who profited from such change by replacing the city's excellent system of electric trams with less-efficient gas-burning buses in constant need of new tires.

Whatever kept Ray and Cissy moving, one senses that there may have been something addictive in the need to continually gravitate toward something unknown or new. And all those moves made it possible for him to become familiar with various parts of L.A., eventually contributing to the indelible portrait of the sprawling, many-faceted city that one finds in his books.

Ray was making a very good salary at Dabney Oil—something like a thousand dollars a month at a time when a decent apartment could be rented for about fifty dollars per month. He and Cissy could easily have bought a house and settled down; they apparently contemplated doing just that and looked at a lot near Huntington Palisades, but they decided it was too windy and bleak out there. Real estate sales were exploding in L.A., subdivisions were opening up everywhere, and land schemes of all varieties—some legitimate, some bunko scams—were flourishing, yet the Chandlers chose to live modestly and move often. Ray was suspicious of being conned, careful with his money, and perhaps this kept him from entering the real estate market. But there was also this: Ray himself admitted that he and Cissy were "very fussy" people, and I'm sure it wasn't difficult for them to find something wrong with wherever they lived—barking dogs, nosy neighbors, street traffic, nearby construction—compelling them to constantly move in search of something better. He also had a contemptuous view of the petit bourgeoisie with their attachment to consumption and ownership, and this may have played a part in keeping them on the move. None of these explanations, however, to my way of thinking really could account for the fact they seemed incapable of staying in one place for any length of time.

From Longwood Avenue they moved to a larger apartment on Highland Avenue, a busy thoroughfare just west of Hancock Park. It was during the time that they were living in the apartment on Highland Avenue that Chandler left Cissy and moved into the Mayfair Hotel on West Seventh Street, not far from his office in the Bank of Italy building, where he holed up to drink and ruminate on the increasingly unhappy state of his life.

I drove down Seventh Street, not expecting to find the Mayfair Hotel still standing. But there it was, bedecked with colorful flags and still very much in business in what had become a kind of shabby no-man's-land at the edge of downtown. I parked and went inside and checked out the lobby, which appeared to have been restored and looked quite lovely. It had towering pillars and a high ceiling that opened onto a mezzanine where there was a restaurant—I could hear the sound of glasses and silverware clinking up there. I picked up a brochure from the front desk and learned that the Mayfair was built during "the Roaring Twenties" and that it had been newly renovated to reflect the "grandeur of the era with the glass etchings, brass fixtures, skylights and friezed pillars that adorn the lobby atrium."

Although it was a little late for lunch—almost two o'clock—I climbed the wide staircase, which took me straight to the dining room and was greeted by an elderly maître d' with a rather bad comb-over and a courtly old-world manner. The room was nearly empty. Also, there was an odd and rather unpleasant smell. It appeared as if they were closing, but the maître d' quickly assured me that I still had "fifteen minutes" to eat and he said, "Come, come, I show you." and led the way across the room to where a buffet had been laid out on two long tables—platters of cold cuts and orange cheeses and silver chafing dishes in which concoctions bubbled and steamed (and also gave off that somewhat cabbagey-cafeteria smell I had noticed earlier). "All this," he said, making a grand sweeping gesture toward the buffet, "all for you!" He seemed unhappy when I told him I didn't think I would stay, but perhaps I would come back later, another day. "Okay," he said and shrugged, looking as disappointed as if I had walked out on a dinner party he'd organized just for me.

I went back downstairs and asked the woman at the front desk if I could see a room. I said my sister was coming to town and I was looking for a place for her to stay and I told her I'd like to look at a room on an upper floor because my sister wanted a view. I don't know why I felt compelled to tell this lie, but once told I had to elaborate because the clerk began asking me questions—just when was my sister coming? And exactly how long did she plan on staying? Really I just wanted to see a view from a room. I wanted to see what Ray had seen when he stayed here. I wanted to look out a window like the one he had threatened to pitch himself out of. I knew this was morbid, but it was true.

A bellhop took me up to the ninth floor and opened a room for me to look at. The room was small and not very pleasant. Everything was gray, no color anywhere. I walked over to the windows, which looked east, straight down Seventh Street, toward downtown and the Bank of Italy building. I stood there for some time, looking out over the city. I could feel the bellhop becoming impatient and I avoided turning around and looking at him.

"Room okay?" he finally asked.

"Yes, fine."

"You like the view?"

"Yes," I said. "Nice view."

"Nice view," he repeated.

"Yes."

"Very nice view."

"Yes."

I wasn't making it easy for him. I knew he must have things to do. But I didn't want to leave that room just yet. I was thinking of the misery Ray felt at that point in his life, when he had stayed in this hotel and made those calls to his friends threatening to kill himself.

I looked down. It was a very long way to the sidewalk.

I wondered what had brought him to such a low point, aside from the alcohol, which inarguably was a depressant. Did he feel trapped once again, as he had in the years when he'd worked at the L.A. Creamery and lived with his mother, mired in a job he found uninspiring and caring for a woman who was no longer healthy? Had the guilt and shame of betraying Cissy with another woman become too much for him to bear? Did his marriage feel dull and disappointing? "You know how it is with marriage—any marriage," he wrote in *The Lady in the Lake*. "After a while a guy like me, a common no-good guy like me, he wants to feel a leg. Some other leg. Maybe it's lousy, but that's the way it is."

For a man like Chandler—a moral man who regarded marriage as almost sacred—there was a high price to pay for that kind of straying. He explained this once, in a letter to his agent Helga Greene, in which he also revealed some troubling thoughts on how he might have compared sexually to Cissy's previous husbands.

It's difficult enough to accept that your wife, or mine, had two other husbands, one of whom at least may have been a better lover than I. But to accept infidelity when one is committed is very very difficult. That is, if one regards marriage as a serious business. I personally, and am probably quite wrong, don't think infidelity is a matter of much importance if one has a casual view of marriage. But if you find an ideal and an inspiration, you don't cheapen it. It's not so much that an individual is hurt, but that one's whole level of being is hurt.

Ray regarded marriage as serious business, and it can only have made matters worse that he was cheating not on a young, healthy wife but one who was older and ill. Cissy was succumbing to a lung condition that would plague her for the rest of her life. She suffered from bouts of pneumonia and fatigue—around this time, Chandler makes mention of her illness and a bill he received for medical services, which he felt was too high. ("I wrote that I considered it exorbitant and explained why. The next thing I knew I was served by a collection agency.") For Ray, it was just another opportunity to use his business acumen to demonstrate how he could outfox the opposition, but it also suggests that Cissy's condition required expensive treatment.

He knew he was cheapening his "ideal and inspiration" by cheating on Cissy, and his method of dealing with his guilt was to check into the brand-new ten-story Mayfair Hotel and drink himself to the brink of suicide.

I thanked the bellboy for showing me the room, gave him a tip for his trouble, and left the hotel and drove over to 1024 South Highland Avenue, where Cissy and Ray had moved sometime around 1927 and where Cissy continued to live after Ray moved out and began dividing his time between the apartment he'd rented for his secretary-girlfriend and the room at the Mayfair Hotel.

Throughout the twenties he had continued to write poems, many of them for Cissy, most composed in the middle of the night as he struggled with insomnia. "Lady, please waken, I long to kiss / those gentle answering lips," began one. Not all of the poems, however, reflect such a sweetly romantic tone. There is one that seems particularly troubling, called "Song at Parting":

He left her lying in the nude
That sultry night in May
The neighbors thought it rather rude
He liked her best that way

He left a rose beside her head
A meat ax in her brain
A note upon the bureau read
I won't be back again.

In the summer of 1927, Chandler was thirty-nine; Cissy was fifty-seven. The years between 1928 and 1932 were the worst years of their marriage. Ray's alcoholism and infidelity, their sporadic separations, his suicide threats and blackouts, the binge drinking and disappearances amounted to a laundry list of problems Cissy had to confront and try to deal with, not to mention her own illnesses. Ray seems to have crashed and careened and drunk his way through these years: in a way it's remarkable he survived at all. "I can remember sitting around with two or three congenial chumps," he later confessed, "and getting plastered to the hairline in a most agreeable manner. We ended up doing acrobatics on the furniture and driving home in the moonlight filled with music and song, missing pedestrians by a thin millimeter and laughing heartily at the idea of a man trying to walk on two legs."

Highland Avenue is lined with tall sycamore trees and graceful older apartment buildings that have for the most part been well maintained over the years. The apartment building where the Chandlers had lived at 1024 South Highland Avenue was still standing. It didn't appear from the outside to have changed very much from the time it was built, except security bars had been added to the windows, and a big green striped awning shading

the entrance looked rather out of place on the Spanish-style
building. The place would have been new when the Chandlers
moved there. It represented a step up for them, a neighborhood
farther to the west, located near the Wilshire Country Club and
the area known as Hancock Park, which, like most neighborhoods
in L.A., had barred Negroes from owning property until the late
1940s, when Nat King Cole fought to become the first black man to
buy a house in the area.

I wanted to see the inside of the apartment where the Chandlers
had lived. I sat in the car in front of the building for a while and
worked up my nerve and then walked up the path to the front
door and peered inside. The door was open and I could see
through the screen door into a darkened interior. I could also hear
what Chandler had once called "the slobbery hum" of a vacuum
cleaner. When the noise finally stopped I rang the bell. A middle-
aged woman came to the door. I told her I was a writer, interested
in the life of Raymond Chandler, the famous mystery writer, who
had once lived in this apartment back in the 1920s. I said I was
sorry to disturb her but I wondered if there was any chance I
might have a look inside—I knew it was a great deal to ask, but if
she didn't mind, I'd like to just have a very quick look . . .

I could tell she had no idea who Raymond Chandler was, and also that she didn't know whether to let me in or not.

"Just a minute," she said. "I'll have to ask my husband," and she disappeared, leaving me standing at the door.

I thought about what she had just said: *I'll have to ask my husband.* It was exactly the sort of thing my own mother would have said. I grew up in a household where the husband made most decisions, large and small. But in 2005 this seemed like an anachronism, that a woman would need to ask her husband if she could allow someone to come into their house. On the other hand, maybe it was wise of her to consult with him before acquiescing to a request from a total stranger.

I was thinking about this when the husband came to the door. He was a big man and he looked like a larger, heavier version of the actor Bruce Willis. He was bald, and as Chandler once said of a character, it looked like his ears had slipped down his head. He regarded me a little suspiciously as I introduced myself and repeated what I had told his wife and apologized for interrupting his afternoon. I could tell he'd never heard of Raymond Chandler either. He told me there'd be no point in letting me come inside because everything about the apartment had been changed. He and his wife had moved in ten years earlier and completely remodeled the place. The previous occupants had lived there for twenty-five years, he said, and left the apartment in terrible shape. I asked him how large the apartment was, and he said three bedrooms and one-and-a-half baths. About 1,400 square feet. Before they remodeled the apartment, it looked like other old apartments, he said—wood floors, old-style bathrooms, high ceilings—but they had changed all that. Now, he said, it was modern. It had carpet. A new kitchen. New tile baths. It made me think of a Chandler line from one of the stories or novels—which one, I couldn't remember right then—about how the all-tile bathroom had become the new standard of civilization.

I thanked him for the information and left. In a way, even though I hadn't been able to look inside, what he'd told me felt useful somehow. The apartment was larger than I imagined: three bedrooms for just two people, and then just one as Cissy continued to live on there alone after Ray split. I turned and looked back at the place before getting into my car. The apartment was on the ground floor and had a large picture window facing the street. For a brief moment, I could imagine Cissy sitting in a chair before that window. Looking out at the street, a book in hand. Waiting. Lonely. Bored. It wasn't a good image.

The long, slow disintegration of Chandler's career in the oil business came to an abrupt end in 1932. By then the Depression had arrived, and with it a new grim reality for thousands of previously party-happy Angelenos. The suicide rate from just one bridge, which spanned the newly constructed Arroyo Seco freeway, had risen to more than seventy a year, forcing the city of Pasadena to post round-the-clock police in an attempt to foil further attempts. A man named C. C. Julian, once the richest oilman in Los Angeles and a scam artist of exquisite skill, had been convicted of bilking investors out of millions of dollars—ordinary folks as well as sophisticated bankers and heads of studios—and had fled the city in disgrace. Everywhere people were witnessing financial collapse. The great wild bubble of the fun-filled twenties had not just burst, it had erupted fatally, in disaster after disaster. Dabney Oil Syndicate somehow managed to survive the bad times, but Raymond Chandler didn't.

For years he had been showing up late for work, sometimes coming into the office on Wednesday instead of Monday, and if that wasn't bad enough, the secretary with whom he was involved often went missing, too. His troubles multiplied, as did his affairs. One secretary was told she would have to leave the company, but Chandler intervened and said he would take care of the matter and the girl stayed on. Still word got out that he had taken an apartment for her where he went on weekends, and their two-day binges were responsible for her failing to show up for work. One of his coworkers, a man named John Abrams who had married into the Dabney family, had taken a great dislike to Ray. He considered him to be not only a "stinko drunk" but also the office "mar-tinet," and he decided to take matters into his own hands.

Disgusted by the way Chandler consistently and flagrantly mis-used his managerial position by having affairs and failing to per-form his duties properly, Abrams drove up to Lake Arrowhead one day to see his boss, Joseph Dabney. He found Dabney sitting on the porch of his mountain house, napping quietly in the sun like any good aged capitalist. Abrams told Dabney what he thought of Chandler and urged him to fire him.

When Chandler heard what Abrams had done, he was enraged. He threatened to sue him in retaliation. But it was too late. His position at the firm had become eroded. Dabney fired him. At the age of forty-four, Ray found his days in the oil business had come to an end, and so had his regular paychecks.

He fled to Seattle for a while, where he stayed with an old army buddy, until he heard that Cissy was once again ill with pneumo-nia and in the hospital, and he quickly returned to L.A. and she took him back. The marriage would have ended, no doubt, had it not been for her loyalty combined, perhaps, with her awareness of her lack of options. They moved in with Cissy's sister Lavinia and her husband, Archie Brown, for several months until Cissy had recovered. Sobered, remorseful, and now out of work, Ray seems to have hit bottom and come out of the crisis by making some difficult decisions: for one thing, he decided to stop drinking. For another, he committed himself to his marriage again. He and Cissy reconciled and began looking for a new apartment, in order to make a new life.

$\mathcal{F}$ive

I n the late spring I decided to make a trip to New York City. I wanted to track down the address where Cissy had lived on Lenox Avenue in Harlem and see if I might be able to discover anything more about her early years in New York and her first marriage to the salesman she had met when she was in her early twenties and working as an artist's model.

The morning I left for New York, it was one of those days in L.A. when the sunlight bleaches the color out of everything it touches. The rains had stopped just short of breaking an all-time record, and we were back to the overexposed world of blistering brightness. It felt like the sort of day Ray had described in *The Little Sister:*

It was one of those clear, bright summer mornings we get in the early spring in California before the high fog sets in. The rains are over. The hills are still green and in the valley across the Hollywood Hills you can see snow on the high mountains. The fur stores are advertising their annual sales. The call houses that specialize in sixteen-year-old virgins are doing a land-office business. And in Beverly Hills the jacaranda trees are beginning to bloom.

The jacarandas were also blooming on Carondelet. I stood on the sidewalk, covered with lavender petals that had fallen from the trees that lined the street, waiting for the taxi that would take me to the airport, with a very particular kind of Southern California luminosity electrifying the atmosphere around me. A group of Mexican kids were playing with a little yellow dog across the way. From a window nearby came the smell of frying garlic and the lively strains of salsa music. I had lived in this neighborhood almost twenty years, and still I knew little about my neighbors, including the people who lived in my building. Once an elderly man in the next apartment had died, and it was several days before anyone discovered his body. Now another elderly woman lived alone in the same apartment, a woman so reclusive and antisocial I almost never saw her. I knew only that she had no phone. She had no friends. And no relatives with whom she was in contact. When she died, how would anyone know she was gone? Alienation, impermanence, anonymity: this was how many people had lived in this city, including Cissy and Ray. After a while all that moving around meant little to them, because the houses or apartments themselves meant nothing, or next to nothing, compared to their real source of rootedness, which was the ease they felt with each other and the self-enclosed world they created together.

The taxi took surface streets to the airport—down Hoover to Jefferson and over to La Cienega. It was an eerily quiet ride. All along the route the sidewalks were empty of pedestrians. Yet there was nothing surprising about this. "There is an air of Sunday vacancy; here where no one walks," Truman Capote had once observed about L.A. In this city, every day was Sunday.

The cabbie drove down La Cienega, past the old rusting oil derricks that lined the road, still pumping after all these years and looking older and more out of place all the time—pterodactyls dipping their beaks into the crude again and again, as if driven by an insatiable thirst.

On the airplane I found myself drifting off into a kind of daydreaming in which I felt myself in the presence of either Cissy or Ray, or sometimes both of them at once. I slipped into rooms with them. I heard the way they talked to each other. I felt I was coming to know them in the way I had known an aunt and uncle of whom I had been particularly fond as a child, and now I was remembering them many years after their deaths. In the apartments and buildings—the addresses where I had gone searching for some trace of them—I had glimpsed only surfaces and exteriors, and yet in my daydreams I often imagined them inside these rooms, decorated not unlike the rooms in Ray's early stories:

> It was a small living room with bright overstuffed furniture, a red floor lamp with a cluster of French dolls at the base, a gay carpet with large diamond shapes in it. Two curtained windows with a mirror in between them.

The floor lamp with the cluster of French dolls at its base turns up in several of Ray's stories. Most likely Cissy owned such dolls and propped them up like that, at the base of a lamp where the light would fall on them, illuminating them in such a way as to make them seem more animate, like Freud's automata. Perhaps she carried these French dolls from place to place with her, along with the stagily erotic trappings of her "French boudoir."

At some point in her life, not long after she married Ray, she stopped allowing photographs to be made of her. As far as I knew there were no photographs in existence showing the two of them together. The last image of her seemed to have been taken around the time of their reconciliation. She wears a lacy dress with a plunging neckline that shows a little cleavage, drop earrings, and a thin chain around her throat, and she looks serious—a little tired would perhaps be more accurate—yet she is still beautiful, sensuous, womanly. This was the photograph of her that Chandler kept on his desk, and which, after her death, he carried with him and showed frequently to both friends and people he had just met. It was also the image of her that I thought of when I saw her in my daydreams, though I really didn't need photographs to conjure either one of them: their faces were fixed in my mind. In any case there was something much stronger than a mere physical idea that connected me to a feeling of being in their presence.

Of course I had read many descriptions of how Ray dressed and behaved at different points in his life, how he wore outrageously patterned ties and favored tweeds and flannels, how he could be sensitive and kind, often seeking out the one person at a party or gathering who appeared to be the shy or awkward outsider, how he could also be abrasive and boorish, petulant and rude, excessively opinionated and elitist, a natural mimic and an entertaining storyteller, how he retained his English accent and public school manners throughout his life. Depending on his mood, he could be both bawdy and courtly. With Cissy I felt he was mostly courtly and that their life together had a very old-fashioned and mannered quality. I imagined them in small apartments, and later in their house in La Jolla. I saw Cissy in lace-trimmed dresses or dressing gowns, in some shade of ecru or pink, like those she wore in real life (no mannish tailor-made suits for her, such as those worn by so many of Chandler's fictional female characters). Lace and cleavage, fluffy blond hair framing a pretty face, eyes outlined in kohl for drama, lips well defined, Cissy emanated femininity, as well as the sultry aura of another age. People who met her later in her life commented on how she seemed forever frozen in an earlier period, sometime closer to the turn of the century.

In these rooms where I saw the Chandlers, Cissy has always taken pains with her appearance. She sits and reads; she files her nails; she listens to music and gazes out a window at the sea; she converses with Ray about meals to be fixed, what to serve with tea, about her sister Vinnie, who occasionally visits. She is often tired and moves about, when she moves at all, with a rather languid air. Ray dotes on her. She reclines on a couch. She is droll and witty but often lethargic. They gossip. They discuss all sorts of things—letters he's gotten from editors and agents, the need to hire a new cook, occasionally some aspect of his work, whether he should agree to be photographed for a book cover, or reveal his age to the public. Taki, their beloved black Persian cat, is always with them, commanding their attention, amusing them, curled up between them on the sofa, which they do not call a sofa but a *davenport*. Cissy is calm and patient, unless she is in pain, and then she is fretful and uneasy. Ray performs the daily domestic chores without complaint, always solicitous of her. She slips from room to room in silk robes and pretty little pink slippers, taking her time. She sleeps late and sometimes hardly leaves her bed all day. At night, he stays up after she falls asleep and writes long letters to his many correspondents, most of whom he has never met, or sometimes he dictates them into the machine. Often she wakes up at midnight and comes into the living room and sits with him, and he fixes her tea and they sit on the davenport, next to one another, and look out at the night through the big bay window, at the moonlight on the sea and the flecks of stars and the little colored lights curving down the coast toward San Diego.

I could close my eyes and be with them.

It was late afternoon when I finally got into the city and checked into the Washington Square Hotel. I unpacked and then went out for a walk. The streets were filled with people. I walked over to Washington Square Park and stood near a crowd watching a magician perform tricks. There were people with dogs and people with guitars, people with briefcases on their way home from work, children with their parents, people of all ages and races, and I was struck by the vivid and vibrant public life of New York City and the graceful little neighborhood park that served as a magnet for gatherings. In L.A. people would be stuck in their cars at this hour, creeping slowly forward down crammed freeways, ensconced in a deadening state that alternated between boredom and anxiety. One person to a car, four, six, eight lanes in each direction, everyone trapped, alone in their humming metal carapace.

I sat down on a bench in the park and opened my notebook and read over notes I had made on the plane.

What about the idea that Cissy was supposed to have been the model for a nude painting that hung for years in the bar of the St. Regis Hotel (or was it the Plaza)? Could I possibly track it down? Would the hotels have old photographs I could look at that might show this painting? And would I be able to recognize Cissy, naked, at such a young age? Nobody really seems sure this painting actually exists. It could be just a rumor, a story that seems to have surfaced around the time when Ray went to work at Paramount Studios in the early 1940s when there was a lot of speculation about him and his much older wife. Ray himself may have floated this story. Who knows. He did own some nude photographs of her. I wonder if he carried them with him, or ever showed them to anyone? Maybe the idea of a nude painting of Cissy hanging in a hotel like the Plaza gave his wife a certain allure at a time when it was widely rumored she was old and beyond appearing in public. Maybe those pictures of her with her beautiful body increased her cachet, made her seem exotic and mysterious. They certainly must have given him ideas for Carmen Sternwood and the plots for his books, women being blackmailed over nude photographs.

I turned back farther in my notebook to something I had copied down from an interview with Billy Wilder, conducted sometime after Ray's death, by the screenwriter Ivan Moffat. Wilder, who had worked with Ray on the script of *Double Indemnity*, based on the novel by James M. Cain, was asked what Chandler thought about the finished movie, which Wilder had directed.

WILDER: In the first preview we had in Westwood Village, James Cain was standing in the lobby and he put his arms around me and said that it was the first time that somebody had done a good job on any of his stuff, and he kissed me. Chandler sneaked out because he did not want to be seen with his wife.

MOFFAT: Why?

WILDER: Because she was a grey-haired lady.

MOFFAT: He was ashamed of her, was he?

WILDER: People would kind of turn to him and say, "Oh, is this your mother?" You know. That kind of situation.

MOFFAT: Was she sort of a mother figure?

WILDER: No, she was a mother image, she *looked* like a
  mother.

There was something about Wilder's recollections that didn't ring true to me. For one thing, that bit about Cissy being a "gray-haired" lady. As far as I knew, Cissy had always dyed her hair blond, right to the end: she wouldn't have been caught dead (literally) with gray hair. And the implication that Ray was ashamed of Cissy and that's why he left the screening early, in order to avoid being seen with her, also felt off the mark, although it was true that by that point he had become very sensitive about her age. But it's just as likely that he left the screening early because he wanted to protect her and spare her the embarrassment of being compared to the beautiful young women who accompanied men like Wilder who, after all, in the same interview boasted of "fucking a lot of girls" during the period when he was making *Double Indemnity*.

It was fine for Wilder in his midthirties to be having affairs with starlets who were sometimes still in their late teens. That was normal. But it was an entirely different thing, a curiosity and an oddity, for Chandler to be with a woman eighteen years older—his mother image, as Wilder put it. I wondered if Wilder ever imagined himself as looking like a father to one of his young girls. It didn't seem likely.

For some time I had been thinking about the double standard that existed when it came to older women and younger men, and how this had complicated life for Cissy and Ray. After Ray was fired from Dabney Oil and Cissy took him back, they had become more reclusive, shutting themselves off from outside life, and I felt that largely was due not only to the fact that Ray became more solitary as he began to transform himself into a writer but also because of Cissy's age. I think Ray found the idea of the older woman as an experienced, nuanced, and attractive lover very appealing in the beginning, but I also think that at this point in his life, he well understood that Cissy was much older than she had claimed (but how much older? he must have wondered), and he realized he needed to protect her. One way of protecting her was simply to retreat into the safety and privacy of the domicile.

Sitting in the park, watching the steady stream of pedestrians stroll past my bench, I began to think about the older women who had been famously involved with younger men—Marguerite Duras, Edith Piaf, Simone de Beauvoir (who had a three-year affair with Claude Lanzmann, seventeen years her junior), Colette, and Georgia O'Keeffe—all women who were successful in ways their younger lovers hoped to be. Duras, Beauvoir, Colette, and Piaf were all French, and it seemed to me that the French might have a greater regard for older women as viable, vibrant, attractive lovers than Americans did and that it had been this way for a very long time.

In Colette's linked novels, *Chéri* and *The Last of Chéri*, the beautiful middle-aged courtesan at the heart of the story, Léa de Lonval, and Frederic (also known as Chéri) begin an affair when Chéri is only nineteen. Léa is twenty-four years older and a friend of Chéri's mother. But Léa, like Cissy, makes a secret of her date of birth. And also like Cissy, Léa is a woman of refined taste—this is in part what draws younger men to her. Léa knows she is aging, but she is still beautiful and careful never to let her young lover catch her untidily dressed, or with her blouse undone, or in her bedroom slippers during the day. "Naked, if need be," she says, "but squalid, never!"

What was Léa's appeal for her young lover? "Complete trust, a self surrender to confessions, candors, endless secrets—those hours in the depths of the night when, in almost filial gratitude, a young man unrestrainedly pours out his tears, his private likes and dislikes, on the kindly bosom of a mature and trusted friend." At the beginning of their affair Léa considers Chéri to be a passing fancy—a "liaison" or "adoption," like other young lovers in her past, but in time she falls so completely in love with Chéri that she is devastated when his mother arranges for him to marry a woman his own age. Chéri, for his part, never quite recovers from the affair with Léa. His marriage pales in comparison, and he begins to obsess about his former mistress. He confesses to a friend he would have married Léa "if it hadn't been for the question of age . . . but," he adds ruefully, "there *was* the question of age." Léa keeps the affair going as long as she can, pulling out all her tricks to emphasize her best physical qualities ("I have now to wear something white near my face, and very pale pink underclothes and tea gowns"). Her beauty is like Cissy's, and like most beautiful women, she experiences a moment of panic when it begins to fade. She had always attracted younger men (Colette tells us that Léa "has never soiled her hands or her mouth on a withered stick"). She needs to feed off "youthful flesh" and she is proud of the thirty years she has devoted to "radiant youths and fragile adolescents." But after Chéri's marriage, Léa realizes she has lost him, and she undergoes a change and decides at long last to forgo the pleasures of love and romance. She gives in to aging, becoming a plump and gray-haired lady who acquires a kind of sexless dignity.

Chéri does not see her for many years, but his obsession with her does not diminish, and finally he pays her a visit and is repulsed by what he finds—an old woman! How has it happened that his lovely Léa has grown so grotesque? He cannot hide his disgust. "Forgive me, Chéri," Léa says to him, in a kindly attempt to comfort him and explain the inevitable. "I've loved you as if we were both destined to die within the same hour. Because I was born 24 years before you, I was doomed, and I dragged you down with me." Léa tells Chéri to go back to his wife: "It's her turn to tremble; but her misery will come from passion and not from perverted mother love." Chéri leaves her, "like a man escaping from a prison." But his obsession continues to doom him, and the novel ends with him lying on a sofa in a friend's apartment, surrounded by pictures of the youthful beautiful Léa, before which he commits suicide.

Colette herself was fifty-three, the same age as Cissy, when she met her second husband, Maurice Goudeket—who like Ray had just turned thirty-five.

The light was failing in Washington Square Park and yet I didn't feel like going back to the hotel just yet. The question I was trying to answer was this: was Colette right in suggesting that a relationship between an older woman and younger man involved a component of perverted mother love, and was that, as Wilder suggested, part of the appeal of Ray for Cissy (and vice versa)? And why was there a stronger taboo (or at least bias) against older women having romantic, sexual relations with younger men? Could society's uneasiness be based on a whiff of incest or child violation by a maternal force? Or was it simply a case of sexism, that same old boring reaction to women asserting status and power? In youth-conscious America, where women were constantly objectified in vulgar ads, was a woman's aging body judged more harshly than an aging man's? And if women had a long history of traditionally holding the money—the political power and inheritance rights—wouldn't older women, like older men, become greater magnets for younger suitors?

I walked back toward the hotel thinking about these things, which on the one hand seemed to have rather obvious answers. As far as I knew, Cissy had never expressed a longing for children— not with her first or second husbands, and certainly not with Ray, where her age made the question moot—but I knew so little, really, about what she had or hadn't wanted. Yet everything about the way she'd led her life when she was in her childbearing years suggested she was more interested in having fun than having kids.

I stopped at the hotel bar and ordered a gimlet, the drink I always ordered now. I realized I was developing a fondness for this drink, as if I believed it might connect us somehow. But the truth was I already felt connected to Ray.

I rose early the next morning and caught the subway train to Harlem. I had never been to Harlem before, a place that for me evoked jazz, Billie Holiday, the Cotton Club, the Apollo Theater—a whole world of black music and culture. Though it had become the most famed black region in America, Harlem didn't start out as an African American community. It had been an upper-middle class residential suburb—Manhattan's first true suburb—when Cissy lived there in the 1890s. A real estate boom, fueled by the extension of New York's subway lines north to Manhattan's upper reaches, had taken place in the early 1890s, and rows of brownstones and exclusive apartment houses had appeared almost overnight. The developers overbuilt, however, and sometime around 1915, when the speculators and realtors realized they had a glut of housing on their hands, they decided to rent to Negroes in order to save themselves from financial ruin. At this point, blacks had no geographical community of their own but were dispersed throughout New York. For the first time in the city's history, they were offered decent living accommodations and they flocked to Harlem, alarming white residents, who saw this as a "Negro invasion." The sons and daughters of slaves who had been freed only twenty-five years earlier—and many freed slaves themselves who had come north after the Civil War—finally had the possibility of a community of their own. Within a decade this consolidation produced a flowering of black art and culture known as the Harlem renaissance. By then, however, Cissy had left Harlem. She had already married her second husband, Julian, and was living in the diasporic conglomeration of L.A.

It was raining hard when I left the hotel, and even harder when I emerged from the subway at 125th Street. Hurricane Frances had moved north from the Florida coast and was pounding the Atlantic seaboard, and the worst part of the storm was expected to hit that day.

I began walking down 125th, one of the main thoroughfares of Harlem, huddling under the umbrella I'd bought from a street vendor. People hurried by, trying to shield themselves from the pounding rain. Some huddled under black plastic bags in lieu of raincoats. A few older women had fashioned rain bonnets out of white shopping bags that billowed in the wind like living, breathing things.

Lenox Avenue, where Cissy had lived, was a long walk from the subway station, especially in a downpour, but somehow I didn't mind the walk or the rain. It wasn't cold, just wet, and everything around me was vibrant and active. The streets were crowded on a Saturday morning, in spite of the weather. Clerks stood under awnings in front of small stores, watching the rain come down to the accompaniment of the rap music that blared from speakers, and sometimes they nodded to me or said hello as I walked by. I passed the Apollo Theater with its large marquee announcing the Apollo Amateur Night: ONE MIKE, ONE STAGE, ONE CHANCE, EVERY WEDNESDAY NIGHT AT 7:30 P.M. A STAR IS BORN, A LEGEND IS MADE.

The apartment building where Cissy had lived, at 333 Lenox Avenue, was just around the corner from the Apollo, near the Porgy and Bass Seafood restaurant, an attractive red brick building, four floors, with tall windows facing the street and an empty beer bottle sitting in a paper bag in the doorway. There were buzzers near the entrance, one for each of the four apartments, and I considered pressing one to see if someone might let me in, but then I thought better of it and huddled in the doorway, with the rain blowing and spitting against me and peered into the lobby, which was dimly lit by a circular neon fixture that sputtered on and off. Immediately inside the doorway, a steep stairway ascended to the upper floors, and beside this, a long dark hallway led to the apartments on the ground floor. I imagined Cissy climbing those stairs to her apartment, a well-dressed young woman from Ohio, on her own in the city, perhaps returning from a modeling session or a piano lesson, maybe in the company of a gentleman friend. The neon fixture on the ceiling flickered a few times more and then went out, leaving the hallway in darkness, and my glimpse into the interior ended.

"We are both pretty much overfastidious," Ray had once said of the two of them, "but we can't help it." I wondered if her overfastidiousness had been there from the beginning. It seemed to me these kinds of habits were set early and that one's neatness or slovenliness really didn't much change over a lifetime. A number of times in his letters Ray had taken pains to comment on Cissy's excellent sense of style and her impeccable taste. "The trouble with my wife," he once said, "is she has too much good taste for this generation."

Across the street a couple entered Sylvia's Queen of Soul Food restaurant, which was doing a lively business in spite of the rain. Lenox Avenue had been renamed Malcolm X Boulevard. Most of the buildings on the street were old, from the era when Cissy had lived here, and many were in poor repair. Horse-drawn carriages were the primary mode of transportation during Cissy's stay on Lenox Avenue. She had lived through a time when the world was remade by electric lights, refrigeration, the automobile, telephone, television, and airplanes. What would she have made of the Starbucks across the way, on the corner of Malcolm X Boulevard and 125th, and the fact that a cup of coffee had become fifty times more expensive, or the leisurely and obsessive way in which it was now consumed all day long by the cultish aficionados?

After Cissy married Leon Brown Porcher in 1897, they moved to an apartment on West 123rd Street, just two blocks away from Lenox. I didn't have the address for that apartment, but I walked over to 123rd, past run-down apartments with boarded-up windows and chained entryways. The chains hadn't managed to keep the squatters out: here and there, on an upper floor, I could see an open window and a figure peering out or sitting on the window ledge, smoking a cigarette. On the side streets, off the main thoroughfares, entire blocks of old apartment buildings appeared abandoned and decayed, areas so derelict it looked as if a bomb had exploded in the neighborhood and the residents had fled. I kept walking, past the Crossroads Baptist Church and the Muhammed Mosque #2 and Dee's Hair Braiding Salon, until I came to 123rd Street, and from there I made my way back to the subway station and the hotel, and a hot bath and dry clothes.

When night had fallen I sat in the darkness of my room on the top floor of the Washington Square Hotel and listened to the stormy gusts buffeting the crowns of trees. From afar came the rumble of thunder, which seemed to reverberate loudly through the city, as if caught in the deep canyons created by the tall buildings. The last of the weakened hurricane moving through. Palest sheet lightning erupted now and then in flashes of soft brilliance, like bombs in old war films.

I thought about Cissy smoking opium and posing nude for artists and photographers during her Harlem years and wondered how these photographs had been used and whether any had ever been published anywhere. I had found only one photograph of her from this era, a blue-tinged image of her in an artist's studio, holding a classical pose, draped in what looks like a long flowing toga.

Had other photographs of her found their way into the magazines featuring semiclothed women that began to appear around the turn of the century? Burlesque had by then become a popular form of entertainment, stage shows emphasizing legs—especially legs clad in tights—and featuring other carefully exposed parts of women's bodies. It's hard to imagine now just how titillating the sight of a woman wearing tights had been, but such shows were often banned, considered too racy for the general public. Pictures

of nude women had to be consumed in secret. Even reproductions of classical Greek sculpture were considered outré, but in the 1890s, magazines such as *Munsey's* and *Nickel* and *Metropolitan* began to carry reproductions of nudes in works of art, justifying these pictures as a mark of maturity and civilization.

The era in which Cissy was posing nude for artists marked the beginning of a more libertine element finding its way into the wider culture, in the form of burlesque shows and erotic photographs, including cabinet cards (small photographic images that could be propped up on a shelf or carried in a wallet). Around this time magazines began to present well-endowed "pinup girls." In *The Big Sleep*, set in the 1930s, Marlowe uncovers a ring of pornographers who work out of the back room of a bookstore that supposedly deals in rare books. By then erotic images were not so uncommon: all you had to do was know the right people in what was still a secret and closed world.

I sat up late, watching the rain out the window. At about midnight, the storm suddenly intensified and the windowpanes rattled fiercely for a while. Then the wind died down. I opened the window and leaned out into the cool storm-filled night. The rain had stopped, but below the water gurgled in the overflowing gutters and everything glistened with shards of light falling from the streetlamps. New York had been washed clean, and it smelled fresh and beautiful.

The next morning I took a taxi to the Church of the Transfiguration at Fifth Avenue and Twenty-ninth Street—also known as The Little Church Around the Corner—where Cissy Hurlburt had married Leon Brown Porcher in December 1897. It was raining again, and the heavy mist lay thick over the brown brick church nestled prettily among trees and green foliage. The church had been built in 1848 as part of the Oxford Movement, which, in response to the age of the Industrial Revolution and increased urbanization, held that the Anglican revival should focus its ministry on modern cities such as London and New York. When other churches in the area had refused to conduct funeral services for an actor named George Holland, owing to the "disreputable" nature of his profession, his friends were told that "the little church around the corner" might accommodate their needs, and thus a long relationship between actors and the church was born, and it acquired its charming nickname. For over a century it had also been a favorite place for weddings, but would there be any record of the marriage of Leon Brown Porcher and Cissy Hurlburt?

A young woman in the rectory offered to look up the records for the date I had for their wedding but cautioned it would take at least an hour to do so and asked me to come back later. I waited in the main chapel to avoid the rain still falling outside. A thin, balding man sat at the organ, practicing hymns, and the heavy notes reverberated throughout the chapel and animated everything. Even the chairs and the floor vibrated with the music. Dark, heavy oil paintings hung in the recesses of the room, polychrome crucifixion scenes, marble figures of Madonna and child.

Though a native of Ohio, Cissy did have familial ties to New York. She was related to Clarence Day, the humorist and longtime *New Yorker* writer noted for his affectionate books about his upper-class family, the best known of which was *Life with Father,* which also became a play and a 1947 film. Clarence Day had grown up in a sophisticated, well-to-do household at 420 Madison Avenue at Forty-eighth Street, in the sort of old New York family who sent their sons to Yale and had their name on the end of their own pew in St. Bartholomew Church. But their roots went back to Ohio. The money came from Wall Street and early railroad ventures.

Clarence Day, who was born in 1874, just four years after Cissy's birth, started out as a broker but was stricken with rheumatoid arthritis in 1899 and gave up the business world, retiring first to a ranch in Arizona that the Day family purchased for him and his epileptic brother, Harold, believing the dry climate might help them both. But the ranch had no effect on Clarence's health, and he returned to New York and became a writer. His godfather was Nathaniel Currier, famed for his lithographs and for the firm he founded with James Ives. Day experienced his greatest success in the 1920s with such books as *This Simian World*, a collection of off-beat observations that speculated on a world with an alternative evolutionary history, and *Life with Father*. He was good at delivering lines such as, "If your parents didn't have any children, it's likely you won't either." The books seem dated now: they describe a world that has largely disappeared, romantic and foppish.

Chandler made only one reference to Cissy's connection to Clarence Day, in a letter once, remarking that Cissy's sister Lavinia had been named for Day's mother. There is no indication that the Chandlers and Day ever had any contact (Day died in 1935, just at the time Ray was beginning to publish his first stories). It is possible, however, that Cissy may have had contact with Day and his family during the time she lived in Harlem, though later they appear to have lost touch. Cissy and Ray were like orphans, people for whom any notion of family was almost nonexistent. Ray still had relatives living in England. They included a cousin, Dr. Loftus Bor, a specialist in native Indian grasses who was also assistant director of the Royal Botanic Gardens, Kew, but Ray made no effort to keep in touch with them. Later in his life, however, after Cissy's death, when Ray was making regular trips to England, Dr. Bor contacted him at his London hotel and invited him to Kew Gardens for lunch and a tour of the grounds, and Ray accepted his invitation, accompanied by Helga Greene. By and large, however, Ray had no use for his extended family and he cut them off rather mercilessly. According to what he told Helga, Ray "loathed" his relatives. When she attempted to contact some of them after his death in an effort to learn more about his childhood, she was rebuffed, particularly by Ray's aunt Ethel, his mother's sister, whom Ray had particularly disliked. Ethel told Helga Greene she would not talk to her about Ray's childhood because that was the past and the past "wasn't interesting." As Helga also discovered, there was an incident involving Ray that may have prejudiced the family against him. The story, as told to Helga by Dr. Bor, was that Ray refused to vouch for Dr. Bor's brother (Ray's cousin) when he applied to emigrate to America and needed Ray to provide a letter of recommendation, saying that he didn't really know him and therefore couldn't vouch for him. The family as a whole thought this was bad form, but Dr. Bor himself laughed about it and told Helga Greene it would have made no difference, because his brother was slightly "touched in the head" anyway and suffered from a persecution mania; he would have been persecuted in the United States by his imaginary demons just as much as he had elsewhere.

Aside from his mother and the genial Dr. Bor, Ray's relatives appear to have been a rather mean-spirited and small-minded lot. He once told a story about his uncle, the same uncle who had paid for his education at Dulwich, whom he described as a man of rather evil temper. "Sometimes when dinner did not suit him," Ray wrote, "he would order it removed and we would sit in stony silence for three quarters of an hour while the frantic Miss Groome [his uncle's housekeeper] browbeat the domestics below stairs and finally another meal was delivered to the master, probably much worse than the one he had refused; but I can still feel that silence." English snobbishness was a strange and puzzling thing to Ray, and he never quite recovered from the effects of being treated as a poor relation. The humiliation he and his mother experienced early on at the hands of relatives would leave a lifelong mark and instill in Ray a sense of pride and determination to never again succumb to belittlement, a feeling he later transferred to his creation Philip Marlowe, whom he once described as a lonely man whose "pride is that you will treat him as a proud man or be very sorry you ever saw him."

After an hour in the dim, dank chapel, I returned to the rector's office. The secretary had located the marriage registration book for 1897, the year I had requested. She led me to a back room where, on an old wooden desk, a large leather-bound book had been left open to the page listing the marriages for the month of December. And there, halfway down the page, were the names of Leon Brown Porcher and Pearl Eugenia Hurlburt entered in a neatly uniform script.

Several things about the entry were of immediate interest to me. The first was that Cissy had given a false name for her parents, listing their surname as Gray instead of Hurlburt (Gray was in fact her mother's maiden name). Second, instead of providing their true address in Perry, Ohio, she had supplied her own address on Lenox Avenue in the space provided for "Parents' address." (Leon had done the same, listing his address on 123rd Street in Harlem for his parents.) It appeared as though they wished to keep their wedding a secret from their families by providing false names and addresses. No friends had witnessed their marriage, either: the people who were listed as witnesses—Howard Burton and Fanny Gettings—had also witnessed half a dozen other marriages that week, suggesting they were simply people who could be called on to witness weddings on short notice. On the surface at least, Cissy and Leon's marriage looked like a secretive and perhaps hastily arranged affair.

But most interesting of all was the column in the registry where the bride and groom's ages were listed. Leon had put his age at twenty-one; Cissy had listed hers as twenty-three. But in 1897, Cissy was actually twenty-seven. She had deducted four years from her official age. Just as with her marriage to Ray, she had felt compelled to lie about her age, even then, when she was still in her twenties. Obviously she had always wanted to be taken for younger than she actually was, even at an age when it wouldn't have seemed necessary. Would Leon have really cared whether she was two years older than him, or four? Maybe not. But Cissy certainly cared. She cared enough to invent a new age for herself and then to go on inventing new ages as she grew older.

I took a cab up to the Plaza and made my way through the vast, labyrinthine lobby, past the Palm Court and the concierge desk and the bookstore to the wood-paneled bar, which overlooked Central Park. As I walked through the hotel I scanned the walls and the paintings that hung there, looking for a nude of a young nubile blonde. I didn't really expect to find it. Even if it had once actually existed I had the feeling that it was now long gone, replaced during a remodeling or maybe purged on a puritanical urge. Still I felt a little hopeful as I entered the bar and looked around. But there was no painting of a nude blonde hanging in the bar. The only painting in the room was a dark, muddy rendering of a Central Park scene, the sort of painting you could look at once and never see again.

I ordered my usual gimlet from a white-coated waiter, and when he delivered it I asked him if by chance he remembered a nude painting of a blond woman that might have once hung in this bar. He said no, he did not remember such a painting, but he had worked there for only thirteen years, so maybe it was before his time. Was there anyone who had worked there longer? I asked. He said yes and pointed to another waiter standing near the bar, a small, dark-skinned elderly man who even from a distance appeared to have a rather formal and elegant manner about him.

"Would you like to speak to him?" my waiter asked.

I said I would, and when the man arrived at my table I asked him the same question I had asked the first waiter: Do you remember a painting hanging in this bar—a nude picture of a beautiful blonde?

"No," he said. "No painting. But they made a movie here once, with a beautiful blond actress. Maybe that is what you mean?"

No, I told him, it was a painting I was looking for.

"How long have you worked here?" I asked.

"Thirty-two years," he said. "A long time."

It was a long time, but not long enough. The painting I was looking for was painted a century earlier. If it really existed it may have hung here in the early decades of the twentieth century—too long ago, I felt, for anyone alive now to remember it. And where was it now?

I thanked the elderly waiter. The day was fading outside. Through the large windows at the end of the bar I could see the horses and carriages lined up at the south end of Central Park, waiting for customers. The horses dozed on their feet, their heads dropped and haunches cocked. A couple near the window were kissing. She kissed him with a kind of lingering moist passion while he twisted his head rather awkwardly to receive her kiss. I thought of the passion Ray had felt early on for Cissy. He once said of Cissy, "I don't know how I ever managed to get her," as if only a fluke could account for his luck. Another time he said, "Cissy was a raging beauty, a strawberry blonde with skin I used to love to touch." His adoration of her lasted many years—many years of touching that lovely skin. In spite of her preoccupation with age, she does not seem to have been one of those beautiful people who live for the splendor of their appearance and the regard it evokes and who are often destroyed by its passing. Yet Ray was not unaware of the cruelty of aging. In a fragment of an uncompleted story he lamented the effects of time on great beauty: "There are women so fair that one despises what Gods let them grow old; there are faces so exquisite that one loathes the years that change them."

As much as I wanted to find the nude painting of Cissy as a young woman, what I really would have liked to discover was a picture of her as an old woman. I wanted to see a photograph of the woman Ray had still loved at the end of her life, when she was eighty-four. But as far as I knew, no such photograph existed.

Cissy's marriage to Leon Brown Porcher lasted seven years, and it appears to have ended badly. A document I later unearthed, dated May 21, 1904, signs into effect a divorce judgment in favor of the plaintiff, Pearl Eugenia Hurlburt, stating that her husband has not "appeared, answered, or demurred to the complaint" filed against him. Did Porcher, the traveling salesman, simply disappear? The divorce decree goes on to state that while each is freed from the other, it will be lawful only for Pearl to remarry, in the same manner as if Leon were dead, but that it will not be lawful for Leon to marry again until Pearl "shall actually be dead."

Why, I wondered, was it the case that Pearl could marry again, but not Leon? Was this legal punishment for his having failed to respond to the affidavit filed against him?

The document goes on to state that Pearl was free now to resume her maiden name. But she did not do this. Seven years later, when she married Julian Pascal, she was still legally using the name Pearl E. Porcher. They were married before a justice of the peace in Greenwich, Connecticut, and this time Cissy's mother, Maria, was the witness to the ceremony. What Cissy was doing during those seven years between the time she divorced Leon and married Julian we don't really know, but it seems likely that she was studying piano and that one of her teachers was Julian Pascal. Less than a year after their marriage, Julian and Cissy moved to California. He was a fragile man, older than Cissy. In Los Angeles, Julian met the Warren Lloyds through musical circles—since Alma Lloyd studied singing, this would have been a logical connection. And through the Lloyds, Julian and Cissy met Ray and his mother, and all became a part of The Optimists.

Six

C handler once said that when a civilization is in the process of going rotten, you will always find the symbols of this rotten-ness in the suburbs, in the lives and homes of supposedly decent people.

Los Angeles was (and still is, as the trope goes) nothing if not a vast collection of suburbs (all that rottenness in search of a cen-ter). To become the capital of noir, all L.A. needed was the perfect bard—the poet of the common who, rising out of the sleaze and junk material of the city, could capture it with a voice like no other. And it found him, in the owlish, bespectacled former accountant who, after his sacking from Dabney Oil and humiliat-ing fall from grace, was ripe for reinvention.

In 1932, many Americans were feeling crushed by the hard heel of the Great Depression. Cissy and Ray were not untouched by that hard heel. Ray had no job. They had no income. Reunited, they rented a one-bedroom apartment in a graceful little building on Greenwood Place, just off Vermont Avenue in the Los Feliz dis-trict of Los Angeles, not far from Griffith Park. They did have some savings they could live off for a while, if they were careful, if they lived simply, which is what they began to do.

I drove over to Greenwood Place and parked on the dead-end street lined with tall eucalyptus shedding their bark in long ragged flesh-colored strips and walked back to 4616, the address where the Chandlers had lived. The building was still there, surrounded by big avocado trees that cast a watery green light across the stucco facade. It was a lovely old building, laid out like a Spanish hacienda. A graceful little archway with the words EL PUEBLO painted across the top led to an interior courtyard strung with little colored lights that had been left on even in the daytime. Very quietly, making every effort not to attract any attention to myself, I unlatched the metal gate and slipped inside and walked back through the archway to the little protected courtyard. It was nice back there, very peaceful and quiet. Ivy climbed up one wall, and strelitzia were blooming in the little patches of garden encircling the courtyard. There was a wrought-iron bench and a small table with two chairs. I sat down on the bench, as if I belonged there, as if this were my building, my apartment complex, my little private patio. I took out my brown leather notebook and set it on the bench beside me and settled in for a while.

I tried to imagine what this place had felt like in 1932 when Cissy and Ray moved in. I could easily see them here, in this private, quiet little world. Ray had understood something about this city and its residents, how, unlike New Yorkers, Angelenos don't really want to bond together as urbanites or take undue pride in

their city, even if they could, even if such pride were an option. Mostly they want to be left alone. They want to live secluded lives in gardenlike settings. They like the privacy of their cars. They take an almost perverse pleasure in L.A.'s centerlessness—and in what D. J. Waldie has termed its "sacred ordinariness," a kind of blatant celebration of the banal (muscle boys, valley girls, surfer dudes, restaurants in the shape of hats and hot dogs). The gleeful embracing of popular culture and the spawning of endless tackiness is an industry in this town, and Ray understood that. In a vacuum of values, in this world of lateral possibility, people could nurture their extravagant myths of private gratification and self-realization. Driving along the Pacific Coast Highway you could almost believe you were in Italy or Greece, some place with traditions instead of tract housing, and you could dress the part—any part you chose. He knew there was no use sniping at the place; instead he recognized its contradictions, a city both vital and greedy, lost and beaten, full of emptiness and beauty. In the loneliness and vacuity of this smog-laden bowl between the mountains and the sea, Ray understood that L.A. was the perfect place to reinvent himself: he set out to become what he had always wanted to be.

With no job any longer to go to, and no demands on his time, he and Cissy began taking long drives up the coast. Some mornings, when they awoke in vital, greedy, wayward L.A., newest city in the world, city without a past, scene of such numerous options, they dressed with their usual fastidiousness, packed a small suitcase, and set out by car to explore the California coastline, as if their romance with each other and with the sunny, languorous, mobile world of Southern California were starting all over again. They put the top down on the Packard convertible and drove up Highway 1, the Pacific Coast Highway. The stretch between Santa Monica and Oxnard had just been opened in 1929, making it possible to drive all the way up the coast to Santa Barbara, and a beautiful drive it was, past the pristine Malibu ranch and all the pretty little coves and beaches, the jutting headlands and the whales spouting offshore, the sea otters lolling on their backs amidst the ropes of blistered kelp. Ray not only loved to drive, he loved to drive fast if the road was good, but on the Pacific Coast Highway he did not drive fast. They took their time motoring beside the sea, stopping for lunch or tea and passing nights in roadside inns or small hotels. And on one of those nights, in one of those little hotels, Ray had an epiphany. Later, he described that moment in a letter to a friend:

> Wandering up and down the Pacific Coast in an automobile, I began to read pulp magazines, because they were cheap enough to throw away and because I never had any taste at the time for the kind of thing which is known as women's magazines. This was in the great days of *Black Mask* . . . and it struck me that some of the writing was pretty forceful and honest, even though it had its crude aspect. I decided this might be a good way to learn to write fiction and get paid a small amount of money at the same time.

I decided this might be a good way to learn to write fiction.
It was so simple. Why not try to write what you enjoyed reading, especially when you could see a definite form you could copy and when you felt you might even be able to do it better than the fel-

lows you were reading? In that hotel room, lying in bed with Cissy next to him, he read a story in *Black Mask* and turned to her and told her that he thought he could write a story like that and maybe even write it better.

Why don't you then? she said.

He enrolled in a short-story writing class in Santa Monica, a class taught at night by an instructor who gave one-page assignments such as "create a scene," or "create a character," or "create a sense of atmosphere" and who awarded him As and Bs for his efforts, the first of which did not yet in any way resemble the "pretty forceful and honest" prose he had discovered in *Black Mask,* nor did it reflect that "crude" aspect except in the blatancy of the forced lyricism. In these exercises, he was looking back, to England, with its mists and moats and hedges, rather than at the raw material of the modern city that surrounded him. One of his first exercises began:

The walls of the Castle of Innifrath were vast and grey with that greyness which remembers dark deeds and a moon too pale to be friendly . . . and in its black and scummy moat dwelled shadow the sun had never reached.

He had not yet figured out that he could look around him, at the shadows that dwelled in the vast scummy world of L.A. and the sprawling centerless lack-of-soul atmosphere where corruption was endemic in almost every institution, from the police to the press, and in the puritanical but brutal citizenry that often took delight in scamming one another. It would take some time before he understood that he could tell stories that captured the tribal mind of America by examining one of its most prominent features—the endemic violence and corruption of big-city life, the lost dreams of little people, the failed ventures, the numerous stopgap schemes for saving the penniless and fallen victims of the rapacious boom cycle that had so recently, and so resoundingly, busted. But when he did find his voice, it came straight out of the landscape of L.A. and the world of the working class.

All the years he'd been living in L.A. he'd been listening to the way people talked—the wildcatters who worked the oil fields, the secretaries who hailed from the Midwest, the rough-and-tumble elements of society he encountered on the streets of downtown L.A., the women and men he'd met in bars, the peepers and creeps who haunted porn shops and the illicit gambling joints. And then there was the endlessly amusing landscape itself, the sunny lurid city he'd been studying for years, with its faux-glam aura, the lean Hollywood cowboys and fey lover boys, the girls who yearned for fame, the old men who'd gotten rich peddling oil and myths and plots of land, and the children they couldn't control.

The first story he sold to *Black Mask* in 1933 was called "Black-mailers Don't Shoot," which he later cannibalized to make the novel *The Big Sleep*. The story took him eight months to write, and he got paid $180. From the rural romance of Castle Innifrath and its dark moat, he made the leap to a hardened urban landscape peopled by sleazy porn dealers, blackmailers, naked girls, drug addicts, con artists, and rich people with dark family secrets— combinations of corruption that would serve him well in many stories to come. He discovered his formula very early on: a heroic man, working alone and with little pay and even less respect, agrees to seek justice for an ordinary citizen who has no one else to turn to. The man works for himself, he's a loner with a shabby office—no wife, no kids, no family, no background, usually not even a friend—just a calling, as a kind of white knight seeking jus-tice for the vulnerable and maltreated. And though it was a man's world he described, there were plenty of women in it: blondes, brunettes, redheads, most of whom needed rescuing or straight-ening out. And he, Raymond Chandler, knew just how to rescue them. Because he was, at least in his version of the story, the young knight who had rescued his own damsel Cissy from what he would continue to portray throughout his life as an unhappy marriage.

He read Hammett and Hemingway, attracted by the swiftness and simplicity of their prose, the clean, sharp sentences and the cool, hard surface of the masculine world they depicted. Hemingway and Hammett: each in his own way understanding the need for terseness and direct forcefulness, for a prose of terrible urgency. From Hemingway Chandler learned to keep his sentences short and swift—sometimes very short, and very swift, as in "He drank." Or, "He sat."

From Hammett he took the detective, a hardened hero like Sam Spade. But whereas Hammett had simply described the lone man walking in the rain, Chandler made us hurt for that man. His lonely man was more likable than Spade, less harsh and brittle, more *human*. He exposed the man's wounds, his longings, his fears, and the biggest wound of all was the man's haunting, endemic, incurable, ever-present loneliness. An existential separation oozed from the writing, like something dark seeping from an unseen place. It takes an existentialist to know one, and Chandler was our first, our best, our own homegrown existentialist, admired even by Camus.

Ray took something else from Hammett: a sense of the wisecracking humor of *The Thin Man,* which came out the year Ray published his first story. His Marlowe owes a lot to Nick Charles—the cool, suave, imperturbable cosmopolitan who tosses back his first drink with breakfast and keeps going to midnight and somehow never gets a hangover but just grows wittier and more clever as the day wears on. In some ways, Marlowe was Nick without Nora, the more streetwise Angeleno version of the more effete San Franciscan, but what connected these characters was the love of the bon mot, the fast repartee, and a good manly capacity for liquor. Neither Hammett nor Chandler was particularly good at depicting crowd scenes. They focused on the intimate one-on-one. Chandler once said he could never manage a roomful of people in his fiction, but give him two people snotting at each other over a desk and he was a happy man.

I heard a car pull up out front of the apartment building on Greenwood Place, and a man sat at the wheel, staring out the windshield for a while. He seemed to be looking at nothing. Once or twice he glanced at me, as if he were waiting for someone to emerge from one of the apartments, someone he didn't know but had arranged to meet. It was as if he thought that person might be me, but he wasn't quite certain. There was an air of vacant expectation in his look, of an unspecified uncertainty, an eager anxiety he kept projecting my way. He had a large handsome face on which a beautiful blankness was written. He sat at the curb for a while, the car idling, and then suddenly he pulled away, gunning the engine and racing off with a little squeal of tires.

The string of colored lights overhead stirred in a light breeze. They suddenly seemed so fakely festive in the light of day, so forlorn and out of place. I thought of some lines from *The Little Sister*, from the wonderful scene where Marlowe goes for a drive one night, over Cahuenga Pass to the San Fernando Valley, the cars so few their headlights hurt, and eats a lousy meal in a second-rate diner, and then he keeps driving, the way Maria, the character in Joan Didion's *Play It As It Lays*, will later do, endlessly and mechanically driving as if being driven in turn by some unseen manic force. Marlowe drives all the way to Oxnard, a hundred miles round-trip, just a little jaunt for an Angeleno, until he hits the Pacific Coast Highway and turns south, with the traffic flowing against him, the big eight-wheelers streaming north and hung over with orange lights, and on the right the great fat solid Pacific trudging into shore like a scrubwoman going home. And all during this driving he keeps thinking, *You're not human tonight, Marlowe,* as his disgust bubbles up, his sneering contempt for everything he sees or thinks about, even the lazy California surf, which has none of the harsh, wild smell of the Atlantic, just a big, thick odorless and waddling kind of ocean—*California,* he thinks, *the department-store state, the most of everything, the best of nothing*—and then he passes Malibu, and he grows cranky again—*more movie stars, more pink and blue bathrobes, more tufted beds and Chanel No. 7, more windblown hair and sunglasses and attitudes and pseudo-refined voices and waterfront morals*—and again, he stops himself, *You're not human tonight, Marlowe*—and then finally he comes into L.A., which he smells before he gets to it: it smells stale and old like a living room that has been closed up too long, but the colored lights fooled you, he thought . . . the lights were wonderful . . . the little colored lights. Sitting there in the courtyard, I remembered how when I returned from a recent flight and stepped off the plane in L.A. I smelled that smell he had talked about—stale and old, like a living room that had been closed up too long . . . and I thought once again, as I had so many times before, my God, how did he get so many things *so* right?

And yet that wasn't the real question. The real question was how did an accountant for an oil company transform himself into one of the most interesting and original writers America has ever produced?

Natasha Spender—now Lady Spender, wife of the deceased poet Stephen Spender—provided a part of the answer when I called her in London one day and we spent over an hour on the telephone, the first of two long conversations I would have with her. She had become friends with Chandler late in his life, in the years after Cissy's death when Ray made several trips to London and even lived there for months at a time. When I spoke with her, she was in her late eighties, yet she demonstrated a remarkable memory for events and details from the distant past, and she had a very lively and amusing way of speaking, especially when she talked about Ray, of whom she had been very fond.

I have always thought, she said, that when Ray lost his job with the oil company and he began to try to write that really he became like a schoolboy again. It was as if he were a child again, going back to school. That's how he approached it, as if writing were just another subject to be learned. He was the schoolboy, and Cissy was like his mother, there to help him and take care of him. He felt quite proud of the fact that he had taught himself to write, and he used to talk at great length how he had done this, by reading and studying the work of other people.

Chandler taught himself the formula of detective fiction by taking the plots of some of Erle Stanley Gardner's stories and rewriting them. Later he would write to Gardner,

> I forgot to tell you that I learned how to write a novelette on one of yours about a man named Rex Kane, who was an alter ego of Ed Jenkins and got mixed up with some flowery dame in a hilltop house in Hollywood who was running an anti-blackmail organization. You wouldn't remember. It's probably in your file No. 54276–88. I simply made an extremely detailed synopsis of your story and from that rewrote it and compared what I had with yours, and then went back and rewrote it some more, and so on. In the end I was a bit sore because I couldn't try to sell it. It looked pretty good.

He understood that every writer imitates in the beginning, what he called (quoting Robert Louis Stevenson) "playing the sedulous ape." He emulated Gardner and Hammett and Hemingway and the writers he was reading in *Black Mask*. He credited Hammett with helping him understand the importance of using real people, the crooks who appeared in newspapers every day. Hammett, he said, took murder out of the Venetian vase and dropped it in the alley. In most English detective stories, murder was still an affair of the upper classes, the week-end house party and the vicar's rose garden but Hammett, he said, gave it back to the people who commit it for reasons, not just to provide a corpse. He put these people down on paper as they were, and he made them talk and think in the language they customarily used for such purposes.

In his stories—even the earliest ones—Ray made people think and talk in the language they customarily used. Not the English of Dulwich College but of the oil fields of Signal Hill. He said he had to learn to write in American English. He became a student of slang and prison jargon and the language of pickpockets and racketeers, making lists of such terms in a notebook he kept for that purpose.

When he began trying to write mystery stories (which were often of a length to qualify as novelettes), he said he had no "fancy notions" about what he was doing. He could let himself go as a writer and overcome his tendency to intellectualize. For a formal man like Chandler this was important. He wanted to have fun with his writing, to insert an "element of the burlesque," and was surprised that Americans ("of all people," he said, "the quickest to reverse their moods") seemed slow to understand that this element of burlesque was intentional.

He felt free to experiment, having nothing to lose, nothing to prove. Later he would say, "I began to realize the great number of stories that are lost by us rather meticulous boys simply because we permit our minds to freeze on the faults rather than let them work for a while without the critical overseer sniping at everything that is not perfect."

The sort of writing he was doing didn't have to be perfect. It could even be funny.

He read the pulps, and he wrote stories, and then he began to sell them. What helped him more than anything was his desire. He deeply *wanted* to be a writer, and he believed he might make himself into one if he worked hard enough. He thought that "any writer who cannot teach himself to write cannot be taught by others. Analyze and imitate," he said. "No other school is necessary."

He brought the accountant's sense of discipline to the work. He believed in the necessity of adhering to a strict schedule if you were going to be a writer, and of writing from the gut.

I believe that all writing that has any life in it is done with the solar plexus. It is hard work in the sense that it may leave you tired, even exhausted. In the sense of conscious effort it is not work at all. The important thing is that there should be a space of time, say four hours a day at least, when a professional writer doesn't do anything else but write. He doesn't have to write, and if he doesn't feel like it he shouldn't try. He can look out of the window or stand on his head or writhe on the floor. But he is not to do any other positive thing, not read, write letters, glance at magazines, or write checks. Either write or nothing. It's the same principle as keeping order in a school. If you make the pupils behave, they will learn something just to keep from being bored. I find it works. Two very simple rules. a. you don't have to write. b. you can't do anything else. The rest comes of itself.

Either write or nothing. That is what he did.

Cissy nurtured the sense he had of himself as her white knight whose task it was to stand as the moral force in the corrupted universe, of which Los Angeles, with its rapacious entrepreneurs, its crooked cops and biased press, its sleazy politicians and fantasy film industry, was perfectly emblematic. He would not have become the writer he did had he not had this vision of himself to impart to his fictional hero, and he needed Cissy to fulfill this idea, just as he needed Los Angeles to provide him with atmosphere and stories.

Cissy did not particularly care for the kinds of stories he began writing, even though she read each one carefully when it was finished and sometimes even helped him type them up—these stories filled with violence and sleaze and tough-talking men. She did not like the stories because they were brutish, too violent for her taste, though she did like the style in which he was writing. Her argument was that he could do much better. She told him he should quit writing out of the corner of his mouth. That was her advice to him.

Quit writing out of the corner of your mouth.

A few months after I sat in the courtyard of the apartment on Greenwood Place, I would go to Oxford in order to look through the Raymond Chandler archive in the Modern Papers Room of the

Bodleian Library, and my suspicions about Cissy's influence would be confirmed. (It's interesting how his archive, like the man himself, is divided between two countries: half of Ray's papers ended up in the Bodleian, bequeathed by his English agent and literary executor Helga Greene and her son Graham Greene, and the other half are in L.A. in the Special Collections Department at the UCLA library.) In Oxford, I discovered many items that were useful and which excited me—photographs I'd never seen, including a photograph that astonished me, showing Cissy and Ray together (I had thought there were none). I found notes written in Cissy's hand as well as other personal information, including nicknames that Cissy and Ray had used for each other. He had called her "Double-Duck," or more tellingly, "Momma." I had known that she called him "Raymio," owing to his deeply romantic nature, but at the Bodleian I discovered she gave him another private name, the secret name "Gallibeoth," which appeared on notes she wrote to him and sometimes at the edge of photographs. This name immediately intrigued me. It seems to have been a made-up name she assigned to him while they were still conducting their affair—she had written it, for instance, along the bottom of a photograph of Ray taken in Golden Gate Park in San Francisco in 1920, the year her divorce from Julian became final and four years before their marriage. The name invokes the Arthurian figure of Galahad and suggests that from the very beginning he played the role of white knight with her. I felt this was important because it indicated that the character of Philip Marlowe, who is so obviously associated with the idea of the knight, was a persona that arose straight out of Ray's own personality, and that this aspect of his personality had been nurtured, if not outright created, by Cissy herself, many years before Chandler began writing mysteries.

While living on Greenwood Place, they got a cat, a tiny black long-haired Persian kitten, which they named Taki—a variant spelling of the Japanese word for bamboo—and they brought her home to their apartment and put her in a little basket, lined with white cotton eyelet, that looked like a baby bassinet. They took her picture—a little black puff of fur with two glittering eyes. She became their adored, darling Taki, as dear as any child to them and as indispensable to their happiness. A cat that would grow to weigh eighteen pounds, whose huge size pleased Ray enormously. In the years to come, throughout all their moves from place to place, Taki would accompany them, and according to Ray she would remember all the places she had been before and would feel at home anywhere except for one or two places that got to her—he did not know why—and she would not settle down in these places and after a while they knew to take the hint. Chances are, Ray said, there was an ax murder there once and we were much better off somewhere else. Thus Taki became an accomplice to their rootlessness, part of the system of signs and omens forecasting a change.

Ray's pleasures and desires were specific. He loved his pipe. He adored animals—all animals, but especially cats. He would have liked to keep a dog, he said, but dogs were more work, and he had enough work as it was, teaching himself to write. He did however begin to acquire a collection of tiny animals, glass figurines that Cissy called his "amuels." She had a collection of amuels as well, but much smaller than Ray's. His was vast, extraordinary, a Noah's Ark of amuels, each of which had been given a name. In Oxford, in a file at the Bodleian Library, I discovered a list compiled by Cissy—her handwriting had become easy to identify, as she always used a distinctive color of turquoise ink—but this list was typed on five-by-seven-inch cards, under the heading "Raymio Amuels." Very carefully, she had listed each amuel by its name and what kind of animal it was, sometimes even indicating the color of glass. The vastness of this amuel collection astonished me, and even more impressive—perhaps the word is obsessive—was the fact that each of the tiny animals had been named: there was Pavlova the winged swan, Sally the salamander, Larina the green frog, Irwin a blue rabbit and Baby a small yellow glass rabbit, a chicken called Butterball, Snowflake the white tortoise, Seabiscuit the green tortoise, Sasabonsum "a very pretty green glass" crocodile, Glencannon a small Scotty dog, Dappelgrimm the giraffe, a bad dog called Faithful Fido, and many elephants—Kashinmore I and II named after a poem Ray had written—as well as Mandalay, Tharagaverug, Araby, and Sunshine; little Three Legs was a bone-colored dog, Bamboo a "pussy," Violet a goat, Walter a squirrel, Henry the bear, Samuel the Camuel, Winston the Lion and Mañana the mule, Polyphemus the owl, Anatole Penguin, Farouk Camel, and Yamashita Tiger, Quon Mane mountain goat, and Sequoia blue deer. The list went on and on, almost fifty amuels in all.

Imagine, I thought when I discovered the list, collecting all those glass figurines and moving them each time they changed residences. Packing up Samuel the Camuel, and Henry the Bear, and

Pavlova and Tuonela, the winged and wingless swans, Whirlaway the horse, and Mr. Pettigrew the pig. It seemed to go beyond a mere collection—as if these figures were talismans, intimates in a world largely free of human friends or acquaintances, a magical assortment of beasts to provide company for a solitary couple.

Cissy was the keeper of the magic, the recorder of names and of certain stories, and the amuels were part of the magic and stories. Part of the invented, insular world they carried from place to place.

At Oxford, in the Modern Papers room, in going through the eighty-three boxes that make up the Chandler archive, I opened a box of photographs one day to find lying on top a picture of Ray as boy, a studio portrait taken at Brands Studio in Chicago. In this photograph, he looks to be about three years old. He is sitting on a brocade sofa, which is partially covered by some kind of fur rug, and he is holding a doll with both his hands, standing it in front of him at the edge of the sofa, as if presenting the doll for the camera. Both Ray and the doll wear similar dresses. Ray's dress has a scalloped collar and his hair is cut in straight bangs and falls to his collar. At the top of the photograph, Cissy has written "Ray with Alfred" in her turquoise ink. On a separate sheet of very thin paper, she has also provided a short paragraph to accompany the photograph:

Ray with Alfred who fell overboard but miraculously swam the Atlantic and arrived at the hotel a few days later.

I came across this sheet first, Cissy's handwritten paragraph, and the little story confused me; I wanted to take it literally. Who was this Alfred who swam the Atlantic? And then I saw the picture of Ray holding the doll—Alfred the *doll*—and I realized this was a story from Ray's childhood. A story about his "friend" Alfred. This was the story he made up about Alfred's "miraculous" reappearance after falling overboard. A story imbued with magic and heroism. The lost Alfred swimming the Atlantic! Suddenly reappearing at the hotel! This was a story about finding what you have lost, about never really losing anyone because he will miraculously reappear. This was also a story that Cissy had preserved. It was Ray's boyhood story. But it was Cissy who had taken the trouble many years later to write it down. And for whom? What imagined posterity? She did not write down her own childhood stories (or maybe she did, and they were among the letters and journals he had burned), but she recorded Ray's adventure with Alfred. Because she was the keeper of stories, of talismans and amuels, the maker of lists, and the collector of the magic that kept their private world together. As someone who met them would later say, *she was his entry into his world of fable.*

In the same folder there was another picture of Ray taken a few years after the picture with Alfred. In this photograph, he is perhaps seven or eight. He wears a white shirt with a large bow tied at the neck—another studio portrait, but this one looks to have been made in Ireland or England. The look on his face is so extraordinarily sweet, so open and innocent and endearing: a somewhat serious little face, with large soft eyes and sensitive mouth. This photograph shows him at the age he was shortly after his father left him forever. There is no Alfred here. In this picture the story has changed. People do disappear. And they have.

What a charming boy he must have been—you can see it in this picture—and how kind he must have been to his mother, how devoted. Very early on the pattern was set. It was Ray's job to take care of a needy, vulnerable woman, and it was a job he would embrace, one that would absorb him for life. It was a job that he *needed.* And in truth, one he came to love.

He really was the most incredible fantasist, Natasha Spender said to me. He would concoct these elaborate tales about various things that had happened to him and even though you knew they were lies, they were terribly entertaining.

You could have been an actor, Cissy used to tell him, if you hadn't become a writer. He was so good at dramatizing things, making up stories, acting out parts, assuming different voices. A brilliant mimic, people said. An amusing man.

He was fond of drama, and of exaggeration. Toward the end of his life, after Cissy was gone and he was rarely without some sort of female involvement, Natasha Spender told me he had taken an almost perverse delight in fostering contention between the women in his life. Perhaps it made him feel more fully alive, more desirable, to see his women friends at odds with one another, with him at the center of the action. Jean refusing to meet Natasha, of whom she was jealous. Kay and Jean at odds. Helga and Jean increasingly suspicious of each other. The wonderfully named Fay Crooks, who had briefly been a girlfriend of his, colluding with Jean against Helga. Always a spot of female trouble to keep things lively. As Natasha told it, it wasn't always easy to stay neutral among the many women around him, because he had an almost devilish way of wanting to put one up against the other.

When it came to women, he was highly excitable. He was drawn to their beauty, but they made him nervous, overly anxious to please; they caused such an excess of emotion, an intense response. With Cissy there had been less of that, at least after the excitable beginning: she was attracted to his devotion, he to her wisdom and beauty, the mutual fascination of a mature woman and a much younger man. In her he found the solace and steadiness of a devoted friend and ally. With Cissy, as with Florence, there had been the safety of the domicile, the gentle round of domestic chores to balance the rigorous hours spent writing, the warm and steady company to offset the emotional vacillations. He had a partnership with Cissy, a symbiotic attachment, a sense of compatibility and domestic purpose, and what he would later call a loving presence in the home. With Cissy, as with his mother, he could be his true self—Raymio, Gallibeoth, the gallant gentleman, there to serve and please.

Cissy. Flossie. These were his ideal relationships. Women who needed his care as well as his affection and who in return were willing to devote themselves to him.

. . .

He knew he had treated Cissy badly during his drink-sodden Dabney days, and during the decade of the thirties he seemed bent on making it up to her. Even though they were required to live frugally, he still filled a room with red roses every year on their anniversary and bought her presents of jewelry and perfume and champagne. He wrote love poems for her, including this one, which he composed for her birthday on October 29, 1935.

IMPROVISATION FOR CISSY

You who have given me the night and the morning,
The stillness of your eyes, the softness of your lips,
The murmur of your heart like a steady sea,
And a voice like chanting in an Attic glade
What have I given you?

Lear years slinking by at the edge of dusk,
Gaunt with memories, hollow with old pain,
Silences into which come the voices of forsworn desires,
And the colors of unattainable delights,
These I have given you,
And of them you have made jewels to wear in your hair.
This is what love is, this is what love is.
When love is this, how can there be despair?

The old pain he speaks of is, of course, the old pain of past arguments, his affairs and drinking, leaving her lonely, ill, abandoned. So the bastard world he begins writing about in the *Black Mask* stories, the world where people behave badly and exploit and abuse one another, is in part his own corrupted universe, his selfishness he's had to face, and he invents his early heroes, and then finally Philip Marlowe, as a correcting influence, a chaste and moral man, if not exactly a sober one—champion of underdogs and defender of women, except of course those bad women who must be punished if not outright killed.

Writing was like anything else: you just had to learn it. And learn it he did, working away at a typewriter in the apartment complex on Greenwood Place, while Cissy shopped and cooked, fixing him lunches and dinners that were far better than anything they could get in restaurants.

Ray was proud of her cooking. Throughout his life he praised it. After her death, he saved her recipe box and carried it with him from place to place, until it became part of his own archive. I found it at the Bodleian Library—a dilapidated black and white speckled cardboard affair, the size of a shoe box, crammed with four-by-five cards on which she had written out recipes for some of Ray's favorite dishes—Mystery Meatloaf and Cissy's Fried Chicken, Cissy's Ham Goodbye, and Perfect Rib Roast, Never-fail Dumplings, Crepes Suzette with Sherry, as well as Glamorous Cherry Pie and Vanilla Ice Cream, a recipe on which she had written "Raymio likes it." Many of her recipes had been clipped from women's magazines—canapes made of liverwurst; a frankfurter pickle spread; a cocktail made of tomato juice, Tabasco, and lemon; but some had been passed down from her mother, Marie's Soup, for instance, or Mama's Chili Sauce, while others came from friends who lent their names to the dishes. Sometimes there's a reference to Ray on the recipes, such as "Applesauce for Gallibeoth" or "Raymio's Favorite Pancakes." These recipes are above all quintessentially American; like Cissy herself they seem to have come straight out of the heartland, and yet (also like her) they often have that yearning for elegance—the Lobster Thermidor from Town Lyne House in Massachusetts, and the Palace Court Salad recipe clipped from a San Francisco paper in 1932, which must have come from a trip they made to the Bay Area during the time they were living here on Greenwood Place.

In many ways the 1930s were their best years, even if these were the *lean years slinking by at the edge of dusk / filled with silences into which come the voices of forsworn desires* (no more affairs, he must have promised her, no more boozing). *This is what love is, When love is this, how can there be despair?* The thirties were perhaps the most contented period of his life—and the most even and sober, which may account for the feeling of well-being. You can see his happiness in the photographs of him taken during this period. A number of these photographs appear to have been taken by Cissy. Pictures of Ray standing in the yard of one or another of their rented houses.

Many show Ray with Taki—Taki draped around his neck like a fur stole. Taki sitting on one of his shoulders. Taki cradled in his arms like a big black hairy baby. One shows Ray with a little light-colored cat: he's standing in a backyard near another little building with a stairway leading to an upper floor. On the back of this photo Cissy has written, "Ray and Twink near Ray's shack, Santa Barbara, 1936."

Ray's shack. Santa Barbara, 1936. Did *shack* refer to the place where he wrote? I had not known they ever lived in Santa Barbara until I saw this photograph. Just another address, one more residence, to add to my ever-growing list.

For a time during the midthirties, Ray was involved with a group of other writers who called themselves The Fictioneers. The group had about twenty-five members, all pulp and movie writers, who met once a month in a private dining room at Steven's Nikobob Café at the corner of Ninth Street and Western Avenue, in order to discuss their craft, but according to one member, the real purpose of these evenings was to get comfortably drunk and then en masse attend one of the local burlesque theaters. One of the things that attracted the men and held the group together was that most of them were working in the same markets—all trying to sell their stories to the same magazines. As one of the founders of the group said: "In the East there was a lot of backbiting among competitors, but in Hollywood, because we were three thousand miles from our markets, we clung together, passing on any information that might help the other fellow." At these meetings of The Fictioneers, Ray was described as "a very retiring person who would sit at dinner after the table had been cleared, sucking on his pipe and offering very little comment." "Most writers like to talk about their own work (which is the reason for a writers' club)," one of the members said later, but he added that Ray seldom discussed what he was working on. Another of the writers reported that Ray was hard to get close to. He described him as "a professorial type, more of an intellectual than most of the other pulp writers I knew. He was a quiet man at that time, did not drink, and was older than most of the rest of us."

Occasionally he and Cissy would accept an invitation to dinner at the home of one of The Fictioneers, but they always kept their distance. Ray would consume many cups of coffee and smoke his pipe and converse very little with other guests. He was standoffish and cool. Often he was more interested in the hosts' cats than the human guests. One woman remembered inviting the Chandlers to dinner, and when Ray learned that the couple's cat had been exiled to a trailer out back for the duration of the dinner, he insisted on visiting the cat and spent considerable time consoling the animal. The hostess sensed he was more interested in spending the evening with her cat than joining the lively party going on inside.

These outings were few and far between, but they demonstrate that the Chandlers did occasionally go out during the time when Ray was just beginning to publish his first stories, even if they rarely seemed to connect with other people.

From Greenwood Place they moved to Santa Monica, to an apartment that is now the site of a trailer court beneath a freeway underpass, and from Santa Monica back to the city center, to half of a duplex on Redesdale Avenue in Silverlake, and from Redesdale they moved to Pacific Palisades, then to Santa Barbara, and then back to Pacific Palisades, where the snapshot of Ray with Taki was taken in 1936. In all these photographs from the thirties he is smiling. Later he will not be smiling. After Cissy's death, in every photograph I ever saw of him except one, he is scowling. When I spoke to Natasha Spender, she mentioned this, how she once scolded Ray for always looking so grumpy in his photographs. He should smile more often, she told him. He needn't look so grim.

In the 1930s no one needed to tell him to smile. It came to him naturally. He smiled for the camera, and for the woman who held it. He held his beloved black cat, his pipe clenched between his teeth, and he smiled, at his handsome cat, at his shutterbug wife, at the sunny palm-tree-studded world in which he found himself. Because life was good. He was writing. He was publishing his stories. And, very important, he was sober. He had given up drinking completely. And he had done it all on his own.

The morning fog was beginning to burn off, and still the air was a diaphanous soup that felt strangely primeval. In the small leafy garden on Greenwood Place, the high sun strained through a vague soft grayness. There were other apartments I wanted to see, other addresses to track down, and I stood up to leave. As I walked back toward the front gate, I passed again through the covered archway, and this time I noticed something I had missed earlier, a row of old metal mailboxes built into the stucco wall. The mailboxes were rusted closed, long unused—nine mailboxes, one for each apartment. On the last mailbox was a small slip of paper that had one word written on it, in an old-fashioned script, and that word was the name CHANDLER.

At first I couldn't quite believe my eyes. The light was rather low and I bent down for a closer look. And there it was, most definitely, the name *Chandler* written in a delicate script. The paper was yellowed with age. Was it possible, I wondered, that Ray had written his name on this slip of paper and put it here on this mailbox and it had been left untouched all these years? It seemed unlikely. And yet there it was. And the mere sight of it gave me a little buzz of excitement. But it also confused me. Did it actually date from 1932, when Ray and Cissy had lived here?

I was thinking about this, feeling distracted as I headed for the front gate, when I bumped into a woman who was struggling to open the gate while carrying several bags of groceries. I held the gate for her, and on an impulse I introduced myself and told her about my interest in Raymond Chandler and asked if she lived in the building. She said that she did. She knew that Chandler had once lived here. One of the other tenants in the building, a great Chandler fan, had told her this when she first moved in. Her name was Lisa, and it turned out that she lived in the same apartment where Chandler had lived. If I wished, she said she would be happy to let me come inside and have a look around.

I helped her with her groceries, and she led the way to the ground-floor apartment. As she opened the front door, two cats bolted past us, and she hurriedly put her groceries down and raced off down the sidewalk after them, calling out that I should go ahead and have a look around. I stepped inside a cool, dark living room with wood floors and a low ceiling. Blinds covered the windows, and a low slatted light fell on a few pieces of furniture and on the dark wood floors—a noirish light, I thought, low and atmospheric and banded in dramatic stripes. It was a small apartment, one bedroom, one bath, much smaller than the place Ray

and Cissy had rented on Highland Avenue when he'd worked for
Dabney Oil. It felt like the kind of place where a man trying to
become a writer might live. I was glad to see it hadn't been remodeled. The kitchen still had the old black-and-white tile from the
1930s, and the wooden cupboards showed evidence of many layers of paint. At one end of the kitchen was a little breakfast nook of
the sort Chandler often wrote about. It looked like a lot of apartments in L.A. Nothing terribly distinctive about it. Except Raymond Chandler had lived here once with his wife. He'd sat up at
night writing poetry to her. He'd eaten breakfast with her in this
little nook, and here Cissy had cooked him breakfast and dinner.
It was the kitchen, especially, that seemed to hold their presence.
I got my camera out and took one picture, standing at one end of
the kitchen. By then Lisa had returned with the fugitive cats. They
were both black, like Taki. I asked her how long she'd lived in the
apartment. Just a year, she said. She had moved to L.A. from Mis-
souri. She didn't say why and I didn't ask. Maybe she was in the
film business. She was pretty and young and fresh-faced, like a
would-be actress, the sort of person Ray might have written
about, a girl from the Midwest, attractive and open, the kind
who'd let a stranger into her apartment because she was so trust-

ing, or because she simply didn't know any better. Did you know, she said, that some episodes of the television series *Melrose Place* were filmed in this apartment building? I said I didn't. But it didn't surprise me. This was L.A., after all, where the lines between the fictive world and the real one were always blurred.

I thanked her for letting me have a look around, and then I left, but not before taking one last look at the mailbox and the tiny hand-lettered *Chandler*, written in faded black ink on the wavy yellowed paper.

Redesdale Avenue is one of those narrow streets in the Silverlake district of L.A. that winds up into the hills above a reservoir, twisting and turning as it snakes higher and higher, with views of tall buildings in downtown L.A. opening up now and then as you round a bend. I had no trouble locating the apartment where Ray and Cissy had lived in 1933. In the Bodleian I had come across a note from Erle Stanley Gardner, written to Chandler while he had lived here in Silverlake. Both he and Ray had stories in the December 1933 issue of *Black Mask*—it was Ray's first published story— and Gardner was deeply impressed with his debut. Right away, he said, he sensed that Raymond Chandler possessed a "special talent." He wrote to Ray and invited him to come by for an evening, saying he'd like to meet him. Ray's response was typically sardonic:

I should consider it a great privilege to meet Erle Stanley Gardner, even though a man who uses three secretaries and has to be flagged as he whizzes through, would undoubtedly be far too fast company for anyone of my rather pensive habits. Also I am the merest beginner in writing and spend most of my time looking out the window and trying to think of something to write about . . . but I appreciate your kindness in asking me to drop in just the same and shall hope to call you up very soon and pay my respects. I live not far from your address.

Ray did drop by, and it was the beginning of a long friendship between the two men. Even Cissy liked Gardner. They were both lunar telescope enthusiasts, and in later years, the Chandlers would occasionally drive down to Gardner's ranch in Temecula, an hour and a half south of the city, to visit him, sometimes spending the night so Cissy could look at the moon through Gardner's telescope.

The Chandlers had lived at 1639 Redesdale, a duplex apartment built to look like a kind of thatched English cottage. The neighborhood, a maze of narrow streets, seemed eerily quiet on a Monday afternoon. Nothing but the sound of the wind in the trees. No pedestrians. No sidewalks. No movement at all, except for an occasional passing car. The duplex sat on the corner of Redesdale and Rotary, and the apartment Chandler had lived in was on the left-hand side of the building and included a small covered balcony, situated over a garage, and covered with that ubiquitous California plant, the scarlet bougainvillea.

I parked at the curb in front of the duplex and sat there for a while, staring at the heads of two plastic pink flamingos that had been buried up to their necks in the front yard. The place had a slightly neglected feel—an untended garden and overgrown trees badly in need of trimming. I got out and walked up and down the curb, looking at the duplex from different angles. Somebody peered out from behind a curtain and stared hard at me, then quickly disappeared. Did I seem like a suspicious character? Probably so Walking in this neighborhood would be enough to make you suspect. A delivery truck pulled up and a man pounded on the opposite door of the duplex and then when he didn't get an answer he drove away. Then a man opened the other door and looked at me angrily, as if he thought I was the one who'd done the pounding. He was the same man who had peered out from behind the curtain at me, and he lived in the half of the duplex where the Chandlers had lived. I started up the steps, thinking I might introduce myself and tell him about Chandler, that he'd once lived in

his apartment, but he gave me such a hostile look it stopped me in my tracks, and then he slammed the door. I guessed I wouldn't ask him for a look inside after all. There'd be no point.

In the early stories, Ray used different names for his heroes—Mallory, Walter Gage, Steve Grayce. Marlowe hadn't yet been born, though those early incarnations shared many of his qualities. From the beginning, the stories were written in the first person, with only one or two exceptions, establishing the intimate voice of a narrator who speaks straight to the reader. They were populated by a wide array of characters who always included a good number of moral defectives, nasty creatures who inhabited a cold, half-lit world where the wrong things always happened, never the right. From the beginning his narrators were bards of urban decadence. There was a sense of sleaze—flea-bitten hotels, night clerks with dirty fingernails, characters in rumpled suits in need of a shower. The early stories were as coolly dispassionate as the later novels, and the hero was just as sardonic, just as detached. Yet the evil was never gratuitous. The violence and corruption was always rooted in the complexities of the human personality. That's where the stories got their power. From the characters. And individual scenes that never felt rushed, rather than mere plots.

The trademark qualities of Chandler's writing seem to have emerged from his mind early on, rather than developing slowly over time or as a result of his having gradually learned his craft. The moral hero, the wisecracking man who spoke the language of the street. The direct voice, and brilliant similes and slang. The Dantesque underworld of L.A. The blondes, the bimbos, the weary PI who runs afoul of the cops. These were all a part of his early literary landscapes.

He wrote about the sort of women who turned up in news reports in the Los Angeles papers in the 1920s and '30s, stories he certainly would have read. There was, for instance, "Broken Blossom," as the press called her, a drug addict who surfaced in Los Angeles after being cast out of Chinatown in 1929. The daughter of a wealthy Pasadena family, she had given up home, friends, family, and a possible career to live for many years as a "slave" with the Chinese, who kept her in line by supplying her with drugs. This was the sort of story Ray would have liked, the wayward daughter of the rich Pasadena family, a girl addled by drugs and kept as a sex slave. He could do something with that. Just as he could with another prominent story of the time, this one featuring a woman dubbed Tiger Girl who murdered her best friend, whom she suspected of having an affair with her husband and was sent to San Quentin for the crime, though she escaped and was later found living in Honduras. "Bad" women sold newspapers, and there seemed to be no shortage of them in L.A. in the free-for-all years of the 1920s and '30s.

The women in Chandler's stories were complex—maybe not so much complex as troublesome. They fell into three categories: the witches, and the bitches (usually rich), and the bumpkins or innocents. Carmen Dravec, of the early story "Killer in the Rain," who becomes Carmen Sternwood, the thumb-sucking nymphomaniac in *The Big Sleep*, is the prototype for the witch, the sexed-up female, high on dope and low on morals. Her sister Vivian, played to hauteur perfection by Lauren Bacall in the film version of the novel, is the model for a long line of rich bitches—cool, icy, man-bashing blondes who often dressed in "mannish" outfits. And Orfamay Quest, the dumpy little liar from Kansas in *The Little Sister*, is the model for the bumptious midwestern innocent who gets shipped back home when the big city becomes too much for her. Marlowe never really had to treat these women as anything more than the tropes they were meant to represent, because he never really got involved emotionally with them. His emotions, as it turned out, were usually reserved for men.

I went back to my car and got behind the wheel, but I didn't drive off. I just sat there for a while, staring at the buried plastic flamingos. Something was troubling me. Something someone had said to me when he discovered I was writing about Raymond Chandler.

So, he said, are you going to finally answer that question we're all curious about?

What question is that? I asked.

Was Raymond Chandler really gay? he said, and then he laughed.

Raymond Chandler *gay*?

The person who asked me this question was a mystery writer himself. A big burly guy who got a smirk on his face when he threw the question out, as if he wouldn't mind taking the Big Man down a notch by making him a closeted homosexual.

I don't know, I answered. I'll have to think about that. And I did.

I thought about it when I went back and reread some of Ray's early stories and discovered scenes and descriptions that seemed rife with homoeroticism.

In "Pearls Are a Nuisance," the suave and rather effete hero Walter Gage befriends a rough-looking character named Henry Eichelberger whom he suspects of having stolen an old lady's pearls but whom, in one of many plot twists, he also takes on as a partner in solving the crime. Walter is certainly a foppish character—he speaks "like Jane Austen writes," and when he talks he waves an "airy hand." At one point the rough-talking Henry says to Walter, "Don't pansy up on me," when Walter hedges the question as to whether or not Henry is handsome. After a day of hard drinking, they end up in bed together:

> At five o'clock that afternoon I awoke from a slumber and found that I was lying on my bed in my apartment in the Chateau Moraine, on Franklin near Ivar Street, in Hollywood. I turned my head, which ached, and saw that Henry Eichelberger was lying beside me in his undershirt and trousers. I then perceived that I was also as lightly attired. On the table nearby there stood an almost full bottle of Old Plantation rye whiskey, the full quart size, and on the floor lay an entirely empty bottle of the same excellent brand. There were garments lying here and there on the floor . . .

Henry and Walter are an odd couple, Henry with his brutish manners, and Walter with his beautiful wardrobe and his highbrow, witty way of speaking. "What makes you always talk so funny?" Henry asks him. Walter replies: "I cannot seem to change my speech Henry. My father and mother were both severe purists in the New England tradition, and the vernacular has never come naturally to my lips, even while I was in college."

Walter lends the rough-hewn Henry a suit when they go out together one evening to confront a bar owner they think might have been involved in the theft: "Henry looked almost handsome in my second-best dinner suit, with a fringed white scarf hanging over his shoulder, a light-weight black felt hat on the back of his head . . . and a bottle of whiskey in each of the side pockets of the summer overcoat he was wearing." Later, back in Walter's apartment after they have knocked back a few more drinks, Walter says, "You would not care to pass the night here, Henry?" "Thanks pal," Henry replies, "but I'm O.K. back at the hotel . . . I guess I'd better change my duds back to where I can mix with the common people." Walter misses him after he's gone: "Henry left me then and I felt suddenly very depressed and lonely. Henry's company had been very stimulating to me, in spite of his rough way of talking. He was very much of a man."

Walter does have a girlfriend, who works for the old lady from whom the pearls were stolen, but for most of the story she's not speaking to him because she's angry about his excessive drinking. By the end of the story, the low-life Henry has earned not just Walter's friendship but his affection, as Walter realizes in the final scene as the two men stand together in the moonlight:

> I moved over beside him and watched his averted face, insofar as I was able to see it in the dim light. A strange melancholy came over me. In the brief time I had known Henry I had grown very fond of him.

The whiff of homosexual attraction hangs over this story like a cloud of cheap aftershave, as it does in other stories from the period. Consider "Pickup on Noon Street," for instance, and this scene in which Pete Anglich, a hard-drinking undercover cop, is taking a shower in a cheap hotel when he is surprised by a "Negro intruder":

> He went into a dim, dirty bathroom, stepped into the tub and turned the shower on . . . he soaped himself, rubbed his whole body over, kneaded his muscles, rinsed off.
>
> He jerked a dirty towel off the rack and started to rub a glow into his skin.
>
> A faint noise behind the loosely closed bathroom door stopped him. . . . Pete Anglich reached for the door and pulled it open slowly.
>
> The Negro in the purple suit and Panama hat stood beside the bureau, with Pete Anglich's coat in his hand. On the bureau in front of him were two guns. One of them was Pete Anglich's old worn Colt. . . . The Smiler let the coat fall to the floor and held a wallet in his left hand. His right hand lifted the Colt. He grinned.
>
> "Okey, white boy. Just go on dryin' yourself off after your shower," he said.

Pete Anglich toweled himself. He rubbed himself dry, stood naked with the wet towel in his left hand.

The Smiler takes Pete's money from his wallet, but the naked Pete foils the robbery by flicking the wet end of his bath towel straight at The Smiler's eyes and, in the ensuing struggle, the two men grapple and fight for the gun, which "slides" over Pete's flesh in a blatantly erotic manner until, bodies still entwined, Pete manages to shoot The Smiler, then "let him down on the floor and stood panting . . . and put his underclothes and socks and shoes on."

The entire scene between the white man and the black takes place with the white man naked. A good deal of bodily contact occurs, flesh pressed against flesh as the two men struggle. What did the readers of *Detective Fiction Weekly* think of this story when it was published in 1936? Or for that matter, Chandler's description of another male character, who turns up later in the story and is evoked in the kind of lush prose usually reserved for femmes fatales?

John Vidaury was six feet two inches in height and had the most perfect profile in Hollywood. He was dark, winsome, romantic, with an interesting touch of gray at his temples. His shoulders were wide, his hips narrow. He had the waist of an English guards officer, and his dinner clothes fit him so beautifully that it hurt.

"Not getting the girl" in Marlowe's case is never really a misfortune because it's never really a goal. When he does finally "get the girl" in *The Long Goodbye*, by going to bed with the millionairess Linda Loring, he shows not a shred of real erotic desire or emotional feeling for her. In fact, the next morning when Marlowe discovers one of Linda's long dark hairs still clinging to the pillow, he pulls the bed apart and remakes it, as if to remove any trace of her.

For Marlowe a warm erotic feeling toward a woman never seems a possibility—with the exception, as Natasha Spender pointed out to me, of one woman, Anne Riordan, in *Farewell, My Lovely*, whom he declines to sleep with on moral principle but whose hand he holds and then lets go of "slowly as you let go of a dream when you wake with the sun in your face and have been in an enchanted valley." Anne is a redhead like Cissy, and out of all the women in the novels, she seems to engender the tenderest feelings in Marlowe. He can be attracted by women, but strangely the lust always ends up feeling mechanical, as if he resents even having such desires. Often the women he's most attracted to have certain masculine attributes, either in manner or dress—like Mrs. Eddie Mars in *The Big Sleep*, who wears a platinum wig to cover her own hair, which is clipped as short as a boy's, and who wears a dress with a masculine cut. And although Marlowe appears to fall for Mrs. Mars, the description of their brief physical contact is less than warm:

> Her face under my mouth was like ice. She put her hands up and took hold of my head and kissed me hard on the lips. Her lips were like ice, too.
>
> I went out through the door and it closed behind me without a sound, and the rain blew in under the porch, not as cold as her lips.

When Marlowe does become aroused, it's by the women who have committed the most brutal murders—like Mrs. Grayle in *Farewell, My Lovely*, who kills Lindsay Marriott, beating him until he has brains on his face. Or Eileen Wade in *The Long Goodbye*, for whom Philip Marlowe is "as erotic as a stallion," and who later is revealed as a murderer who has pounded her female victim's head into a bloody sponge. In six of the seven novels, a murder is committed by a woman. The men in the novels, even such criminals and mobsters as Moose Malloy and Eddie Mars, engender in Marlowe a kind of admiration, and often an appreciation of their physiques (in *The Lady in the Lake*, Chris Lavery has "a terrific torso and magnificent thighs"—"so long, beautiful hunk" Marlowe says when he parts from him). Marlowe gets kissed by women, and he kisses them, often and usually with a kind of hardness and urgency, but the subsequent disengagement is immediate and rather thorough, as if the physical contact is gratuitous, indulged only because it's expected.

In the case of the Sternwood sisters, in the space of the same night, Marlowe makes out with one (Vivian, dressed in a low-cut gown) in the front seat of her car, only to go home and find the other (Carmen) naked in his bed and, repulsed by her, tosses her out. The next morning he wakes feeling repelled by all women: "You can have a hangover from other things than alcohol," he says. "I had one from women. Women made me sick."

It would be very easy to explain Marlowe's distance from women by simply evoking the limits of the mystery story in the 1930s—it was a man's world, and a man's genre, and there was really no place for much romance in that world. A good hard kiss was about as romantic as it got. Chandler's decision to make his heroes unavailable to any real emotional engagement with a woman not only reflected the "rules" of the genre but must have in some way reflected his own deeper feelings.

In his own lifetime Chandler had to confront the charge that Marlowe was susceptible to male charms. An American writer named Gershon Legman wrote to Chandler in 1949, accusing him, as Chandler put it, of "homosexualism." Legman found evidence of this in certain descriptions scattered throughout the stories and novels, such as the description of Red Norgaard ("probably the nicest man I ever met," says Marlowe) in *Farewell, My Lovely*:

> He had the eyes you never see, that you only read about. Violet eyes. Almost purple. Eyes like a girl, a lovely girl. His skin was as soft as silk. Lightly reddened, but it would never tan. It was too delicate . . . he was not as big as Moose Malloy, but he looked very fast on his feet.

Moose Malloy, the big oafish goon who hires Marlowe to "find his Velma" and who in the first few chapters of *Farewell, My Lovely* manages to break a man's neck and strangle a helpless old woman, still has a "voice that is soft and dreamy, so delicate for a big man that it was startling. It made me think," Marlowe says, "of another soft-voiced big man I had strangely liked."

It was the word *strangely* that Legman seized on to "prove" Marlowe harbored homosexual inclinations. In his book *Love and Death: A Study in Censorship*, he wrote:

> No matter how "strangely" Chandler's detective, Marlowe, moons over these big men, they are always beating him up ... The true explanation of Marlowe's temperamental disinterest in women is not "honour" but his interest in men ... Chandler's Marlowe is clearly homosexual—a butterfly, as the Chinese say, dreaming that he is a man.

Ray dismissed Legman's charge by refusing even to acknowledge the letter in which it was made. Later Ray wrote to a friend, saying, "Mr. Legman seems to belong to that rather numerous class of American neurotics which cannot conceive of a close friendship between a couple of men as anything other than homosexual."

There was always the possibility that if Chandler—and by extension Marlowe—did harbor any homosexual inclinations they might have been so deeply repressed as to never have been acknowledged, leaking out instead, via the unconscious, in certain passages of prose. I remembered something Natasha Spender had said to me in one of our phone conversations regarding her first impressions of Chandler, how she and a group of close women friends who had befriended him had all simply assumed he was a closeted homosexual, for reasons she was only too willing to discuss.

Natasha met Raymond Chandler in April 1955, a few months after Cissy's death and a few weeks after Chandler, distraught over his loss, had tried to commit suicide. In March of that year, while drunk, he called the La Jolla police, telling them of his plan to kill himself, then took a loaded revolver into the bathroom of the house in La Jolla that he had shared with Cissy and discharged the revolver twice. The police arrived just as the shots were fired and rushed into the bathroom only to find Chandler sitting in the shower stall unharmed. Somehow he had managed to miss himself, and so had the ricocheting bullets. The news of this episode (what he himself later referred to as the world's most inept suicide attempt) was widely reported in the press, and in the wake of the publicity, Chandler fled to London, and it was there, not long after he arrived, that he met Natasha and Stephen Spender at a luncheon given for him by his publisher, Hamish Hamilton, and Hamilton's wife, Yvonne.

Natasha recalled how she had sat next to him at that luncheon and how she sensed the "aura of despair" that still clung to him. At the time, Natasha was an up-and-coming concert pianist in her thirties, with two young children, an attractive woman who took an immediate liking to Ray. Knowing of his recent suicide attempt, she decided to take him under her wing, and with a group of her close women friends, she formed a kind of rescue brigade whose mission it was to keep Chandler occupied with female company. They figured he was such a gentleman that if he had a date with a woman he would not fail to show up and thus could not consider harming himself.

These women, as they got to know Chandler, came to believe, "without a second thought," as Natasha put it, that Ray was a repressed homosexual, "a perhaps too facile conclusion," as she admitted, but one based on certain observations. For one thing, they thought only a strenuous repression of his own homoerotic tendencies could account for the "alert and vehement aversion he always went out of the way to express toward homosexuals." (Since Stephen Spender had written about his own homosexual past, as a young man in the 1930s in Berlin, where he had gone to live with his friends W. H. Auden and Christopher Isherwood, one assumes that Natasha was perhaps more keenly sensitive than most people to homoerotic tendencies, though she later claimed, in a conversation with me, that she "was always the last to know about these things.") There was also the fact that for all Ray's "jolly talk about sex," he never made the slightest advance toward any of the women who made up the rescue brigade, nor did he show any interest of that sort in any of the women they introduced him to. Natasha believed that Ray's upbringing—his "swine" of a father and "saint" of a mother (these were Ray's own terms)—and the way he spoke of his own character of "exceptional sexual purity," engendered by the stultifying atmosphere of Dulwich College and the Victorian rectitude surrounding his childhood, had all conspired to create a condition of repressed sexuality in him. In an essay about Ray, "His Own Long Goodbye," published after his death, she wrote:

> From his reminiscences it seemed clear that at far too early an age he was made to feel he was "the man of the family" in this household of women, at the same time protecting his mother and sharing the humiliations she suffered from the moralizing condescension of his aunt and grandmother. Clinically this pattern of childhood situations is often recognized as a determining factor for later homosexuality.

There is also, of course, the clichéd picture of the homosexual man who marries the beautiful, much older woman, after living with his mother until she dies. But still, I found all this to be conjecture.

The last time we spoke on the phone, Natasha told me a story about a luncheon she had once given, to which she had invited Ray and several friends, one of whom was gay and who brought along his younger lover. At the end of the luncheon, her gay friend complained to Natasha that during the meal Chandler had "made a pass" at his lover. "I was surprised," Natasha said, "since I hadn't noticed anything."

Another time, she said, her husband introduced Ray to a writer he'd discovered named Frank Norman, at a luncheon he'd arranged for the two of them. Spender was then editing a literary magazine, *Encounter*, which was publishing some of Norman's prose, and he thought Ray would be interested in meeting Norman, a very unusual character. He had been a habitué of the Soho underworld and spent some time in prison—experiences he later wrote about. Ray was excited by the prospect of meeting a "hardened criminal," as he put it, and was immediately taken with Frank Norman, whose life as a thief he found very romantic. The lunch was a great success, in spite of the fact that Ray had arrived quite drunk. Later Spender reported to his wife that during the lunch Ray's attraction to Frank Norman (rather like the educated Walter Gage's attraction to the rough Henry Eichelberger) was so pronounced as to amount to a flirtation.

I didn't know what to make of these stories about Ray. I wondered, in fact, whether I had any right even to be pondering his sexuality. And yet didn't such an inquiry have a place when it came to trying to understand his marriage?

It seemed to me that Ray never resolved the question, What did Marlowe want? Marlowe had a dual impulse: to protect women, honor them, put them on a pedestal and at the same time keep them separate, lest he might be contaminated by their otherness, which he had only a vague reason for fearing. In *The Long Goodbye*, the novel in which Marlowe develops the most intense feeling for another man, Terry Lennox—unquestionably the tenderest relationship in the entire oeuvre—Lennox is given a speech in which he rails against women: "The goddam women," Lennox says, "waving their hands and screwing up their faces and tinkling their goddam bracelets and making with the packaged charm." "Take it easy," Marlowe replies. "So they're human . . . what did you expect—golden butterflies hovering in a rosy mist?"

When Chandler wrote *The Long Goodbye* he had already received Legman's letter accusing Marlowe of being a "homosexualist," and perhaps that was why he went to some length in this novel to explore the subject. Marlowe and the alcoholic writer Roger Wade have a rather long discussion about homosexuals while Wade is drunk

"Know something?" [Wade] asked suddenly, and his voice suddenly seemed much more clear. "I had a male secretary once. Used to dictate to him. Let him go. He bothered me sitting there waiting for me to create. Mistake. Ought to have kept him. Word would have got around I was a homo. The clever boys that write book reviews because they can't write anything else would have caught on and started giving me the build-up. Have to take care of their own, you know. They're all queers, every damn one of them. The queer is the artistic arbiter of our age, chum. The pervert is the top guy now."

"That so? Always been around, hasn't he?"

He wasn't looking at me. He was just talking. But he heard what I said.

"Sure, thousands of years. And especially in all the great ages of art. Athens, Rome, the Renaissance, the Elizabethan Age, the Romantic Movement in France—loaded with them. Queers all over the place. Ever read *The Golden Bough*? No, too long for you. Shorter version though. Ought to read it. Proves our sexual habits are pure conventions—like wearing a black tie with a dinner jacket. Me, I'm a sex writer, but with frills and straight."

He looked up at me and sneered. "You know something? I'm a liar. My heroes are eight feet tall and my heroines have calluses on their bottoms from lying in bed with their knees up. Lace and ruffles, swords and coaches, elegance and leisure, duels and gallant death. All lies. They used perfume instead of soap, their teeth rotted because they never cleaned them, their fingernails smelled of stale gravy. The nobility of France urinated against the walls in the marble corridors of Versailles, and when you finally got several sets of underclothes off the lovely marquise the first thing you noticed was that she needed a bath. I ought to write that way."

"Why don't you?"

He chuckled. "Sure, and live in a five-room house in Compton—if I was that lucky."

.   .   .

A car crawled past on Redesdale Avenue and stopped just ahead of me, and a man and a woman got out and climbed the stairs and disappeared into the duplex where the Chandlers had lived. They shut the front door with a bang, and in the silence that followed, the neighborhood seemed even more quiet, deathly quiet. Even the wind had died down. Not a thing moved. Except the heat. You could see the heat bending the air into crenellated and transparent waves floating up off the asphalt.

In a letter written in 1957 to his English solicitor, Michael Gilbert, Ray refers to the "fancy boys" that abound in Hollywood:

> I admired your acute remarks about pansies, queers, homos, whatever you want to call them, but at the risk of being thought trying to be the Great American Male (which I am not) I rather disagree with you that they cannot be judged. Of course judgment is not the right word. These are sick people who try to conceal their sickness. My reaction may be uncharitable: they just make me sick. I can't help it. My dead wife could spot one entering a room. Highly sexed women invariably seem to have that reaction.

My dead wife could spot one entering a room.

Had Cissy really had such an aversion to homosexuals, and if that was the case, was it because she disliked them? Or did she sense the threat they might present to her?

Earlier in the spring I had gone to interview Don Bachardy, the artist and longtime lover of Christopher Isherwood. Bachardy and Isherwood had known Chandler toward the end of his life. They once spent a weekend together in Palm Springs, in January 1957, along with Natasha Spender and her friend Dr. Evelyn Hooker, an early pioneer in gay studies (in the early 1950s, Dr. Hooker was the first psychologist to conduct clinical psychological studies and compare test results from gay and straight men, enabling her to report no evidence whatsoever of greater maladjustment or psychological problems in either of the two populations). Bachardy took a 16mm movie camera with him to Palm Springs and shot some footage of the weekend, including images of Chandler fooling around on a diving board. It was the only footage of Chandler known to exist—just a few minutes of film that showed Ray at the hotel pool, putting on a display of his diving prowess for Natasha and Evelyn Hooker (he would ask them to rate his dives, from one to ten). The footage of Chandler was proving to be elusive to track down—I had been unable to locate it among the items included in the Isherwood archive located at the Huntington Library—and I had gone to see Bachardy, to ask about the film and whether he might help me locate it.

I arrived around ten in the morning. We sat in the living room of the house in Santa Monica Canyon that Bachardy had shared for many years with Isherwood. Out the window I could see the view of the long curving sweep of Will Rogers State Beach and the coastline that stretched north toward Malibu. It was a clear, bright day, and the light at the beach seemed infused with tiny silver ions subtly vibrating in the brilliant sunshine.

"Chris did genuinely admire Chandler very much," Bachardy said as we settled down to talk over a cup of coffee. "He anxiously awaited the new Chandler novel. He couldn't get enough. He even reread Chandler and he would never read a book a second time unless he really admired the writer. There was fun in Chandler. Chris liked that."

I read him a quote by Chandler, in which he said that Christopher Isherwood was the "only queer I have felt entirely at ease with."

"He said that?" Bachardy laughed. "I did feel from Chandler that hostility toward homosexuals. He seemed grumpy and distant with me. But I could see him melting for Chris, in spite of himself. When Chris made up his mind he could charm anyone."

Bachardy said that had often happened over the years. People would take out their dislike of homosexuals on him rather than Isherwood, because of who Isherwood was—he was famous, and also charming, whereas Bachardy was very young when they met (he was still in his teens; Isherwood was in his forties) and many people disapproved not only of their homosexuality but also their age difference. Homosexuality was still listed as a mental disorder, and fear and discrimination were rampant. "People could 'swallow' Chris," he said again, "because of who he was, so the abhorrence got directed at me. When I met Chandler I realized immediately that there couldn't be any real exchange between him and me."

Bachardy stopped and took a sip of coffee and smiled at me. He still had the boyish good looks of a young man, even though he was in his seventies. He was a fit, lean, and attractive man, but the most attractive thing about him was his spry, rather gnomish nature—his lightness of spirit.

What he said next surprised me, though perhaps it shouldn't have. "The funny thing about Chandler is that when Chris and I first met him, we both had the feeling he might possibly be gay himself." They had sensed it, he said, during that weekend in Palm Springs.

"But he was married for many years," I said.

Bachardy raised his eyebrows and laughed, as if to say, *So?*

Bachardy knew very little about Cissy or Chandler's personal life, and so I filled him in, explaining how Ray and Cissy had met and fallen in love when she was still married, how they had married two weeks after his mother had died, how Cissy was eighteen years older but had lied about her age, something she had done even when she was in her twenties.

"She was just planning for the future!" he said, and laughed.

I told him that Chandler and Cissy had stayed married for thirty years, and that from all accounts he had adored her.

"Men don't know what they're missing in an older woman," Bachardy said. He named a woman, an actress friend of his, who he said was married to a Frenchman twenty years younger and how happy they were. (Of course, I thought, it would be a Frenchman . . .)

I told him that for much of his life Chandler had professed a great dislike of homosexuals, that he had often displayed an excessive reaction—the "alert and vehement" aversion he'd gone out of the way to express, which Natasha mentioned. Though I understood that this could indicate a strenuous effort to reject his own impulses, I felt it could also mean that he had simply been a victim of the prejudices of the day. I repeated Chandler's remark that his wife had perhaps an even greater dislike of homosexuals than he did and that she could "spot" a homosexual when she walked into a room.

Bachardy's face lit up. "Well, it's perfect, isn't it?" he said. "He married his mother. A woman who hated queers. It's the perfect cover. How much more self-protective can you get?"

I had sat so long at the curb in front of the duplex on Redesdale that the light had begun to change and a pearly pink glow had fallen over the city. The more I thought about Ray's sexuality, the less I felt I knew what he had really felt toward men, and the less I felt it was my business. What difference did it really make if he was a repressed homosexual, or the red-blooded male he had believed Marlowe to be? And at this stage in the game, who could ever know the truth? The one thing I knew for certain was that he had adored women all his life. He had worshipped his wife. He had pursued relationships with many different women after her death, longing to make another commitment, to fall in love, to have a woman companion again, though it seems these relationships were largely, if not completely, sexless. Perhaps he may also have had longings for men. Women were so complicated. Men were comfortingly simple in comparison, and a man's world is an emotionally safe world. In *The Long Goodbye* there's simply no question Marlowe had loved Terry Lennox—he moons over him after he's gone, indulges in little rituals of pouring him a cup of coffee in absentia, lights a second cigarette for his ghost, as if keeping a romantic flame kindled, but when I thought about these scenes, they seemed somehow so innocent. It felt like platonic love. The safe kind of emotional feeling that would not have become physical. It was the love of an achingly lonely man for one true buddy, a soul mate of the same sex. There may have been erotic feelings for men, but in Ray's time, only foolhardy souls or very brave men could admit to them, let alone act on them. Whatever his desires, I think his puritan impulses were constantly at war with his sexual impulses and that his feelings about both women and homosexuality reflect this. At heart, what he feared was what he called "the ordinary vices" that homosexuals reminded us we all possessed. In 1949, shortly after receiving the letter from Legman accusing Marlowe of being homosexualist, he makes this clear in a letter to a publishing colleague:

> The mob impulse to destroy the homo is like the impulse of the wolf pack to turn on the sick wolf and tear him to pieces, or the human impulse to run away from a hopeless disease. This is probably very old and very cruel, but at the bottom of cruelty is a kind of horror . . . All cruelty is a kind of fear. Deep inside us we must realize what fragile bonds hold us to sanity and these bonds are threatened by repulsive insects and repulsive vices. And the vices are repulsive, not in themselves, but because of their effect on us. They threaten us because our own normal vices fill us at times with the same sort of repulsion.

I read that to Don Bachardy—he laughed at the phrase *normal vices* and the idea that homosexuals threaten us because they represent some deep repulsion about our own sexual natures. I'm sure Ray didn't see the contradiction in that phrase: how could something normal also be a vice?

Seven

"I have been asked," Ray once commented during an interview,

> why so many of my books have been set in Los Angeles; in
> other words what there is about that extraordinary city that
> made me want to write about it. There is a very simple
> answer. I wrote about it because I lived there from 1912 until
> 1946 and no one had really written about Los Angeles; about
> its particular flavor, about its gradually increasing toughness
> and criminality, or about the peculiar world of motion pic-
> tures. Half the writers in America live there now, but none of
> them lived there when I began to write about it. Every large
> city in America inevitably has its crime element. In Los Ange-
> les we have never had enough police.

It wasn't quite true that no writers lived in L.A. when Ray began
to write his first stories. John Fante lived there, and so did
Nathanael West, and each would publish a novel (*Ask the Dust* and
Day of the Locust) in 1939, the year Ray published his first novel,
The Big Sleep. But in many ways, he had the city to himself. From
the beginning it was the "crime element" in L.A. that intrigued
him. Sometimes he had to do little more than read the newspaper
to come up with a story.

In the 1930s, he wrote nineteen hard-boiled detective stories, most of them for *Black Mask* but a few for *Dime Detective* magazine. The stories had titles like "Spanish Blood" and "Killer in the Rain," "Finger Man," "Smart-Aleck Kill," "The Man Who Liked Dogs," "Pick-up on Noon Street," "Red Wind," and "The King in Yellow." Hammett was also writing for *Black Mask*, and he and Chandler met once at a dinner for *Black Mask* writers and were photographed on the occasion, standing at opposite ends of the back row. It would be the only time they would meet; of all the people portrayed in the photograph, only they would go on to have enduring reputations.

In 1939, Cissy typed up a few pages of notes Ray had made, outlining his hopes for the future. He had just completed and published *The Big Sleep*, and it's clear he hoped to move beyond the mystery novel into "straight" fiction. "Since all plans are foolish," he wrote, "and those written down are never fulfilled, let us make a plan, this 16th day of March 1939, at Riverside, Calif."

He then outlined his plan. Over the next few years he would write "three more detective novels," using parts of stories he had already published. He would also write a "dramatic novel—a short, swift, tense, gorgeously written story verging on the melodramatic," based on notes he had made for a story called "English Summer." ' The surface theme is the American in England and the dramatic theme is decay of the refined character [an Englishman] and its contrast with the ingenuous honest utterly fearless and generous American of the best type."

He intended to write some "short-long stories" as well:

a set of six or seven fantastic stories . . . each a little different in tone and effect from the others.

The three mystery stories should be finished in the next two years, by the end of 1940. If they make enough money for me to move to England and to forget mystery writing and try English Summer and the Fantastic Stories without worrying about whether these make money, I tackle them. But I must

have two years' money ahead, and a sure market with the
detective story when I come back to it, if I do. If English Summer is a smash hit, which it should be, properly written, written up to the hilt but not overwritten, I'm set for life. From
then on I'll alternate the fantastic and the dramatic until
I think of a new type. Or may do a suave detective just for
the fun.

When she had finished typing up these notes, Cissy wrote at the
bottom of the page:

Dear Raymio, you'll have fun looking at this maybe, and seeing what useless dreams you had. Or perhaps it will not
be fun.

Some have found this comment to be evidence of the couple's
closeness when it came to Chandler's work, an indication of the
intellectual intimacy and frankness that bound them together.
Others have thought Cissy's comment unnecessarily harsh and
damning, reflecting a kind of needling on her part, a reminder to
her husband that his dreams of producing "real" literature were
useless. "Perhaps I'm reading more into this than I should," wrote
one critic, Robert Kirsch, "but this little note strikes me as terrifyingly cruel."

Terrifyingly cruel? Or simply intimate and frank? Cissy was doing
what she had always done for him, and what she would continue
to do for him until the day she died. She was injecting humor and
lightness into a situation. She was being playful and affectionate.
She was reminding him of something he surely knew but often
ignored—the fact that the best-laid plans often went awry. She
knew he was overestimating what was possible (three novels in
two years? Plus six or seven short stories? And a gorgeously written literary novel?) Her note wasn't cruel. It was in fact just the
opposite, a tender reminder that later he should look kindly, and
with wry amusement, upon his overly enthusiastic memo.

Several times over the following months and years Ray took the trouble to answer Cissy's question as to whether or not he'd find it amusing to look back at his plans and see what "foolish dreams" he had.

In September 1940 he wrote next to her comment, "It was not."

In February 1941 he reaffirmed this with one word: "Check."

Nine months later he wrote, "Double check."

In April 1942, "God help us!"

And then, in his last comment on the subject, dated March 1944, he changed his mind and wrote: "Yes it was because I had now achieved it, although not with these stories."

They did not make it to England in 1939, nor did they go in 1940 or 1941 as he had hoped to. War broke out, and he and Cissy continued their pattern of moving constantly from place to place.

When he published *The Big Sleep* he was fifty-one years old; Cissy was almost seventy. The book was written over a period of three months. The decision to use the first-person voice of Philip Marlowe gave the book undeniable power, for in Marlowe's voice there comes through what Chandler called the controlled half-poetical emotion that lies at the heart of the book. The novel brought him attention and also a contract for a second book with Knopf. But many critics didn't think the book worthy of notice. Some found it "dirty." A critic from *The New York Times* wrote that the language in the book was "often vile—at times so filthy that the publishers have been compelled to resort to the dash, a device seldom employed in these unsqueamish days." The *Times* critic went on to deem *The Big Sleep* "a study in depravity" and pointed out that Marlowe was the only fundamentally decent character in the whole book.

The *Times* critic was not inaccurate: crooked cops, a homosexual blackmailer, pornographers, nudity, a drug-taking nymphomaniac, as well as mobsters and adulterers and alcoholics all show up in *The Big Sleep*. And yet, given the real events unfolding in 1930s Los Angeles, one could hardly accuse Chandler of exaggeration.

There wasn't an element of the political and social scene in L.A.

that wasn't tinged by rottenness—the police, the local government, the business community, even the press, including the city's main newspaper, the *Los Angeles Times*, were all riddled with bribery and influence-peddling, and nowhere was this made clearer than in an episode involving Clifford Clinton, the owner of Clifton's Cafeteria, the pay-as-you-can populist eatery located next door to Chandler's onetime office in the Bank of Italy building, where Ray used to have lunch.

Clinton, a former missionary in China and a man of conscience, was disgusted by the dishonesty among elected officials. As an anticorruption reformer, he helped organize a group called Citizens Independent Vice Investigating Committee in an attempt to expose the corruption in all levels of city government. He and his group went after city hall, filing a report in 1937 that charged Mayor Frank Shaw and members of his administration with accepting campaign contributions from organized crime, being politically influenced by the underworld, and protecting the racketeers who ran the city's gambling joints.

City hall struck back with a vengeance. Clinton was verbally attacked by the mayor as well as the chief of police and the district attorney, all of whom labeled him public enemy number one. Soon the attacks went beyond mere words. Clifton's Cafeteria was stink-bombed. His family was threatened, and his taxes were raised without justification. Much of the campaign against Clinton was directed by Capt. Earl Kynette, chief of the Los Angeles Police Intelligence Bureau, who conducted a standing investigation of the reformers and personally oversaw repeated efforts at harassment.

But Kynette went too far. On October 18, 1937, Clifford Clinton's home on Los Feliz Boulevard, just a few blocks from where Cissy and Ray had lived on Greenwood Place (and where I had discovered their name on the mailbox), was bombed. Clinton and his family survived the attack but were severely shaken by the violence. Then another reformer was blown from his car as he tried to start it, but he, too, miraculously survived and lived to testify against city hall. Captain Kynette and Mayor Shaw were eventually implicated in these bombings, and their connection to the racketeers was disclosed. Clinton, shown here on the right at a hearing at the city attorney's office, was not afraid of fighting for what he believed in and in that respect, he was like Marlowe.

The *Los Angeles Times* had opposed Clinton from the very beginning and joined the attempt to discredit him, claiming that he was giving the city a bad name. But it was Mayor Shaw and the police department who were eventually discredited. The mayor was defeated in a recall election, and the racketeers, no longer feeling as welcome as they once had, began moving their operations out to a little windblown, desolate, sun-baked desert town called Las Vegas, where they found they could operate openly.

In *The Big Sleep*, Chandler made use of the corruption exposed by Clinton and the reformers, through characters like Eddie Mars, the club owner and racketeer, and the DA who does the bidding of the rich General Sternwood, the newspaper that keeps stories out of print, and the corrupt cops who do what they're told and to hell with legality. In L.A., as Ray once said, the law was where you could buy it. The rich made the rules, and the mobsters kept officials in their pockets. Politicians and law enforcement existed not to protect ordinary citizens but to profit from their power. Into this vacuum of justice stepped Philip Marlowe, private investigator—the man who couldn't be bought, not by the powers that be anyway. But for $25 a day and expenses, he could be hired, though he tended to be picky about the cases he took. Like the gunslinger of the Old West, the lone man who stood up to the rustlers and thieves and land and railroad barons on behalf of the frightened citizens, Marlowe was there to help the little guy who had nowhere else to turn. He wasn't afraid of the bad cops and the threatening DA and the bad boys of city hall. He took on the mobsters and gamblers and hired guns, invading their own dens to confront them. And he did it with humor and a cool head, undeterred by the beatings and the abuse he inevitably suffered. As Ray once said, Marlowe had an innocence that could seem almost immature, if being in revolt against a corrupt society can be considered immature. He was a lone wolf, and he liked it that way. He neither wanted nor expected much for himself. He seemed to exist in a perpetual present, without memory or thought for the future or his own happiness. He believed in nothing except his own ability to tell right from wrong. He was more than just the cowboy of the American myth. He went back much further than that. He was the perpetual redeemer of humanity. He was Galahad of Arthurian legend. He was Cissy's Gallibeoth, the noble moral enforcer, born in the brain of her husband as the seed of himself, the fantasy nurtured by her from the beginning of their relationship and played out daily with each other. She was the key to his imaginary self, because she brought out his chivalry, that heroic side of his personality that he lent to his creation. This Galahad/Gallibeoth theme is made clear in the opening paragraphs of *The Big Sleep*, in the description of Philip Marlowe as he approaches the front entrance of the Sternwood mansion, summoned by General Sternwood himself to help extricate his bad-seed daughter from a blackmailer's scheme:

The main hallway of the Sternwood place was two stories high. Over the entrance doors, which would have let in a troop of Indian elephants, there was a broad stained-glass panel showing a knight in dark armor rescuing a lady who was tied to a tree and didn't have any clothes on but some very long and convenient hair. The knight had pushed the vizor [sic] of his helmet back to be sociable, and he was fiddling with the knots on the ropes that tied the lady to the tree and not getting anywhere. I stood there and thought that if I lived in the house, I would sooner or later have to climb up there and help him. He didn't seem to be really trying.

He didn't seem to be really trying.

Philip Marlowe would become the figure who would *try*. He would try to rescue not only the damsels but anyone else in need. He would become a new kind of American hero, one who would say, Look here, just under your clean shining surface, can you beat all that dirt?

Cissy and Ray began drifting farther from the center of L.A., spending time in the nearby mountains and desert. They discovered a small town in the San Bernardino Mountains called Big Bear Lake, then a quiet little resort, built around a pretty lake, where a furnished cabin could be rented very cheaply. Ray loved life in the mountains. He liked the cool, sweet air and the smell of pines. He liked chopping wood and building fires at the end of the day, and taking walks along the lakeshore. In Big Bear, he worked on a draft of *Farewell, My Lovely* and started another story, "No Crime in the Mountains," which would later become the basis for his novel *The Lady in the Lake*. He worked hard at his writing. He was a professional. And what was there to distract him? In Big Bear, very little.

Cissy kept herself busy, shopping, and planning and cooking three meals every day. Their mealtimes were civilized affairs, unrushed, replete with little rituals. When Ray had finished writing for the day, they sat in the sunshine and read books together. Sometimes they did nothing at all. Ray was worried about the prospect of war and followed the events unfolding in Europe; he even tried to reenlist in the Canadian army but, at fifty-one, was turned down. From Big Bear, he wrote to Blanche Knopf, whom they had recently met for the first time when she and her husband, Alfred, joined them for lunch in nearby Lake Arrowhead, "The effort to keep my mind off the war has reduced me to the mental age of seven. The things by which we live are the distant flashes of insect wings in a clouded sunlight."

One imagines them sitting on the porch of a cabin in the late afternoon, the forest rising around them, a solitary and friendless couple, with nothing to do and nowhere to go, quietly watching the light shift upon the fleeting wings of the bees and butterflies.

In the fall, when the weather changed in the mountains, they moved back to the city, renting an apartment at 818 West Duarte Street in Monrovia, a suburb northeast of downtown L.A. When the rains let up I drove out to Monrovia, past Glendale and Pasadena, along the base of the San Gabriel Mountains. The air was so clean I could see all the way to the San Bernardino Mountains, snowcapped from the recent storms. Nestled below those peaks was Big Bear, an hour or so away. I passed the turnoff for the Santa Anita racetrack, and tall utility towers, the massive conductors of the city's electricity looming over the landscape. Monrovia must have felt more like a village when the Chandlers lived here—an urban village, a kind of California Mayberry populated by ordinary folk who cooked up big Sunday dinners, loved their wives and kids, worked hard at their jobs, paid their bills on time. On the hills above the freeway, the white stucco houses looked clean and sharp against the vivid green, and it was all so neat and tidy, set-piece middle class.

West Duarte was a busy street now, one of the main thoroughfares of Monrovia. I found the address but not the apartment where the Chandlers had lived. It was the same old story. It was gone. Torn down. Replaced by a cheap white stucco apartment building, its facade streaked with ribbons of rust stains, metal grating over windows and doors. Birds-of-paradise with yellowed split leaves were having a last go at life beneath the first-story windows as a Mexican man hosed down the sidewalk out front with a studied lethargy. The gardener. Watering the sidewalk beside the ratty dry foliage.

By the time they moved here to Monrovia, Ray had already completed a draft of his second novel, but, unhappy with the results, he had thrown the whole thing away and started over. He once said he could never simply rewrite a story he didn't like; he had to discard it and begin anew.

What attracted them to Monrovia? It felt so nowhere, so boonies, so faux-ranch and stucco box, a little appendage of a town stuck to the soiled hem of L.A. Maybe it was cheap rent. Maybe a wish to become further isolated, or copy that small-town feeling they'd found in the mountains. Maybe the place had more charm than I was giving it credit for. They stayed in Monrovia for only a couple of months, then they packed up again. Moved down to La Jolla for Christmas and rented a place at 1265 Park Row for a month. It was their first extended stay in the seaside town, and Cissy loved the place. She told Ray she wanted to live there. They couldn't afford to do so yet. But he promised her they'd come back, maybe even buy a place in La Jolla one day.

The coastal climate didn't actually agree with him, nor did he much care for the people. Women with skins like burnt oranges and smiles like gashes. Men with speckled skin, sporting gauche clothes. From La Jolla he wrote to George Harmon Coxe, a fellow detective writer and contributor to *Black Mask,* thanking him for his letter and the photo he'd sent of his house: "It must be nice to have a home. We haven't had one in so long that I look back with a touch of nostalgia to any place we have stayed in as long as six months. I don't think we shall be here long either. Too dear, too damp, too elderly, a nice place . . . for old people and their parents."

He went on to tell Coxe that he'd had to throw his second book away, referring to the first version of *Farewell, My Lovely.* "So that leaves me with nothing to show for the last six months and possibly nothing to eat for the next six. But it also leaves the world a far far better place to live in than if I had not thrown it away."

In the damp climate of La Jolla he developed a rheumatic right arm, and they begin looking for a new location, planning yet another move. Their continual search for a home was becoming almost painful: "We have not yet found a place to live but hope to soon," he wrote to Blanche Knopf, "and when there is a little peace in a world which knows no peace—all I ask is a quiet corner and deaf and dumb neighbors."

Sometime around this time Cissy gave him a gift of a watch, accompanied by a handwritten note: "For my darling Gallibeoth's birthday and if it holds out until his next one maybe his Double-Duck will give him a better one—maybe a green-gold one with jewels inside and a little face that shines in the dark like Taki's eyes." She also copied out some lines from one of his own poems and gave it to him: *I think of you in that most lonely hour . . . I think of you when dreams have spent their riot . . . and all the gods I made are dead and quiet, til drugg'd with longing on your breast I fall, and then at last I need not think at all.*

They were close during this period—very close. And in spite of all the moves, and worries about war, they seem to have been happy. Just the two of them. Floating along in their Packard, with all their belongings in boxes.

In January 1940 they moved to Arcadia, yet another suburb of L.A., immediately adjacent to Monrovia. In fact the apartment they'd left in Monrovia a few months earlier was only a short distance from the one they now rented in Arcadia, a separate unit in a bungalow court complex at 1155 Arcadia Street.

That place, too, had been destroyed, as I discovered when I went looking for it. It was now the site of a large condominium complex, built in a faux-Bavarian style, all fake timber and boxy stucco. Next door, however, nestled amid the larger apartment blocks, was an old bungalow court apartment complex, a little cluster of slightly shabby units that must have been very much like the place where Cissy and Ray had lived. Great oaks with thick leafy bowers lined the street, and it was in the trees that I felt the history in the landscape, the only continuity connecting my age with Ray's. Looking at them I thought, I am seeing what he saw—*trees*. And everything else is different.

Arcadia felt homogenized and dull, an anywhere kind of suburb, indistinguishable from so many outlying areas of L.A. It was hard to reconcile the dullness of these suburbs with the edgy, exciting stories Ray had been working on when he lived here.

Later Jack Kerouac would capture some of the tedium of Arcadia. In *On the Road*, his character Sal Paradise ends up marooned in Arcadia with a Mexican woman named Terry. After a night of partying on L.A.'s Central Avenue, the main "colored" area lined with jazz clubs (where Chandler also set the opening of *Farewell, My Lovely*, the novel he was rewriting while living in Arcadia), Sal and Terry decide to take their last five bucks and hitchhike to New York. They take the Red Car as far as Arcadia, and start thumbing:

It was night. We were pointed toward the American continent. Holding hands, we walked several miles down the road to get out of the populated district. It was a Saturday night. We stood under a road lamp, thumbing, when cars full of young kids roared by with streamers flying. "Yaah! Yaah! We won! We won!" they all shouted. Then they yoohooed us and got great glee out of seeing a guy and a girl on the road. Dozens of such cars passed, full of young faces and . . . I hated every one of them. Who did they think they were, yaahing at somebody on the road just because they were little high-school punks and their parents carved the roast beef on Sunday afternoons? Who did they think they were, making fun of a girl reduced to poor circumstances with a man who wanted to belove? We were minding our own business. And we didn't get a blessed ride. We had to walk back to town, and worst of all we needed coffee and had the misfortune of going into the only place open, which was a high-school soda fountain, and all the kids were there and remembered us. Now they saw that Terry was Mexican, a Pachuco wildcat; and that her boyfriend was worse than that.

With her pretty nose in the air she cut out of there and we wandered together in the dark up the ditches of the highways. I carried the bags. We were breathing fogs in the cold night air. I finally decided to hide from the world one more night with her, and the morning be damned. We went into a motel court and bought a comfortable little suite for about four dollars—shower, bathtowels, wall radio, and all. We held each other tight. We had long, serious talks and took baths and discussed things with the light on and then with the light out. Something was being proved, I was convincing her of something, which she accepted, and we concluded the pact in the dark, breathless, then pleased, like little lambs.

There is in this passage a sense of Arcadia as the last outpost of L.A., a little burb facing the east-lying vastness of the American continent, where the brown halo of smog hanging over the huge desert encampment began to dissipate and the beef-fattened teenagers looked askance at brown-skinned wandering strangers.

Outsiders like Terry and Sal really had no place in Arcadia, and neither did Cissy and Ray. A few months after moving to Arcadia, they decamped again and headed up to Big Bear for another summer in the mountains. Monrovia, Arcadia: neither place ever turned up in Chandler's writings. They were ephemeral stops, their reality reduced to domestic arrangements; they existed only as cipher-cities somewhere beyond the couple's homey four walls.

Farewell, My Lovely was published in May 1940 with even less sales than *The Big Sleep*. If Chandler was bothered by the low sales, he didn't show it much. He simply kept writing. It was the frame that held his life together—writing and Cissy, and there wasn't much outside of that.

Blanche Knopf had written to request a photo for publicity purposes, something he was loath to provide, but from Big Bear he responded:

Sorry I haven't any snapshots to send you yet. I don't know how much time there is. My wife will try to take some, a very agonizing process for both of us, since she is very particular and I am very badly behaved. . . . I am reaching the age where it takes an artistic touch to make anything of me.

While in Big Bear, Cissy did manage to take a photograph of him, and he also took one of her—one of the very few photographs I found of her at the Bodleian, made at a time when she had stopped allowing pictures to be taken. It survived perhaps only because of the angle at which it was taken.

She is shown standing on a trail in the woods, surrounded by tall pines, wearing white slacks and a light-colored blouse, a full-

length shot of her, with her back to the camera. It reveals a still-shapely woman, now seventy-two years old. Her hips are curvaceous and full, her hair is a mass of light-colored curls. She looks fit and trim. On the reverse of the photograph Ray has written, "Cissy from the back."

In the small reading room at the Bodleian Library, I had stared at this photograph for a long time, as if hoping she might suddenly turn around and look at me. The picture seemed a metaphor for the woman herself—an inscrutable yet alluring figure, hiding her face from the world, yet undeniably there, present in full flesh but withholding herself from our gaze. I wondered if she had seen Ray pointing the camera at her, and at that moment turned her back on him? Or was she simply walking ahead of him, and suddenly he lifted the camera and made a picture of her?

The photograph was all the more moving because I knew that by this time in her life Cissy's lung condition limited her energy and activity. Walking any distance wasn't easy for her. They must have gone into the woods that day, armed with a camera, prepared to endure the "agonizing experience" of producing a decent photograph of Ray, and when this was accomplished they walked a little farther, slowly, taking their time, and then she walked ahead of him, and he made the picture, of a solitary woman standing in the pines, looking away from him.

After a few months in Big Bear, when the weather once more turned cool, they moved again, this time to Santa Monica, where they rented an apartment in a newly constructed building at 449 San Vicente Boulevard, just a few blocks from the beach. But they stayed on San Vicente only a couple of months. There were problems there: noisy neighbors, damp air. So they packed up again, resettling in a little rented house not far away, at 857 Iliff Street in Pacific Palisades. From the house on Iliff Street, Ray wrote to Erle Stanley Gardner:

> Good God, we have moved again. . . . Living, if you can call it that, in a big apartment house in Santa Monica, brand new and all that, I longed for your ranch. I longed for some place

where I could go out at night and listen and hear the grass growing. But of course it wouldn't do for us, just the two of us, even if I had the price of a piece of virgin foothill. It's better over here, quiet and a house and nice garden. But they are just beginning to build a house across the way. I shan't mind it as much as the good neighbors bouncing on their bed springs over at the apartment house.

It's a long trip from Carondelet to Iliff, if you take surface streets rather than the freeways. I headed out Sunset Boulevard, past Hollywood High School and the cheap divey motels with the leggy hookers out front, past the Chateau Marmont, where Belushi died of an overdose and the gargantuan billboards loom over the strip, the Marlboro man and his horse like gods high in the sky, past the pink stucco extravaganza of the Beverly Hills Hotel, nestled amid its well-kept greenery, and down the curving road as it meanders through expensive real estate, the turnoffs for Bel Air and Stone Canyon, and over the car-jammed 405 freeway into Brentwood, where Didion and Dunne and O.J. once lived, past all the landmarks and the banal beauty of the fabled route, Sunset Boulevard, Norma Desmond-land, always ready for a close-up, and was there ever a more photographed street? The old Route 66, Edd "Kookie" Byrnes, all the other fantasy figures of the big and small screen. The farther you travel the more the air begins to change and become infused with a marine freshness. A mist develops. A faint fog appears, shot through with sunshine. A hazy light that says you're almost to the beach. You smell the coast long before you see it. You sense you're coming to the end of the land. And then there you are, just before you reach the well-heeled little village of Pacific Palisades, there on the right, opposite Chautauqua and running north, a little street called Iliff, ascending up a hill: and if you take it you'll come to 857, just another address in Chandlerland.

I pulled up and parked in front of the house. A street lined with eucalyptus, that ubiquitous touch of Australia, minus the koalas. A gentle breeze was blowing in from the sea. The long pointed leaves of the eucalyptus drifted in the wind like stiff little pennants. The address was affixed to the front of the little house in big numbers. Of all the houses visible to me, 857 Iliff was the smallest and the most lacking in visible charm. Maybe it was nicer years ago, when Cissy and Ray lived there, before the current resident, or the one before that, had struck on the idea of paving over the front yard in gray concrete blocks interspersed with dying succulents and tiny white rocks.

When they had lived here, most of the houses on the street were no doubt rather small, like this one, but now the little runt was the solitary testament to a more modest past. All the other houses had been remodeled, enlarged into big manly brutes, like houses on steroids. They strained against the borders of their modest lots, looking as confined and uncomfortable as hulky athletes trapped in too-small clothes.

I got out of my car and leaned against the door and stared at the former Chandler residence for a while, squinting against the sun. It revealed nothing except its own modest proportions. I knocked

on the front door, but no one answered. I stood on tiptoe and tried to peer through a small front window. Across the street a woman in a short tennis dress was unloading something from the trunk of her car, and she stopped what she was doing and stared at me. I gave her my innocent look, my hey-neighbor smile. No burglar me, that look said, just an ordinary snoop, obsessed with a couple who once lived here. Once again I was drawn to the trees on the street. The eucalyptus looked old enough and big enough to have been around in 1942 when the Chandlers lived here. But they weren't talking. Whatever they'd seen, it was locked up in their growth rings.

It must be nice to have a home. How wistful that sounded. How I knew that feeling myself, having looked for one for so long. Where did I belong? So many of my friends seemed to have spent a great deal of time trying to answer that question. We were all to some extent cut off from our pasts. The question became, Where should we live? Where do we really want to settle? Where do we really belong? In the new universe of ambulatory possibilities, it could be a daunting question. For some reason, I felt people who lived in the West suffered more perhaps from this sense of dislocation. Maybe it was part of the geography. Or our genetic makeup, a need to leave behind all that was known and established and settled, to explore a new land, and to occupy it, even if it meant misfortune, disappointment, or unhappiness, and with the certain assurance of loneliness.

They had gardened a little when they lived here. Neither of them seems to have had much of a green thumb or stayed long enough in one place to watch a plant grow, but in a letter Ray once mentioned the windiness in the Palisades and how he and Cissy had had to put stakes around the dahlias to keep them from being blown over.

What simple lives they led. They woke. Cissy cooked. They ate.

He wrote. She cooked again. They had lunch. He wrote some more and then stopped. They shopped. Saw a movie now and then. More cooking. Dinner. Bed.

And then another day, *cloître à deux.*

At fifty-four, Ray was still relatively young, with a good deal of energy, though during this time he complained of having bad luck, bad health, and bad disposition for a very long time, the result, he said, of his advancing age. But at seventy-two, Cissy was confronting advancing age, and far more serious health problems than any he could claim. She was struggling with a serious condition, incipient fibrosis of the lungs, with increasingly painful consequences.

He knew her health was failing, even if he did not know her true age, not then, and perhaps never. In the poetry he wrote during these years, some of which was dedicated to Cissy, it's possible to discern the evidence of his concern for her, as well a clear indication that their intimate relations had changed. The poem "Kashinmor the Elephant" (the name of one of his amuels) contains these revealing stanzas:

> They will ride home and wearily creep in
> To their vast bed as huge and soft as sin
> A battleground of love whose wars are done,
> Whose heroes are with Tyre and Babylon.

> His lady is not young
> Her smile is thin and tarnished filigree
> Mascara melts beneath her haggard eyes
> Between her breasts the powder dampened lies.

> They will lie still and yawn there side by side
> A thousand miles apart except by pride
> Think you some love thing after all
> Keeps his heart the echoing madrigal?
> Think you again some lovely dream pure-drawn
> Will make her young beside him in the dawn?

In a later version the mutual yawns in the poem have turned into the woman snoring while the man listens, sleepless and sad. The self-pitying tone is pronounced:

> *He will lie still and hear her snore again*
> *Filling the night with particles of pain*
> *He will lie still and listen to her flute,*
> *A small white tired man, defeated and mute,*
> *With the face of a stillborn child that no one loved*

Of course nothing would make *her young beside him in the dawn.* Nor would the *love thing,* the *echoing madrigal,* ever play as it once had. The *battleground of love*—the bed—had grown quiet. The air of resignation has settled in. Physical change has overcome the lady, and as for the man—small white tired—he's defeated and mute. And perhaps no longer actually capable of consummating his love, should the lady show any lingering interest. Ray's last change to the poem comes at the end, a penciled-in line that reads: "The small defeated man is impotent and wan."

They did not stay long on Iliff either. Maybe it was the construction Ray had mentioned to Erle Stanley Gardner, the new house being built across the way that got to be too much for them. Or maybe they just didn't like the way the wind blew, battering the dahlias. Maybe the stars didn't line up right at night, or the sun didn't shine brightly enough during the day. Whatever the reason, they left Iliff after only a few months. Once more, they packed up their belongings and loaded everything in the car and drove a few miles to another rented furnished house, this one in Brentwood, at 12216 Shetland Lane, and there they unpacked the car, their clothes and books, the few domestic items, the typewriter and files, hauling it all into yet another house, settling in to yet another strange dwelling with their darling Taki. Who, with all the moves, must have been exclusively an indoor cat. How could they let her out and imagine she'd find her way home when home changed so often?

Again, the question arises: how could all that constant moving not have driven them mad? Or was it the case that the moves actually kept them sane, especially Ray, who all his life seemed to need dislocation, which perhaps made him feel more alive, more acutely attuned to his senses and his environment. The moves stimulated his imagination, these continual changes and the constant adjustment to the new. And even with all the moving around he continued to write with a focused dedication, perhaps in fact because he wasn't stuck in one place but continually refreshing himself with new experiences and vistas. In the three years between 1939 and 1942 he wrote three complete novels, some say his best work, in spite of the fact he was ill and feeling uncertain during much of 1940. He needed, in order to keep working, what one critic called "the romance of the ineffable." Did their moving heighten the ineffable? There is in all his wanderings a feeling of something so crucial it lies beyond any simple categorization.

From Shetland Lane, Ray wrote to Blanche Knopf again, revealing his anxiety over the novel he had just finished, which would eventually be called *The High Window:*

> Your letter, kind and charming as always, reaches me at a very bad time. I'm afraid the book is not going to be any good to you. No action, no likable characters, no nothing. The detective does nothing . . . all I can say by way of extenuation is that I tried my best . . . the thing that rather gets me down is that when I write something that is tough and fast and full of mayhem and murder, I get panned for being tough and fast and full of mayhem and murder, and then when I try to tone down a bit and develop the mental and emotional side of a situation, I get panned for leaving out what I was panned for putting in the first time . . . From now on, if I make mistakes, as I no doubt shall, they will not be made in a futile attempt to avoid making mistakes.

The High Window came out in the summer of '42, while they were living on Shetland Lane. He wrote to Alfred Knopf that he thought the book "a very nice job indeed" but added that his wife did not like the photo of him on the back.

> All the photos I sent you were bad, and this is perhaps about the best, except the very first one, which no longer looks like me . . . most writers are such horrible-looking people that their faces destroy something which perhaps wanted to like them. Perhaps I am oversensitive, but I have several times been so repelled by such faces that I have not been able to read the books without the faces coming between. Especially these fat crowlike middle-aged women's faces.

He could be tough on women, especially as they aged—a problem that didn't seem to bother him when it came to men growing older. Both *The Big Sleep* and *The High Window* open with Marlowe paying a visit to a rich person who is interested in hiring him, one a man (General Sternwood) and the other a woman (Mrs. Elizabeth Murdock). Both are found in rarefied atmospheres, spaces created by people with money—Sternwood sits in a steaming greenhouse filled with hothouse orchids; Mrs. Murdock reclines on a chaise lounge in a glassed-in porch. There's a funereal atmosphere in both environments, the feeling of the rich as decaying, morbid specimens of humanity, trapped in their glass boxes. Both General Sternwood and Mrs. Murdock are aged and ailing, but in the description of Mrs. Murdock, humorous as it is, one finds a revulsion not evident in the passages associated with her male counterpart:

> She had a lot of face and chin. She had pewter-colored hair set in a ruthless permanent, a hard beak and large moist eyes with the sympathetic expression of wet stones. There was lace at her throat, but it was the kind of throat that would have looked better in a football sweater. She wore a grayish silk dress. Her thick arms were bare and mottled . . . then she spoke. Her voice had a hard baritone quality and sounded as if it didn't want any nonsense.

A lot of people over the years have accused Chandler of misogyny (as well as racism, homophobia, and anti-Semitism), and there are passages in the novels that could support such accusations. But it seemed much more complex to me. I think Ray actually feared women and held them in awe. Fear and awe—the flip side of the same coin. We fear what has power greater than us, and women had all the power in Chandler's life and always had. In his fiction he often created idealized versions of men—Marlowe feels a deep sense of obligation to General Sternwood, a wish to protect him. At one point he seems ready to continue to work for him for nothing, just so the old man isn't let down. Rich old men—Linda Loring's father in *The Long Goodbye*, and Henry Clarendon, the elderly gentleman who holds forth in *Playback*, and the old gent who owns the movie studio in *The Little Sister*, Jules Oppenheimer—may prompt snide remarks from Marlowe, but he also has a desire to cater to them.

In contrast, Mrs. Murdock, with her reproving voice, as low as a man's, and her grotesquely unattractive appearance, is never anything but repulsive to Marlowe. She becomes increasingly villainous as the novel progresses, a port-sodden old fake picking tobacco shards off her lips, her face as red as a side of beef, who bullies her meek little secretary, Merle Davis. Marlowe feels sorry for Merle; he figures out she's been sexually molested by Mrs. Murdock's husband and that's why she can't stand for a man to touch her. Marlowe treats her as gently as he's ever treated any woman; there's no suggestion of sex, just a kind of brotherly wish to help this woman who, in her physical description, could be a dead ringer for Cissy (coppery blond hair, pale skin with a sort of natural paleness, cobalt blue eyes, lovely arms, and like Cissy she wears dresses rather than the more mannish suits and pants outfits of most of the other women in his stories). At the end of the novel, Marlowe drives Merle all the way back to her parents in Manhattan, Kansas, just to make sure she gets there and to help her get free of old Mrs. Murdock. He rescues Merle, just as Ray believed he had rescued Cissy, and he gives Mrs. Murdock her

comeuppance in the process. He bullies her, just as she's bullied
Merle. Just as Ray's own mother bullied him, forcing him to wait
until she was dead before he could marry Cissy. He never could
say anything bad about his mother, certainly not while she was
alive, but in his complex fictional portraits of women—especially
older women—what often leaks through is loathing, resentment,
revulsion, and fear, while the older men are figures to please and
win over. And ironically, the desire to seek the favor of a rich old
man will have the most poignant, and the most catastrophic, consequences at the end of Ray's own life.

Unlike so many of the areas where Cissy and Ray lived, most of
which had gone downhill over the ensuing years, Brentwood had
only gotten tonier. The house at 12216 Shetland Lane was a sweet
little classic California stucco bungalow with a red clay tile roof. In
the front garden, white roses bloomed—nothing but white roses,
and all in bloom, and the effect was rather magical. A little porch
stretched across the front of the house, with a nice arrangement

of chairs and a table. The place was fixed up beautifully, fully gentrified. For that matter, so was the whole neighborhood. It was calm. Quiet. The street ended in a cul-de-sac. No traffic to speak of. Ray must have liked that. Nothing to bother them here. All the houses were separated by hedges and trees and flowering gardens. And what beautiful houses they were. The air smelled of money.

I walked down the sidewalk to the end of the cul-de-sac and made a loop back to the house. All I saw were a few laughing children playing on a trampoline and some bees poking at flowers. There was a sweet smell on the air. I passed a two-story Spanish-style house that looked so beautiful, so perfect in every way, I wanted to move in and live there. I could imagine what it would feel like, living in a place like that. The honeyed ease of it all in the languorous climate, the quiet and beautiful neighborhood. Los Angeles in so many ways was an absurd place, comic, tragic, banal, but more so to outsiders than those who lived here. When you lived here, you just woke up every morning to the same beautiful weather and you thought, hey, I'm still here, and isn't it great? It's funny, but it was also just your life. When I looked at that lovely Spanish house I felt what it would be like to wake up there in the morning with the birds twittering their heads off and the sunlight falling through the windows and the air perfumed with flowers and the easy, lazy world of L.A. just outside your faux-Mexican door. No mean streets, these. Instead, paradise.

Ray was a bit of a hypocrite when it came to wealth. He liked money. He enjoyed flaunting it and spent it freely when he had it. And he made a point of moving to a town full of millionaires when he finally did buy a house. But he also hated how rich people acted. How they misused their money, behaved as if they were superior, cultivated garish tastes. He especially hated how careless they were in their treatment of others.

I felt quite sure that finances had played a pretty big part in the Chandlers' moving so often. They were still required to live modestly, stretching out the advances he got for his books. He once said as much: "Is there a place a poor man can live? I'm sick of California and the people it breeds. If after twenty years I still fail to like the place, it seems the case is hopeless."

In the same letter, he outlined what he did like:

I like people with manners, grace, some social intuition, and education slightly above the *Reader's Digest* fan, people whose pride of living does not express itself in their kitchen gadgets and automobiles. I don't like people who can't sit still for half an hour without a drink in their hands, and apart from that I should prefer an amiable drunk to Henry Ford. I like a conservative atmosphere, a sense of the past; I like everything Americans of past generations used to go and look for in Europe, but at the same time I don't want to be bound by the rules.

Moving frequently was perhaps, for him, part of eluding the rules, of escaping the kind of predictably bourgeois life he disparaged. California encouraged such a sensibility. The landscape lent itself to rootlessness and exploration, a play on the idea of identity versus a secure location, a place to challenge conventions of all sorts, including how long you ought to live in any one place.

In the summer of 1942 they were on the move again. They had a little more money now, thanks to the sale of the film rights to *Farewell, My Lovely. The High Window* was also selling more copies than any of his other books. Knopf was about to bring out a paperback edition of *The Big Sleep,* which would go on to sell 300,000 copies, in part because it would be shipped to servicemen fighting overseas and introduce a whole generation of American men to Chandler's work and give them a passion for his stories.

They left the house on Shetland and moved to a cabin in Idyllwild, another little resort town, this one in the mountains above Palm Springs. Two months later they left Idyllwild and rented a place in nearby Cathedral City, just below the mountain town, out in the desert. Known as "the poor man's Palm Springs," Cathedral

City lay just east of Palm Springs, connected by the main highway. The topography was more or less the same in both places, mountains rising sharply to the south and in every other direction desert stretching forth in brutal beauty and dryness. In the summer the temperature hit one ten, one fifteen, and the air was bent into wavering distorting curtains of heat.

The winter was another story. Warm and sunny. The kind of climate that had always attracted the plaid-pants-and-white-shoe crowd, as well as Hollywood people. For the Chandlers, it must have seemed as good a place as any to wait out the war years.

The war continued to depress him, and in what was now an established a pattern for him, he grew disillusioned with Cathedral City after only a short time. Nowhere could really satisfy his needs, because not even he knew what those needs were, except he had begun to feel a need for other people, for some kind of social contact that extended beyond his wife and cat. The solitude of his life, like the air in the desert, left him feeling he was caught in a desiccated existence. You can hear his restlessness and longing in a letter he wrote to Alfred Knopf in February 1943, in which he also gives a rather vivid sense of the effects of wartime rationing on their life:

This place bores me. But I've just been talked into sticking out the mountains and the desert for another year. After that to hell with the climate, let's meet a few people. We have a one-store town here, and the meat situation would make you scream. On Wednesday morning the guy opens at 7 A.M. and all the desert rats are there waiting for him to give out numbered tickets. Anybody who delays long enough to wash his face is automatically classed as parasitic and gets a high number, if he gets one at all. On Thursday at 10 the inhabitants bring their bronchitis and halitosis into the store and park in front of the meat counter and the numbers are coonshouted. When we, having a very late number, kick our way up to the collapsed hunk of hamburger we are greeted with a nervous smile that suggests a deacon caught with his hand in the collection plate, and we leave bearing off enough meat for the cat. This happens once a week and that is all that happens, in the way of meat.

Of course we go to Palm Springs. If we didn't, I should not be writing this letter. I should be out in the desert trying to dig up a dead gopher. We happened on a rib roast a couple of weeks back, just walked in and said hello, and there the damned thing was. We ate for six nights running, behind drawn curtains, chewing quietly, so the neighbors wouldn't hear.

He was bored by Cathedral City. He wanted to leave. But he had just been talked into sticking it out for another year, and clearly it was Cissy who'd done the talking. She had persuaded him to stay to their routine of winters in the desert, summers in the mountains, in either Big Bear Lake or Idyllwild. At least it was something she knew, something she could count on. And Ray was working well. He had almost finished his fourth novel, *Lady in the Lake,* set in a fictional version of Big Bear Lake (or perhaps nearby Lake Arrowhead), called Puma Lake in the book. They could live cheaply in the desert and mountains, and even though they had a bit more money now, they were still thrifty. Their habits and lifestyle hadn't been changed by success. What did seem new was Ray's longing to "meet some people." He was lonely. Tiring of his life as a recluse. He was fifty-five, becoming mildly famous, and why should he soldier on in such isolation? The answer was because Cissy wanted it that way. Maybe she understood that a social life for Ray might mean a return to drinking. For over ten years he'd been sober. A sober, industrious man, a devoted husband, a serious student and practitioner of his craft. Now he wanted a change.

It takes about an hour and a half to drive out to Cathedral City from downtown L.A., depending on the traffic. I took the 60 freeway through outlying suburbs, the forest of signs rising up alongside the road in an endless barrage of words and images, a riotous landscape of boxy buildings slathered with advertisements, signs and more signs, bumptious inflatable clowns, familiar logos that need no words now that they have been burned in our brains, bastardized spellings, improbable contractions, the inescapable assault of the advertising world reminding us that to buy is to live. Or is it to live is to buy?

Just past Diamond Bar the suburbs and the signs drop away and the freeway begins winding through green hills and lush valleys. It was raining the day I drove out there. The beauty and greenness of the landscape beyond Diamond Bar startled me. Misty glimpses of lakes shimmering in little emerald valleys. Conical green hills, fields dotted with cows and oak trees. It felt as if the old world were being revealed, the world the conquistadors had discovered when they first chanced upon this land, the commercial crassness rolled back to reveal a more pastoral place, so lushly gorgeous, a Shangri-la of a landscape, a Lost Horizons. It was the rain playing a trick of course. Washing the world clean. Turning everything green. Laying down a misted beauty over the land. If you cared to be transported to another time, now was the moment to do it, and I cared to, and I was. And then I laughed at myself, rolling down the freeway in my gas-hog car, emitting my little noxious fumes, dreaming of The Way It Was. I was rotten with romanticism. Positively punchy on an idealized past.

I drove out past the gigantic white wind turbines that now dot the desert landscape just west of Palm Springs, rain sluicing the sky. Lightning cracked in the distance as the big white wind blades turned and the thunder rolled and the turbines looked alive to me, like monsters marching up and over the hills waving their arms wildly.

Cathedral City wasn't much to look at on a rainy day—on any day, for that matter. What a poor relation to its rich cousin Palm Springs. A lot of empty stores. Abandoned discos with all the charm of a used condom. A white square of an old drive-in theater rising up out of a trash-blown empty lot. This was a town in serious need of some fix-up. Strange how a dead desert town acquires a degree of rattiness like no other.

The address I had for Cissy and Ray wasn't easy to find. I stopped a couple of times and asked directions. Past Frank Sinatra Drive, someone said. Next street. Take a left.

The place turned out to be a shack in a seedy area, just a block or so off the main drag. All the houses were more or less ruins, run-down rentals, nothing more than tumbleweed catchers sitting on bare lots littered with trash. The little house where Cissy and Ray had lived was one sorry-looking place. Surrounded by dirt hard-packed and baked by the desert sun into concrete hardness, protected by a skinny bitch dog tethered on a short chain. She had big teats, so swollen they almost dragged on the ground. A couple of filthy puppies crawled out from a hole beneath the house and attempted to catch on to a swaying teat as the dog lunged on her chain and barked at me. The barking brought a man to the door, big and dark-skinned, with a belly button winking from beneath his undershirt. I started to get out of the car. I gave him my how-do wave. He took one look at me and turned his back and shut the door.

I drove around for a few minutes, trawling the neighborhood like a prospective buyer, or a cat burglar casing the joints. But there wouldn't be much to burgle here. This was desert-rat territory, dead-appliance-ville, old-sheets-for-curtains world, where the unemployed came to roost, and migrants welcome, legal or otherwise, just come on in and pull up a crate and have a seat. In California, this was about as poor as it got. Just a few miles away in Palm Springs, people were popping for two-million-dollar houses and two-hundred-dollar haircuts. Here it looked like two hundred a month would get you a roof over your head.

When Cissy and Ray lived here, these places would have been resort cabins, let by the week or month, nothing fancy, but not the rat-catchers they'd become either. Certainly the area had a little charm then, these clusters of reputable vacation bungalows, each with a little yard, and close to the shops just around the corner.

The shops were all closed now. Out of business. Finito. The adjacent Main Street of Cathedral City was a vision of abandoned plate-glass storefronts, little one-story buildings that looked old enough to have been built in Chandler's time, now bleak, empty, caked with dust blown in off the desert. Perhaps one of them had been their local butcher shop, where they lined up to take a number. Now a ragged area, in a ragged desert town. Farther down the road were some big new businesses, a mammoth cinema complex, a car dealership with hundreds of sparkling new automobiles sprouting in even rows from the blacktop like a freshly grown crop. Movies, cars—unquestionably popular entities, essential now to our culture—and not just little cars but big ones, and not just one movie screen but fifteen. Out with the old. In with the new. And in between lay the old-dead and not-yet-new, like this stretch of Cathedral's City main street.

They must have been living here when Ray got the call from Paramount Studios, offering him a chance to try a screenplay, adapting James M. Cain's novel *Double Indemnity* with a young new director from Europe named Billy Wilder. Ray didn't get the idea of the whole thing at first. When Joe Sistrom, the producer, called and offered him the job, Ray said he could probably do it, but he wouldn't be able to turn in the screenplay for a couple of weeks, and it would cost them a thousand bucks. Sistrom laughed. Was the guy being funny, or was he really that naïve about the way the movie business worked? Sistrom told him he'd be working with Wilder, in an office on the studio lot, that he'd have ten weeks to do the screenplay, and he'd be getting seven hundred and fifty bucks a week. Ray did the math. Ray liked the result. Ray saw the future . . . *maybe we can see some people* . . . and Ray said, Yes. Sure. Why not?

I drove back to the shack where the dog and her pups were now curled up together beneath a skimpy pepper tree. She didn't bark at me this time. I sat in my car for a long while. All around me the wind was sweeping clouds across the sky. Here is where everything began to change, I thought. Here is where the idyll ended. The moment when things began to turn another way.

Eight

I t was the season of wind. The rains had stopped and the Santa Anas had begun, the hot dry winds that came in from the desert and blew all day and night, setting people's nerves on edge, blowing over RVs in the Cajon Pass, leaving the streets littered with the lacquered-red limbs of the fan palms. In his short story "Red Wind," Ray had described such winds:

> It was one of those hot dry Santa Anas that come down through the mountain passes and curl your hair and make your nerves jump and your skin itch. On nights like that every booze party ends in a fight. Meek little wives feel the edge of the carving knife and study their husband's necks. Anything can happen. You can even get a full glass of beer in a cocktail lounge.

In this season of wind, Orange County was burning. A fire had erupted in the Anaheim hills, just south of the city, and was threatening the expensive homes tucked into the canyons and ridges. Over 2,500 houses had already been evacuated. People were shown on the evening news, clutching pets and baby pictures, loading up their cars, preparing to leave their smoke-filled neighborhoods. The long blond hair of the wives blew in the wind and their husbands' shirt collars flapped wildly and in the background the palm fronds flew at ninety degrees while the crimson and orange flames licked at the horizon. Watching the scenes on

TV, you knew that wind was bad for the fire, or rather it was good for the fire and bad for the people. The newscasters all mentioned how this wasn't the normal season for fire. But seasons were no longer things you could count on. Some mornings now you woke thinking about the planet heating up and how this was definitely not a good thing. Hot dry winds in January, raging fires, smoke and drifting ash falling on the city. Then you reminded yourself that there was no particular season for disaster in Southern California. Disaster was the continuous nascent undercurrent to our days.

I kept the long list of Chandler addresses taped to the wall next to my desk where I could see it every day: *Bonnie Brae Angels Flight Bunker Hill Loma Drive Vendome Catalina Stewart Leeward Longwood Gramercy Meadowbrook Hayes Westlake West 12th Highland Greenwood Redesdale Silver Lake Hartzell Woodrow Wilson Drive San Vicente Iliff Shetland Pacific Palisades Brentwood Idyllwild Riverside Santa Barbara Cathedral City Allen Avenue Big Bear Harlow Haven Arrowhead Arcadia Monrovia West Duarte Palm Springs Havenhurst Drexel Camino de la Costa Hotel del Charro Neptune Place Prospect . . .* The list read like a plainsong of wandering, the liturgy of a long search for home, a mini-mass for restless souls . . .

As I visited each address, one by one, working my way chronologically across the years of a marriage and the geography of a city, I checked it off my list. And as I looked for the addresses and the houses and apartments, I also looked again at his books, and everywhere in his stories and novels I saw the evidence of how the neighborhoods where he and Cissy lived had come into his fiction—how Silver Lake had become Gray Lake, and Santa Monica Bay City. Just as everywhere in the city I saw remnants of the world he'd described.

My list was getting shorter now. There weren't that many addresses left to track down. Sometimes I returned to a place I'd already visited because I wanted to look at it again or to see if perhaps I'd missed anything. I went back to Bonnie Brae where he'd started out and the site of the little church and the beauty parlor and Mexican grocery store. I revisited the house in Silverlake where the flamingos were buried out front, and I went back to the apartment on Greenwood Place where I had found the name *Chandler* on the mailbox. I wanted to see if it was still there, and it was. But the name had faded badly. I could hardly read it now. So it was a fake after all, I thought. Chandler hadn't left it there, it hadn't lasted seventy years, it had faded in just a few months. A plant. Somebody's idea of an homage to Chandler. A nice touch though, I thought. I admired the gesture.

I went back to Magnolia Avenue and Twelfth Street, and Longwood Avenue, and Leeward, returning to the area around the old Ambassador Hotel, and I was surprised to discover that most of the hotel had been torn down since I'd last driven by. All that was left was the old crescent-shaped facade of the Cocoanut Grove and a portion of the main building. It upset me somehow to look at it. I felt it personally, the loss of this hotel where I had swum in the lovely old pool. I remembered how I had loved arriving at the hotel in the afternoons on the days when I swam, strolling through the formal gardens, as if I belonged to that older world—the world of Valentino and Garbo and Gable. Now it was gone, demolished, erased—just another piece of lost L.A.

When the Ambassador had finally closed and I couldn't swim there anymore, I moved over to the Sheraton Townhouse Hotel, a dozen or so blocks away, on the corner of Commonwealth and Wilshire, a red brick hotel built in a vaguely Georgian style that overlooked Lafayette Park, just across the street. There was a nice pool at the Townhouse, too, and a swim club I could join. It was a much smaller hotel than the Ambassador, but it had a lot of history. In Malcolm Lowry's novel *Under the Volcano,* it's where the consul's wife stays when she's in L.A. But still it had none of the grandeur or stately elegance of the Ambassador, though it did have a kind of Old World charm and an interesting mixture of guests. A lot of Europeans stayed there—groups of Viennese musicians, and ballet troupes from Russia, and ordinary travelers from France and Denmark and Germany, people who booked rooms in the hotel perhaps without realizing that the neighborhood wasn't so great, that you couldn't really walk anywhere at night. Lafayette Park was overrun with junkies and homeless people who had their own agendas and needs, and they were not averse to occasionally turning those needs into criminal activities.

Sometimes I met some of the guests sitting around the pool or in the sauna, and when they discovered I was a local, they would begin asking me questions. They couldn't figure L.A. out. They didn't know where to go. They went downtown, they said, and there was nothing there, the streets were empty at night, the place felt dead. When they did rent a car, they didn't know where exactly to go or how to get there, and freeway driving felt intimidating. Plus it took so long to get anywhere. Everything was so far apart. Wasn't there any public transportation? they asked. Where *was* the center of the city, anyway? You could see the confusion these people felt about L.A. It wasn't like any city they'd ever been in. They couldn't figure it out. They were intrigued by the parts. But they felt lost in the whole. This was the *anti-city,* an illegible sprawl of freeways and roads, lacking a discernible heart, or even a vantage point from which it could be seen at a single glance. They knew that where they were, the neighborhood surrounding the hotel, was pretty much *nowhere,* but so much of the city seemed this way to them. The guests at the Sheraton Townhouse looked out the windows of their rooms and what they saw were junkies shooting up in the park and people who hauled their entire lives around with them in metal shopping carts, who lived outdoors on the grass. This, they believed, *was* L.A., and in a sense, they weren't wrong. With a population of 80,000 homeless, you could say they were glimpsing a fragment of a sizable constituency—the poorest of the city's poor. The doormen called the guests taxis and they waited beneath the porte cochere in their nice European clothes and looked out nervously toward the park, at the ragged haunted figures eyeing them from across the way and wondered about these citizens and what sort of city it was that let so many of its citizens sleep in the rough. When the riots broke out in the wake of the police beating of Rodney King, the guests staying at the Sheraton Townhouse stood at their windows and watched the stores and businesses burning around them. No one left the hotel then. No one would have even *thought* of leaving the hotel.

Things went downhill after that. The Sheraton Townhouse finally closed. The pool was drained, and the gardens dried up. Razor wire appeared atop the garden walls. Later the hotel was turned into low-income housing, with a wardenlike monitor who sat at a desk in the lobby and saw to it that everyone signed in and out.

When I thought of the neighborhood, I realized how much it had changed—the Ambassador was gone, the Sheraton Townhouse was a project for the poor. Even Bullocks Wilshire, the beautiful old department store that used to cater to the city's elite and which had the most elegant and extensive hat department in the city, had been forced to close, though the lovely art deco building had been preserved and was now the headquarters for a law school. Ray had written about Bullocks Wilshire in one of his novels, and he and Cissy had shopped there and eaten lunch in its top-floor restaurant, which even in my day was famous for being a fun place to meet, where women could still be seen wearing hats and gloves. Above the bronze doors of Bullocks Wilshire were emblazoned the words TO BUILD A BUSINESS THAT KNOWS NO END. But the end had come, not only for Bullocks Wilshire but for many other businesses along this strip of Wilshire Boulevard.

Down the way, on Sixth Street and Carondelet, stood the old Elks Building, where great towering statues of warrior women, several stories high, formed part of the outside facade. It was now a place to rent for movie shoots. It, too, had words emblazoned above its front doors: ALL THINGS WHATSOEVER YE WOULD THAT MEN SHOULD DO TO YOU, DO EVEN SO TO THEM—a motto that in L.A. could be taken in different ways. These buildings had all been built in the 1920s, at the same time as the main library downtown had been erected—and it, too, had inspirational words above its main doors: BOOKS ALONE ARE LIBERAL AND FREE,

THEY GIVE TO ALL WHO ASK. THEY EMANCIPATE ALL THOSE WHO SERVE THEM FAITHFULLY. Among the city's founders, there had been a kind of utopian longing to create a higher civilization in L.A., one that would inspire the citizenry to achieve new heights—build businesses that knew no end, treat one another as they would wish to be treated, liberate the mind through reading and the arts, and you could still see this kind of idealism writ large on the facades of buildings that had failed their promise.

Sometimes when I walked the streets near my apartment, through the old neighborhoods of the city, I felt I was moving through Chandler's imagination, striding down the streets he wrote about and passing the hotels and landmarks, the areas where he and Cissy had lived. Even my own street turns up in his stories. He must have liked the name. Carondelet. With its faint ring of New Orleans.

Some of the lovely big old apartment buildings that were so reminiscent of Chandler's era—like El Royale on Wilshire and Rampart, were now boarded up, but others had survived, including the Ansonia apartments on Sixth Street and Carondelet, and the Asbury just down the way, and the Rampart Arms, the Gaylord, and the Talmadge on Berendo and Wilshire.

I often walked down a street called Lafayette Park, where the DA in *The Big Sleep* had lived in a sprawling mansion (and where Joseph Dabney once owned a grand house), but all the big old houses had long since been torn down. The street was now lined with condos, owned mostly by Koreans. Up the way, at the intersection of Lafayette and Beverly Boulevard, stood the Hotel Lafayette and the Zimba Room, with the painted sign still visible on the side, TWO DOLLARS A NIGHT WITH BATH. These were the kinds of places Ray had written about. But the area had gone badly downhill. The Hotel Lafayette had become a flophouse, and the Zimba Room was now nothing more than a faded sign, but still an aura persisted here: the L.A. of the '20s and '30s felt alive in this neighborhood. If there were such a thing as Chandlerland this was it, and each day I felt surrounded by a kind of shabbier version of that era, a strangely eviscerated ghost of the world I was trying to imagine. When you constantly change a landscape, you erase the collective memory of a city. How can you live without memory?

In 1943, when Ray got offered the job at Paramount Studios to collaborate with Billy Wilder on the screen adaptation of *Double Indemnity*, he and Cissy left their desert retreat in Cathedral City and moved back to L.A. They took an apartment in Hollywood, not far from Melrose Avenue and the studio where Ray would be working in an office in the Writers' Building. They wanted to be close to the studio, and it was only a five- or ten-minute drive to Paramount from the small apartment they rented at 1040 Havenhurst.

The day I drove up to Havenhurst, the fire was still burning in the Anaheim Hills, and a raft of blue smoke floated over the city. Another fire had broken out the day before in Malibu Canyon: now the Santa Anas blew the smoke from the south and the north and the city felt sandwiched by the fumes. It was 92 degrees on January 8. According to the weatherman, we were heading for another record.

I drove west on Beverly to Crescent Heights and cut up to Santa Monica Boulevard. Havenhurst was just a block east of Crescent Heights. Many of the houses didn't have numbers out front, and it took me a while to find 1040 Havenhurst. I mistook a broken-down bungalow with a locked gate for the place I was looking for, then realized 1040 was really next door—a white duplex with overgrown trees and bushes. I stood out front on the sidewalk, looking around at the neighborhood, at the view of the Hollywood hills, which were just faint blue shapes through the smoke. It was cut-rate L.A. No glamour, no glitz, no charm. Mail-order L.A., as Ray once said: everything in the catalogue you could get better somewhere else.

I noticed a sign almost directly opposite the apartment where he and Cissy had lived:

DEADEND 7 P.M. to 7 A.M.
NO CRUISING

When you saw a sign like this in L.A., you knew what it meant: the area was plagued by either drugs or prostitution, usually both, and the cops were trying to control the action by turning the street into a dead-end zone at night. Easier to catch the johns that way. Snag the cokeheads and pimps. Round up the girls and bust them. This area was known for its transsexuals and transvestite prostitution: just a week earlier a fairly well-known movie director had been busted near here, and the article in the newspaper had taken delight in describing what he was wearing when apprehended—a pink miniskirt, gold lamé heels and matching bustier, and a long platinum blond wig.

I opened the little gate in the fence that surrounded the duplex and walked back to 1040, the apartment on the right side where Cissy and Ray had lived. It was just a little one-story unit—maybe two bedrooms, no more. Plain. One might even say ugly. The front door was painted red now, and a faded American flag hung down limply from a weathered pole sunk in the dirt next to the porch. It didn't look like anybody was home. It didn't look like anybody had been home for a long time. The walkway leading to the front door was littered with old yellow flyers and rolled-up newspapers moldering in plastic covers that had leaked rain. The venetian blinds covering the windows were shut tight. The place looked dead.

I sat down on the front steps. It seemed funny to me that they would have moved here, to such a plain little apartment in such an ordinary neighborhood, but that was Cissy and Ray. Never flashy. Never ones to call attention to themselves. Still, for a guy who was suddenly making good money—a screenwriter pulling down seven hundred and fifty a week—it seemed like an odd choice, an apartment that couldn't have cost more than a hundred a month. They could easily have afforded a better place. But maybe they didn't want better. Maybe they wanted modest, unpretentious, *secure*. Because after all, who was to say the Paramount thing would work out?

From the very beginning Ray had trouble adjusting to his new life at the studio. It was difficult working with Billy Wilder, hard being suddenly thrust into the public eye. He was nervous, insecure. He had never tried a screenplay before, and he'd spent so many years as a recluse, with Cissy as his only companion. He felt ill at ease with Wilder, who was a lot younger—brash and sure of himself, a European émigré who had only recently arrived in this country, after completing his first films. Wilder knew much more about screenwriting and film than Ray did and had an arrogance that rubbed him wrong. Ray didn't take to the nine-to-five schedule, either, or working in an office building. It meant leaving Cissy alone all day. He would later refer to the experience of working with Wilder as an agonizing experience which probably short-ened his life, but he also admitted that he learned a lot from him—as much about screenwriting, he said, as he was capable of learning.

There were also things he liked about his new job. For one thing, there were so many young women around all the time, so many secretaries and starlets, so many beautiful girls in the offices and wandering around the lot. He was given his own secretary. It was exciting to him, and distracting. It was more than distracting. It was tempting. He had always been highly excitable around attractive women. And at Paramount, he liked what he saw. After a long dry spell, his sexual interests were suddenly rekindled.

He also began drinking again. Perhaps it was inevitable. Drinking was a part of the film business. The atmosphere of the Writers' Building at Paramount was rife with alcohol. He tried to hide his drinking from Wilder—at first he'd told him he never touched the stuff. But he must have found the stress hard to cope with. He must have realized how easy it would be to hide a bottle in his briefcase and take a nip now and then. Whenever Wilder left the room, he'd pull it out and take a few slugs, oblivious to the fact that of course Wilder could smell the liquor on his breath when he returned. After a while he no longer bothered to hide his drinking.

Sometimes it began early, at ten or eleven in the morning, sometimes it didn't start until three or four in the afternoon, when a group of writers would head for Lucey's restaurant at Windsor and Melrose across the street, where in the leather booths in the darkened rooms they would gather and tell stories.

Ray liked a lot of the writers he worked with: he found them funny, full of wit and bawdy humor—unpretentious guys who liked what they did and weren't as full of themselves as literary writers. In the loose atmosphere of the studio, surrounded by young men and beautiful girls, he became more aware of his lost youth and his aging wife. He was fifty-five. Cissy was seventy-three. And his secretary wasn't yet thirty.

He propositioned his secretary. She said no. But she liked him. She listened to him and became his friend, his sounding board, his confidante, the person he sometimes called in the night when he needed to talk. He told her how unhappy he was with a wife who was so much older. He told her he had married her because she had enough money to allow him to write. But now he felt trapped. This wasn't the truth, of course—at least not the part about marrying Cissy for her money—but it did lend drama to his situation. It did explain how he had gotten into such a marriage. He wanted sympathy from his secretary, and he wanted sex. He told his secretary that he and his wife no longer had sex. He said he was still young and he didn't want that part of his life to end. He said he didn't know what to do anymore. When the secretary asked why he didn't just divorce his wife if things were so bad, he said he felt obligated to her and couldn't just abandon her in her old age.

The secretary listened. She sympathized with his situation. But she still didn't want to have an affair with him. For one thing, he seemed pretty old. For another, there was the matter of his appearance. He had an ashy, burnt-out look. His skin was so pale, so exceptionally white, he looked unhealthy. He dressed in stuffy clothes—tweeds that smelled of mothballs, flannel pants—totally out of place in casual California with its warm climate. He looked like a tweedy professor, a pipe-smoking poet. He had a stooped and shambling walk. To a woman of twenty-five, he was no catch, he was no Romeo. He was an odd duck, awkward, old-fashioned, of nervous temperament—too inhibited to be gay, as his friend and coworker John Houseman once said, and too emotional to be witty. Young women disturbed him, excited him, and brought out a certain coarseness in him. His voice was normally muted, and it was in a husky whisper, so Houseman reported, that Ray would murmur juvenile obscenities about women—the sort of remarks he would have been the first to take offense at had they been uttered by anyone else.

When his secretary refused to have an affair with him, he didn't give up. He pursued someone else. He kept trying until he was successful. He began having an affair with another secretary who worked at Paramount, and soon they were disappearing together,

sometimes for days or even a week at a time. The woman was never named. But at the Bodleian, I found a note Ray had sent to his agent, directing him to please send copies of all his books to a Miss Bea Winters, secretary at Paramount. Maybe Miss Winters was just a friend, someone he wanted to impress. Or maybe she was his lover.

In any case Cissy figured out what was happening. It was like a replay of the old Dabney Oil days. The drinking again. The affair with a secretary. She became intensely jealous. They began to argue. Sometimes they stayed up all night quarreling, like the time he forgot their anniversary because he was off somewhere with his girlfriend.

I sat on the steps of the apartment on Havenhurst, leaning against the front door, protected from the hot dry wind by the thick bushes and thought about this. A couple of doves were cooing in the trees. A spider was making a tiny web from one twig to another. It was quiet, and not in a good way. It was dead quiet.

She must have felt like a shut-in here, I thought. She *was* a shut-in, with deteriorating health and a negligent husband. And yet I knew that when they first returned to the city and Ray began working at Paramount they had gone out together a lot. In an essay recalling his friendship with Ray, John Houseman wrote about how Ray was almost never seen in public without Cissy. James M. Cain called them "Hollywood's happiest couple." But that had changed. It changed when Ray began having an affair. When he started calling his secretary in the middle of the night and asking her to come over so they could talk. When Cissy got jealous and they began arguing and he began disappearing again, driving off in his monumental gray-green vintage Packard convertible and not returning for days. What a rotten situation, I thought. What a lousy life for both of them, but face it, a lot worse for her. At seventy-three she wasn't going to leave him because where would she go? And he clearly wasn't going to abandon her.

He was stuck with his aging, graying Shirley Temple. She could do nothing about his drinking or affairs. It must have hurt. All the arguments. The sneaking around, the confrontations.

When I first read Wilder's description of how Ray had left the premiere of *Double Indemnity* before it was over and the lights came up so he wouldn't be seen with his elderly wife because he was ashamed of her, I had thought Wilder was wrong. I thought Ray might have been protecting her, not wanting to subject Cissy to comparison, or prying eyes or gossip. But sitting there on the porch at Havenhurst, I realized that Wilder was probably right. Ray had become a little ashamed of Cissy, of the way her age reflected on him, of the way his marriage looked to the guys who were scoring with all the young beauties. Hollywood did that to him. Hollywood was a ruthless place. Age didn't play well here, and it still doesn't. Especially for women.

In his own way Ray tried to make it up to her. He was sensitive enough to realize what he was doing to her. He bought her jewelry and perfume. He had the money now to bring her nice gifts. He bought her a new car, but it was so big she could hardly drive it or park it in the driveway, and she rarely went out alone anyway.

Double Indemnity was a big success. In many ways it was a seminal picture, a dark tale about insurance fraud and murder, which injected a new kind of realism into Hollywood movies. The ending, in particular, set a new standard for brute, unsentimental violence. The male star of the movie, Fred MacMurray, who has just murdered the husband of Barbara Stanwyck, his partner in crime, holds her in his arms. But instead of kissing her upturned face, as she is expecting, he shoots her in the stomach. Close range. Just like that. Kills her while he's holding her close. She deserved it, of course. She was definitely the villain. Yet moviegoers knew they were seeing a new kind of picture, and unhappy endings were now most definitely okay. Shooting a woman while holding her in your arms, poised in embrace, was also now on the table.

When interviewed about the movie years later, Billy Wilder said that *Double Indemnity* was really a love story between two men—Fred MacMurray and Edward G. Robinson, who plays

MacMurray's older coworker and boss at the insurance agency. Robinson knows that MacMurray is up to no good, and he tries to save him, tries to keep him from going bad and succumbing to the influence of the evil Barbara Stanwyck. A love story between two men: that's how Wilder described it. That story hadn't really been a part of Cain's novel but was something added by Ray, and by Wilder, who saw the potential there.

The week *Double Indemnity* was released Cissy and Ray went out to the desert. They spent a few weeks in Palm Springs. He was exhausted. He'd become so disgusted with Wilder in the middle of writing the screenplay that he'd written a memo to the front office, detailing his objections to what he considered Wilder's unacceptable behavior. If they were to continue working together, he said, Wilder could no longer strut up and down the room and wave his malacca cane in the air. Wilder was no longer to ask him to shut the door, or close the venetian blinds, or order him around in any such fashion. Wilder was forbidden to call his girlfriends while they were working together and *spend twelve minutes* on the phone.

It wasn't just Wilder that had worn Ray down. It was the whole studio scene, with its constant temptations and frustrations, compromises and demands. During the weeks in Palm Springs he considered kissing Hollywood off and returning to Marlowe, going back to another novel. Once again he wondered if he might not give up the mystery novel for straight fiction and yet somehow still keep Marlowe as the main character. Could he do that? He wrote to Alfred Knopf, laying out his idea for the new book and asking his advice:

It is to be a story about a murder involving three men and two women and practically nobody else. It is to take place in Bel-Air, and all these characters are wealthy people except the protagonist of the story. Here is my problem. I should like to do a first-person story about Philip Marlowe. I wouldn't have to develop him more than I have already because he is the sort of guy who behaves according to the company he is in. But the story is not going to be a mystery, and I hope to avoid its being tagged as a mystery novel. Is this possible if I use a character who is already established in mystery fiction?

Cissy and Ray spent a month together in the desert, in April 1944. The weather was bad. Rain and wind. Chilly days and nights. He didn't write. He didn't do much of anything at all for a whole month. He wrote to James M. Cain, thanking him for a letter, apologizing for not responding sooner: "I was so completely pooped after nine months at Paramount that I couldn't even make myself write a letter. Just sat and stared morosely out of the window at the sand dunes."

Hollywood had swept him up, burnt him out. He certainly had met some people, as he'd longed to do when he'd been cut off from society in Cathedral City. That was a telling remark he'd made to Knopf about how Marlowe was the sort of guy who behaves according to the company he's in. Ditto Ray. When in Hollywood . . . He must have enjoyed the sex and romance after a long dry spell. He must have liked drinking again. He couldn't have done the sex without the alcohol, I was pretty sure about that. The booze and the sex went together, enabled him to overcome his natural shyness and nervy tendencies. But I also think he could play that game for only so long. The *tawdry imitation of domesticity* really did get him down. He had binged. Now it was time to dry out. To cut out the shenanigans. Cissy was still the center of his universe, his Momma, his Double-Duck, and he was her Raymio and Gallibeoth, and this must have become clear to him as he sat in Palm Springs, staring morosely out the window at the dark clouds and shifting sand.

He and Cissy returned to the city in May. He did not start the novel set in Bel Air. He did not start any novel (though he did sometimes work a little on one he had put aside earlier, about a guy who returns from the war to find his floozy of a drunken wife is having an affair). Instead he accepted an offer he couldn't refuse—to return to Paramount and work on film scripts already under way. Paramount upped his salary; they made him a good deal. All he had to do was polish dialogue on a couple of pictures, one a romance, the other a thriller. He had learned a lot about film, what made movies work. It was a visual world, not a verbal one, but what words you did put into a script had better be right. He was a guy who could get them right. He'd done that in *Double Indemnity*. And that was why Paramount wanted him back.

He was a success now, an indisputable success, both as a novel-ist and a screenwriter. Yet his life hadn't really changed much because he had more money and recognition. He had never cared much for the trappings of success or the way Hollywood people lived. "Most movie people are fine to work with," he said, "but I don't like to go into their homes, don't like to listen to the same old talk—pictures and more pictures. Furthermore, I don't want their scale of living, and if you don't live as expensively as they, well, you just don't belong."

He was not living expensively. One look at this neighborhood and the apartment on Havenhurst confirmed that. But he must have sensed it was time to move again. Maybe he was just restless. Whatever the reason, they left Havenhurst a couple of months after they returned from the desert, while Ray was still doing the polish jobs at Paramount. They moved south and west, to a street not far from Fairfax Avenue in the Jewish district of the city. They rented a house at 6520 Drexel Avenue. Still they did not buy.

Drexel was easy to find, a straight shot down Crescent Heights, past Beverly Boulevard to Sixth. Drexel was a nice street. Old sycamore trees, graceful little houses. Not as big as those in nearby Hancock Park, but an attractive mixture of architectural styles, a neighborhood that had only gotten nicer since the Chan-dlers had lived here. The house they occupied was simple, unpre-tentious, a pretty little stucco bungalow with red poinsettias growing up against the pink walls.

I parked in front of the house, decided to take a walk around the block to get a feel for the area. I looked at the trees and the houses that Cissy and Ray had looked at. I passed several well-dressed elderly ladies walking their dogs—all poodles or variations thereof—ladies who smiled and offered up very polite hellos. I passed a man in slippers and a heavy robe who looked like a patient of some sort being taken for a walk by his young male nurse. The patient stared at me as I walked by and hissed, "Beautiful oh beautiful." He managed to make these words sound rather scary. After a few moments I turned around and looked back at him and noticed how his hands were tied behind his back. A mental patient maybe. I kept walking. I passed the ladies and the poodles again. The neighborhood felt good to me—not too pretentious but very civilized. Nice houses. Well-kept gardens. A-list L.A.

I went back to 6520 Drexel. I didn't want to knock on the door. I didn't want to know who lived there now. I just wanted to sit in my car, out of the hot wind, and look at the house and think about what it had been like for Ray and Cissy when they had lived here. Faulkner was writing the screenplay for *The Big Sleep* then, trying to figure out a plot that didn't always make sense (once he called Ray to inquire who, exactly, had killed the Sternwoods' chauffeur, and Ray had replied, "I have no idea"). *Murder, My Sweet,* the film version of *Farewell, My Lovely,* directed by Edward Dmytryk and starring Dick Powell as Philip Marlowe, had just been released by RKO.

Later, much later, when people had begun discussing such things, *Murder, My Sweet* would be recognized as one of the first true noir films produced in Hollywood. It employed all the classic elements—the use of shadows and silhouettes and oddly disconcerting camera angles, the menacing city with its rain-slicked streets, brutal police, corrupt doctors with their fly-by-night clinics ready to dispense druggy shots, the sense of almost universal corruption, the spoiled rich trying to protect their dirty little secrets, and of course the beautiful but deadly blonde. Ray liked the picture. Dick Powell, he thought, came closest to his own conception of Marlowe—he was better even than Bogart, who would portray him later, though he liked Bogie, too. At that point, no fewer than four of Ray's books were either in production or had already been made into movies. And *Double Indemnity* had just earned Academy Award nominations in both the Best Film and Best Screenplay categories.

They got their furniture out of storage and moved it into the Drexel house by far the nicest place they'd ever rented. Cissy had an operation on her foot and was laid up for a while. Ray's contract at Paramount ended, and while his agent negotiated a new one, he began working at home, staying close to Cissy so he could take care of her while her foot healed. They hired a housekeeper. They hired a cook. They began living a little more like real Hollywood people.

He wasn't drinking. Who knew if he was still fooling around. He went to the studio when he felt like it, met up with his old pals at Lucey's. Maybe there was a little thing now and then, a rendezvous or two. Maybe he still saw women. Maybe he even took a few drinks. But most of the time he stayed at home, sober, and took care of Cissy.

They took long Sunday drives in the Packard convertible, some-times alone, sometimes with their friend John Houseman. They drove up the coast to Malibu for lunch and drove back late in the afternoon as the sun was setting over the ocean. They made an increasingly odd couple, as Cissy's advancing age became more apparent. Houseman described them this way: "In Hollywood, where the selection of wives was frequently confused with the casting of motion pictures, Cissy was an anomaly and a phenome-non. Ray's life had been hard; he looked ten years older than his age. His wife looked twenty years older than he did and dressed thirty years younger."

Houseman, like others before him, found Ray difficult to get to know. According to the public school code in England in which they'd both been raised, you didn't ask questions about a person's past. Still, Houseman had heard that Ray had been a bad alco-holic, and he said this was easy to believe: the first impression Ray gave was one of extreme frailty. Not until later, he said, did one discover the peculiar strength that lay beneath his pale, burnt-out look and his "querulous hypchondria."

Ray liked tailored clothes. He could now afford a tailor in Bev-erly Hills. He favored subdued colors. Someone who met him dur-ing this time described him as an "all-beige person." They said he had beige hair and beige clothes and beige skin, and even his eyes were a kind of washed-out brown-beige.

He and Cissy often went shopping together. Cissy especially liked to go shopping for antiques. She liked decorating the new house. One of her favorite pastimes was changing the furniture around, adding a new piece. He had always admired her good taste. They both liked nice objects. They bought several Chinese rugs. They bought a pair of Louis XV armchairs and a good dining room set.

In early 1945, Ray returned to Paramount with a new contract to write an original screenplay that was to be a murder mystery. He wasn't happy about going back on the lot, but Paramount demanded he work at the studio, not at home. "I regret to say I have to go back to work tomorrow," he wrote to a friend on the eve of his return. "The prospect makes me feel low enough to chin myself on the curbing."

It must have been disturbing for Cissy, too. Once again he would be out of sight, beyond her ability to control his activities. He considered Hollywood a way station, a place to make the kind of money they'd need to secure their future. "If it teaches me to turn out books a little faster—and I think it will—it certainly won't do me any harm. I'm probably too old and too hardened to be glamorized."

The studio's biggest star and highest-paid actor, Alan Ladd, was about to be drafted into the army, and Paramount hoped to make a picture starring him in the short few months that remained before he would be called up. The problem was, they had no project, no screenplay, no idea what that picture might be. John Houseman asked Ray if he had any ideas, and Ray said he did. He'd been working on a novel for some time—he had 120 pages—but he wasn't happy with it, and he'd been thinking of turning it into a film script. He invited Houseman to come over to the house on Drexel and take a look at it.

Houseman arrived to find Cissy propped up on the couch "in a cloud of pink tarlatan," her leg in a cast. He sat down and read Ray's pages. He liked what he read, and so did Joe Sistrom, the executive producer, and Paramount gave the green light to the project, paying Ray handsomely in the hope he could finish the script in such a short time. Ray started working on the screenplay that would become *The Blue Dahlia*. In under two weeks he wrote ninety pages of the story, all dictated to his secretary. Veronica Lake was cast as Ladd's costar. George Marshall was selected as director and began shooting the movie with an as yet unfinished script.

Ray found the experience oddly exhilarating—writing under that kind of pressure, producing pages of script that were shot almost as fast as he wrote them—but the studio began to get nervous. Halfway through the filming, Ray still seemed to have no idea who had committed the murder in the story. The brass at Paramount began asking themselves, Could Chandler really finish the script on time? The shooting began to gain rapidly on the script and Ray had no ending, but he didn't seem worried. He would have an artistic revelation, he said, as he always did. But then disaster struck.

One of the studio executives made the mistake of calling Ray to a secret meeting, as Frank McShane described it. Ray was told not to inform Houseman or anyone else about the meeting, simply to show up at 9:30 one morning in the executive's office. Ray spent a sleepless, worried night, wondering what was up. When he showed up the next morning, the executive made him an offer: He said the future of Paramount was riding on Ray's finishing the script and Ladd's completing the picture. He offered Ray a $5,000 bonus if he could deliver *The Blue Dahlia* on time. The executive must have thought that by making such an offer, he was making a cunning move, but he badly misread his man. Ray was not only offended by the offer but shattered. It succeeded in disturbing him in three different ways. One, his faith in himself was destroyed when he realized there was a real question in the minds of others as to whether he could finish the script. Two, he felt the offer insulted him: the bonus was nothing but a bribe to complete a job for which he was already being well paid. And three, he had been told to keep the offer and meeting secret from his friend, Houseman, and this violated the code of honor he felt he shared with his public school mate.

Ray felt he could no longer work on the script. In ten days, Ladd would leave for the army. Marshall had just shot the ninety-third page of the script, and he needed only a few more scenes and of course an ending, including a resolution of the key question of who had committed the murder. Ray ignored the request to keep the meeting secret and went straight to Houseman, after discussing the situation with Cissy. He informed him he was quitting. He had no choice, he said, but to withdraw from the project. He felt he had nothing further to contribute. Furthermore, the humiliating offer had destroyed his confidence, reduced him to a state of nervous despair, and he could not write in this condition. Houseman pleaded with him to reconsider, and Ray left, saying he needed to go home and lie down and discuss the matter further with Cissy.

What did they say to each other that night? Certainly she must have tried to talk him down off the ledge. No one knew him better than she did. Repeatedly she had been there for him over the years, when he had gotten himself into bad situations, and this certainly qualified as a bad situation. His creative powers were wrecked. His honor was at stake. He was damned either way—his own personal code compromised if he accepted the bribe or agreed to return to work, his professional honor destroyed if he didn't complete the job. The episode reveals what a fragile man Ray really was and how the extreme code of honor and behavior he bestowed on Philip Marlowe arose firmly from his own personality. He and Cissy argued over what he should do, and eventually he concocted a plan, a means by which he might be able to finish the screenplay. The next morning he appeared in Houseman's office, looking less distraught but still grim. He said that after a sleepless and tormented night, he had concluded he could not finish the script. He let this news sink in. And then he began speaking again and laid out a proposal. Houseman later described the moment.

I was certainly aware (or had heard it rumored) that he [Ray] had for some years been a serious drinker—to the point where he had gravely endangered his health. By an intense effort of will he had managed to overcome his addiction. This abstinence, he explained, had been all the more difficult to sustain, since alcohol gave him an energy and a self-assurance that he could achieve in no other way. This brought us to the crux of the matter: having repeated that he was unable and unwilling to continue working on *The Blue Dahlia* in the studio sober, Ray assured me of his complete confidence in his ability to finish it at home—*drunk*.

He did not minimize the hazards: he pointed out that his

plan, if adopted, would call for deep faith on my part and supreme courage on his, since he would in effect be completing the script at the risk of his life. (It wasn't the drinking that was dangerous, he explained, since he had a doctor who gave him such massive injections of glucose that he could last for weeks with no solid food at all. It was the sobering up that was perilous; the terrible strain of his return to normal living.) That was why Cissy had so long and so bitterly opposed his proposed scheme, till Ray had finally convinced her that honour came before safety, and that his honour was deeply engaged, through me, in *The Blue Dahlia*.

Houseman was at first horrified by Ray's proposal. The idea that Ray would start drinking and be endangering his life, that he would be entering a state of not quite being in control, seemed like madness to him. He knew the whole thing would be his responsibility if it went wrong, and that he could never tell the studio executives of Ray's plan, which Ray now presented to him in detail, handing him a sheet of yellow paper on which he had carefully itemized his basic logistical requirements:

A. Two Cadillac limousines, to stand by day and night outside the house with drivers available for:
    1. Fetching the doctor (Ray's or Cissy's or both).
    2. Taking script pages to and from the studio.
    3. Driving the maid to market.
    4. Contingencies and emergencies.
B. Six secretaries—in three relays of two—to be in constant attendance and readiness, available at all times for dictation, typing, and other possible emergencies.
C. A direct line open at all times, to my office by day and the studio switchboard at night.

Houseman took the paper from Ray, asked for an hour to consider the possibilities, and left the room. He visited the set, where the director informed him he'd be out of script by the next day. He stopped by the office of the executive producer, Joe Sistrom, and ran the idea past him. They both agreed they ought to give it a try, mainly because they had no choice. They'd concoct some virus story to explain Ray's absence from the studio and privately find a way to meet his demands. Houseman returned to his office, and, dredging up all the esprit de corps, as he put it, and old-boy public school fervor, informed Ray he'd accept his proposal.

Ray was elated. He was instantly cheered by this news and suggested they immediately go to lunch at Perino's to celebrate. He lost no time in launching his plan: over lunch, he downed three double martinis, followed by three double stingers. Houseman then drove Ray, in Ray's open Packard convertible, back to the house on Drexel Avenue, where the two Cadillac limousines were already in position and the first relay of secretaries had assumed their duties. Ray immediately went to work, having just consumed the equivalent of twelve drinks.

I sat behind the wheel of my car and stared at the front of the house on Drexel Avenue and thought, what a scene it must have been here during those days when Ray was trying to finish the script. The limousines parked out front with drivers cooling their heels, waiting to drive pages to the studio. It was a nice touch, specifying Cadillac limousines—only the best for his words. And what did Cissy do, in her cloud of pink tarlatan, her leg still in a cast, while Ray was methodically getting potted and working with his girls? Did it not dredge up the old wounds? I saw the doctor arriving with his black bag and giving Ray his injections. The limo driver taking the housekeeper to shop. The cook fixing the meals that Ray never touched. The maid fixing cocktails. The secretaries fixing cocktails. Ray fixing cocktails. Everybody making the drinks. The secretaries scribbling, Ray talking out scenes while the secretaries took dictation, Ray correcting proofs, Ray passing out, the limos taking pages to the studio, where the director was waiting to film the next scene, Ray reviving, drinking more, dictating the next scene while laid out on the couch with the secretaries seated nearby, the mornings and the nights flying by in an alcoholic haze.

For eight days Ray did not draw a sober breath, nor did he eat a bite of food. He lived on bourbon and vitamin and insulin shots. He worked nights. He worked days. He worked whenever he could. He passed out. He woke up. And always the secretaries were there, waiting, and the Cadillacs were lined up out front, waiting, and somewhere in this house Cissy was also waiting. Waiting to see how this would all come out. She had opposed his plan vehemently, Houseman said. She was dead set against it. It upset her terribly that he'd chosen to begin drinking again. Because in Ray's life, as in his fiction, women were the keepers of order, the ones with the keys to the liquor cabinet, the sane forces that kept men like Marlowe from going overboard. In *Farewell, My Lovely,* after getting beaten up by Dr. Amthor's thugs, Marlowe makes his way to Anne Riordans's house, and she takes care of him, makes him a drink. "Can I have one more drink?" he asks her later. "This is going to be the last," she says, and it is. Cissy hadn't been able to stop Ray from carrying out his plan, and all she could do was watch the craziness unfold.

The first night following the lunch at Perino's he produced three pages of script that revealed the identity of the murderer (the house detective). From then on he turned out a scene or two a day. Houseman regularly visited him to check on his condition. Sometimes he found him passed out on the couch with his black cat by his side. Sometimes he found him awake and alert with empty highball glasses lined up on the table. He was never without a glass in his hand.

Every evening from eight to ten Ray took a break from the work and sat with Cissy in her bedroom, and they listened together to the *Gas Company Evening Concert.* During those eight manic days was she drinking, too? I think so. I think they had cocktails in her room and listened to music. Natasha Spender had said to me, during one of our conversations, that she was quite sure that when Ray drank Cissy also usually did. She felt Cissy was his *enabler*—

"That's the word they use nowadays, isn't it?" she said. "If she couldn't fight him, she joined him."

When he slept it was only lightly, for a few hours at a time, and then he awoke, seemingly in full possession of his creative faculties, and picked up where he'd left off with whichever of the rotating secretaries happened to be on duty. He drank and wrote, wrote and drank until he felt drowsy again, then nodded off on the sofa while the secretaries went into the next room to type up the pages, which he read and corrected. As the last line of the script, Ray wrote in pencil, "Did somebody say something about a drink of bourbon?" And that was how the ending was shot.

The Blue Dahlia was finished with six days to spare. Houseman wrote:

> Ray had not exaggerated when he said he was risking his life for The Blue Dahlia. His long starvation seriously weakened him and it took him almost a month to recover, during which his doctor came twice a day to administer mysterious and reviving shots which cost him a lot more than the "bonus" he was to receive. During his convalescence he lay neatly dressed in fresh pajamas under a silk robe: When I came to see him he would extend a white and trembling hand, and acknowledge my gratitude with the modest smile of a gravely wounded hero who had shown courage far beyond the call of duty.

The Blue Dahlia went on to be nominated for an Oscar, though even Chandler thought it wasn't a very good film. He thought "Miss Moronica Lake" was miscast as Ladd's love interest and that Ladd's wife overplayed her part. Ladd played an officer returning from war in the company of his two buddies, one of whom, played by William Bendix, has been wounded and has a plate in his head and a hair-trigger temper. Ladd's wife, a party girl, has been playing around on him while he's been gone. Worse, she lied to him about how their son Dickie died while he was away, not from diphtheria as she'd told him but in a car accident while she was drunk behind the wheel. They argue; he accuses her of being a drunk and walks out on her. Outside it's raining, a dark, wet night in L.A. As he walks down the street, suitcase in hand, rain running off the brim of his hat, a car pulls up and the driver, Veronica Lake, offers him a ride. She's the sleek pageboy blonde, the cool, sardonic dame, classy and witty, opposite in every way to Ladd's slatternly brunette wife, and of course they're attracted to each other. But Ladd's wife turns up murdered, and Ladd soon becomes the prime suspect. He goes on the lam, and Veronica Lake tries to help him. When she suggests he might have seen her before, he replies, "Every guy's seen you before somewhere. The trick is to find you." She's the dream woman, perfect in every way, not a hair out of place. But Ladd is in too much trouble to think of women, perfect or not. As with all Chandler stories the plot gets complicated, spins off in different directions, features mobsters and gambling clubs, tough cops: the hero is abducted by villains, driven to a remote location, and beaten up; he's knocked out but comes to and escapes. By then he's turned sour on women. "Women," he says, "they're all poison sooner or later."

Possibly the most enduring thing about *The Blue Dahlia* is its legacy of having lent a variant of its title to a sensational killing that occurred shortly after the release of the movie, one of the grisliest murders in the history of L.A.—the slaying of twenty-three-year-old Elizabeth Short, who was dubbed by the press "The Black Dahlia." Short's body was discovered on January 15, 1947, her body neatly severed in two and drained of blood, her female organs surgically removed, her mouth cut from ear to ear in a grotesque smile. She had been dumped near a sidewalk where she would easily be found. Like Ladd's wife in *The Blue Dahlia*, Elizabeth Short was a brunette, someone who went out to clubs, who had a special fondness for men in uniform, and there were a lot of men in uniform in L.A. in 1947. The Black Dahlia murder was never solved, though the killer taunted the police with notes for weeks after the body was discovered. But in 2003, Steve Hodel, a former L.A. police department homicide detective, published a book, *Black Dahlia Avenger*, in which he claimed that his father Dr. George Hodel, a prominent L.A. physician and womanizer (and a friend of Man Ray's and John Huston's) was the man who killed Elizabeth Short—and probably a number of other women as well, a string of murders that had never been solved. The case Steve Hodel made for his father's being the killer was pretty convincing. Ironically before becoming a doctor, George Hodel had been a musical prodigy while growing up in Pasadena and later, in the 1920's, as a young medical student, he had used his musical knowledge to host the *Gas Company Evening Concert*— the same program that Cissy and Ray listened to every night of their married years.

During the late 1920s, L.A. was plagued by a rash of unsolved murders of beautiful single women, crimes that in their brutality exceeded anything Chandler had ever thought of—the first serial killings of their kind in L.A. So many young women began to turn up murdered and missing that a grand jury was convened to investigate the matter, and L.A. was given a new nickname, "The Port of Missing Women."

The Port of Missing Women.

What Ray thought about the title of his movie being adapted to describe the most brutal of all of these serial killings we'll never know, because at least in print he never referred to it. But he must have realized that life in L.A. had overtaken his art in a particularly grisly fashion.

Ray's time in Hollywood had worn him down and left him exhausted: it was hard for him to find the energy to return to writing fiction. To a friend he wrote: "Three years in Hollywood leaves its mark. My kind of writing takes a certain quality of high spirits and impudence. I'm a tired character, a battered pulp writer, an out of work hack."

He was tired of the picture business, sick of it in fact. The affairs and the drinking and the stress of being so public took their toll. They were both in ill health, both suffering from recurrent colds and bouts of flu. Cissy's foot was still not fully healed. Erle Stanley Gardner invited them to come down to his ranch for a few days of rest. He said they could hike or go horseback riding, not understanding they were physically incapable of doing either. Ray wrote Gardner,

> My wife has been under the weather with the flu for ten days, but she wants to come down to your place as much as I do. . . . I don't think my wife or myself could hike or ride. She had an operation on her foot about a year ago and it's still weak. We don't know how to ride. I am a complete nervous wreck and theoretically could walk a few miles, but probably not your kind of walking. Haven't got the equipment anyhow. What we hope to do was just to get down to your place around noon and spend a few hours with you. We have some business in Riverside and were thinking of stopping over at the Mission Inn and then driving to Temecula in the morning.

The atmosphere of the Mission Inn would have suited them: it was grand place, built of stone and laid out in the style of an old California mission with interior patios and a maze of staircases— a lovely old hotel, as I discovered when I drove out there one day, with blooming gardens, shady paths, and graceful colonnades. The cavernous lobby had stucco walls and beamed ceilings and well-worn mission-style furniture. There were a number of areas in the big sprawling lobby where one could sit, and I settled onto a sofa before a small fireplace. I imagined them checking in, handing the car over to an attendant, Cissy still hobbling on a bad foot, Ray being chivalrous. Tipping generously as he often did. I saw them settling into one of the large comfortable rooms. Coming down to the dining room for an early dinner. Both dressed carefully. The difference in their ages hardly noticeable now, with both of them so frail and worn down.

They had come through a hard time. They were no doubt now

solicitous of each other. Careful about what they said and did. There had been pledges. New promises. No more booze. No more secretaries. No more drinking and drabbing with other writers. No more disappearing for days. No more pretentiousness and squabbling over money, no more starlets and strutting producers, snide tricks and tantrums. No more degraded faked-up idealism, as Ray put it, or fear of losing the "fairy gold." It seemed to him the film business (Hollywood he meant) was dangerously rotten and innately corrupting. "It's like one of those South American palace revolutions," he said, "conducted by officers in comic opera uniforms—only when the thing is over ragged dead men lie in rows against the wall, and you suddenly know that this is not funny, this is the Roman circus, and damn near the end of a civilization." He had made it through a time of excess, but barely. They were tired and shaken. Sobered and chastened. I imagined them sitting in the lobby after dinner. In the old Mission Inn, with its moneyed clientele. Just watching the guests come and go. Too tired for anything more strenuous. No hiking. No horses. Just the art of observation, the solace of a companion.

They went to see Erle Stanley Gardner the next day at his ranch in Temecula. They had lunch there and sat outside and enjoyed the quiet and scenic views and then they drove back to Los Angeles. They stayed a few more months in the house on Drexel Avenue. Ray worked a little longer in Hollywood, trying to adapt his novel *Lady in the Lake* for the screen, but he got disgusted with the project and he walked. The movie of *The Big Sleep* came out. He liked the film. He thought Bogart was terrific, so much better than any other tough guy actor. Bogart had a sense of humor that fit with Marlowe. He had his sad good-naturedness.

Ray started work on a new book, but it didn't come easily. He worked at home, but he was unhappy again with his surroundings. For one thing there were a couple of teenagers next door. Always playing their music. Always making noise. He had never cared for kids anyway. Never liked children at all.

They went down to La Jolla in August, just to get away. It was a nice month to be by the sea, and not such a good time to be in the city. They stayed in the La Jolla Hotel. They talked about a change. They discussed leaving L.A.

They began looking at houses in La Jolla. And then they found one they liked. A one-story ranch house on a street called Camino de la Costa, which ran right along the coast.

The house was almost new, just a few years old. It had a big picture window that faced the sea and the coastline that curved south toward San Diego. There was a long curving hallway that led to two bedrooms and a study, and one side of the hallway had windows that looked out on a pretty little interior courtyard. The kitchen and dining room and hallway all opened onto the patio. There was a maid's room. A bedroom for Cissy, and a smaller one for Ray. A private study at the end of the hallway. Just across the street from the house, an iron staircase led down to a little cove and a small beach with big round smooth rocks pocked by tide pools, and when the tide was out you could sit on a little crescent of sand and sun yourself.

Cissy had always wanted to live in La Jolla. They could now afford to do so. He bought the house for her. They moved into it in the fall of 1946. She was seventy-six. He was fifty-eight. They had been married for twenty-two years and had moved over two dozen times. And finally, in La Jolla, they had bought a home. They had left L.A.

Nine

Years earlier I made a trip to La Jolla to see the house on Camino de la Costa where Cissy and Ray had finally settled down after all their years of wandering. There was nothing terribly special about the place, except it was where Raymond Chandler had written much of *The Little Sister* and all of *The Long Goodbye*. The house was just an ordinary one-story California ranch-style dwelling, with rather boring shrubbery growing up thickly in front. But the site itself was spectacular: It sat on a corner, slightly above the street, with an extraordinary view of

the ocean. The water was just across the way, the glittering sea stretching west toward the slightly curving horizon. That first visit I remember thinking that living in that house would be a little like living on a ship, only it was the ship that was steady and stationary, and the sea that constantly coursed and ran, bulging and breaking toward the house. It never occurred to me to disturb the occupants; I simply looked at the house from the street and then climbed down a set of steps nearby and sat for a while on the beach, in a pretty little cove, and looked at the waves.

Since then I've gone back to the house on Camino de la Costa many times. Each time I worked myself farther into the heart of the house, coming closer and closer, I felt, to Cissy and Ray and the lives they had led in that place, until finally there was nothing left to see, because the house was being torn down.

Cissy and Ray moved into their new home in the fall of 1946. They lived there for eight years, until Cissy died, a little after noon on December 12, 1954. After she was gone, Ray sold the house, and once again he became nomadic.

In many ways La Jolla was an odd place for them, given Ray's contempt for the rich, but in other ways it made perfect sense. At heart he was a snob himself, but the sort of snob who could be unpredictable in his behavior, preferring the conversation of postal clerks and warehousemen to the bibulous millionaires he found himself living among. The roots of his animosity toward the rich lay in his childhood, the fact that he and his mother had been humiliated by the wealthier Irish relatives who'd taken them in. But he also liked lovely things, and when he had money he bought them. When he didn't have money, he hoarded and scrimped to get by and still thought himself superior to the bourgeoisie. He and Cissy had always affected an air of to the manner born, like the well-to-do fallen on hard times. In Hollywood he'd become rich, richer than he'd ever imagined he would be, and with that money he bought the house in La Jolla, for forty thousand dollars—a lot of money in 1946.

It was Cissy, I think, who was the real snob, she who affected the upper-class accent and longed for the good life, and who could blame her? She'd stuck with him through the lean times. Now she had her wish, a nice house in the little seaside town she'd always loved. In Hollywood, she had been an anomaly, with her frilly gowns and Shirley Temple curls, but in La Jolla she fit right in. Here everybody was trying to look more youthful, and they had the money to work at it. Money was what mattered in La Jolla: it could get you into any club or establishment, unless of course you were Jewish, and then, well, there were rules.

The problem was that neither Cissy nor Ray was looking for acceptance, not of the country-club kind anyway. In many ways what La Jolla had to offer was just what Ray didn't want—or what he said he didn't want. He didn't want the company of rich people, or a club; he'd never been social, never cared about belonging to any group. He was too old for tennis, the only sport he'd ever really liked besides swimming and diving, and in any case, he refused to join a club that wouldn't admit Jews even if it did have a nice pool. Cissy was pretty much still living her hermetically sealed life, growing more fragile by the year. They may have changed locales by moving from L.A. to La Jolla, but they had simply hauled their reclusiveness south with them and then become just as fussy and dissatisfied with their surroundings as they'd always been.

La Jolla was mostly an escape. It wasn't real—certainly not in the way L.A. was real, with its mixture of sleaze and hype, tinsel and tackiness, the working hordes and racial mixture. It took money to live in La Jolla and maintain their nice new house, and a staff to help them run it, and Ray didn't want to be bothered with those things. He simply wanted to return to writing novels. He was sick of screenwriting. The problem was novels didn't pay the way screenplays did.

Once Billy Wilder was asked, what effect to you suppose working in Hollywood with you on *Double Indemnity* had on Raymond Chandler? And Wilder gave a rather telling answer:

I guess he could never find his way back to novel writing. He could not sit down anymore unless he sort of smelled some kind of activity and studio companionship. You remember how it was on the fourth floor of Paramount—writers sitting around drinking coffee or pinching secretaries' asses, or whatever it was. He found it very difficult, I guess, to go back to a lonely life with just a wife and a typewriter and to switch back again to a completely different medium. And he was making exceedingly good money, not the sort of money that you have to wait for while you are writing a novel—this was instant weekly money.

I guess he could never find his way back to novel writing. . . . This of course wasn't strictly true. Ray wrote three more novels after leaving Hollywood, two of them very good (*The Little Sister* and *The Long Goodbye*) and one a pale imitation of his earlier work (*Playback*). But Wilder was right, I think, about it not being easy to give up the good money, or to return full-time to the wife and typewriter, and the empty rooms where there were no beautiful secretaries with asses to pinch, no bonhomie over coffee, no racy jokes and witty lunches at Lucy's El Adobe. There was only the stationary ship of a house, the restless running sea, the incredibly rich neighbors, and a sobered emptied-out writer and his aging and ailing wife.

The yard needed landscaping, there was furniture to buy, and enough money not to have to worry for a while. But Ray worried anyway. He never needed a reason to worry. He could worry over nothing.

One of the things he began worrying about was whether the novel he had started, *The Little Sister,* was any good. He was out of practice, after five years in Hollywood. But an even greater worry began to creep in, and that was the feeling that perhaps he had made a mistake by moving to La Jolla and buying the house. There had been a reason for his years of nomadism: "If I go somewhere to study new surroundings," he once wrote, "absorb new atmospheres, meet different types of people, you always have at the back of your mind at least a hope of getting some use from it all. I have lost Los Angeles as a locale."

He wrote that in 1957, when he had already lived in La Jolla for over a decade, but he had begun to lose L.A. as soon as he left it, and this sense of his true literary landscape slipping away from him must have complicated his efforts to continue to write about it, as he was trying to do in *The Little Sister*. Whatever else La Jolla was, it was not a gritty setting for his kind of crime novels.

Knowing of his love for automobiles, Cissy toyed with the idea of buying him something sporty—a Triumph or Jaguar—but they found these cars too small and eventually settled for a new Oldsmobile 98. They made a few acquaintances in La Jolla, people who became mostly Ray's friends, including a screenwriter named Jonathan Latimer, whom Ray had met at Paramount and who lived in La Jolla, as well as Max Miller who wrote the screenplay for *I Cover the Waterfront*. He also got to know the children's book author Theodore Geisel, better known as Dr. Seuss, and the journalist Neil Morgan, and as the years passed, during the times when Ray was drinking, the group often met in bars to socialize. Occasionally an agent or someone from the film industry would visit the Chandlers and be invited to dinner, but these occasions were quite rare and often involved strained moments. There was a subterranean tension in their attempts to entertain. Cissy would become overly fussy and make everyone uncomfortable while Ray, ill at ease with the pressure of being host, became stiff and irritable. Once when the director Joe Sistrom and his wife came for dinner, the Chandlers' cook produced a roast that Ray deemed tough, and he berated the cook in front of his guests, just as his vulgar uncle had done. The next evening the Sistroms dined with the Latimers, who inquired how the evening with the Chandlers had gone, and they replied, *Awful*, and everyone laughed.

Sometimes they met people at a restaurant for dinner, and this was always much easier. Often they ate at a place called La Plaza, which served steaks and Mexican food. By this time Ray was wearing white cotton gloves in public to hide the eczema on his hands. The waitresses at La Plaza remembered him well, for the way he

was always so solicitous of his older wife and how he would sometimes tease them playfully about not properly attending to Cissy's
every need. He was an old-fashioned man when it came to his
courtly manners. And he did adore his wife and want the best for
her. But he was also flirting with those young waitresses, having
some harmless fun, and at no time do I think it really occurred to
him that flirting with waitresses over special treatment for his
wife was double-edged behavior.

He had hoped to concentrate on finishing *The Little Sister*
shortly after moving to La Jolla, but he found himself sidetracked
by different projects and ideas. Wilder was right about Ray's
being used to more activity and attention. In La Jolla, with a new
house to attend to, it was easy to become distracted.

In the spring of 1947, Hollywood reached out to him again. He
signed a contract with Universal Studio to write an original screenplay for a fee of $4,000 a week (he was, at this time, one of the
highest-paid screenwriters in the business). He wouldn't have to
work at the studio, he could stay at home in La Jolla, though the
deal also gave him a reason to head north now and then for a few
days in the city, an arrangement that he liked. He began working
on a screenplay called *Playback* set in Vancouver, where he had
spent some time after the war. The story spanned a crucial week
in the life of a girl named Betty who decides to spend it in a tower
suite in a hotel, under an assumed name, her identity concealed,
and at the end of the week to jump to her death—a setup with
a strong echo of his early story "I'll Be Waiting," about the house
detective, Tony, and the red-haired Miss Cressy who is also staying
in a tower room and who tells Tony, when he informs her that the
previous occupant of her suite committed suicide by jumping
to her death, "Redheads don't jump, Tony. They hang on, and
wither." Here's how Ray envisioned the opening scenes with the
"girl in the tower":

During this week the frustrations and tragedies of her life are
repeated in capsule form, so that it almost appears that she

brought her destiny with her, and that wherever she went the same sort of thing would happen to her.

Her husband, a heel with medals on, is dead; he is supposed to have taken an overdose of Nembutal from the effects of a prolonged binge. His family who adored him don't think he took it at all; the police weren't sure enough to make a stink, even if the family wanted it, which they didn't. All *they* wanted was to see the last of Betty, and that went double for her. If you have the money and friends, you can always cover up a suicide, and sometimes you can cover up a murder. The Randolphs had a legend to preserve; they were willing to pay to preserve it. Even to Betty. But that didn't cost them anything.

So Betty arrives at the hotel and her name is now, let us say, Elizabeth Mayfield.

Playback, for all its elements of mystery and intrigue (the plot involves politicians, rivals for control of the city, the most corrupt of whom ends up dead on Betty's balcony) is really a love story between Betty and a Canadian police office named Killaine, the detective who investigates the murder and not only falls in love with Betty but also risks his career by staking his reputation on her innocence.

Ever the romantic, Gallibeoth to the core, Ray was playing out some of his oldest and deepest themes in *Playback*: the sad lonely woman—damsel in the tower—in need of rescue; the sullied rich family ("risen scum," as James Wolcott once put it) who protect their secrets by buying people off; corrupt politicians vying for power; an unworthy husband, and men who end up abusing or betraying the women who count on them (like Ray's own father).

Though he threw himself into the writing, he had a difficult time completing the screenplay by the time stipulated in his contract and he asked for one, then another extension. He told his agent that he didn't care if the delays damaged his reputation because he didn't like screenwriting anyway, and he never would. It was like "scraping teeth," he said. He was doing the job for the money, and it was taking him a long time, because, as he put it, "I am not very well and I don't have the steam."

Cissy was not well either, and it is not hard to imagine the stress and strain in their lives being exacerbated by Ray's disgruntled view of their new surroundings, even though the place could be amusing to him. He enjoyed the local eccentrics, including two gnomelike females who dressed in large felt hats and bunchy shapeless garments and carried walking sticks and who looked to him like characters out of a Grimms' fairy tale as they walked past his house each day, never abreast, but one several paces behind the other, as if, he said, they were not on speaking terms but held together by some unbreakable tie.

He also enjoyed driving into La Jolla village every afternoon to fetch the mail and do the shopping, chatting with the postman and grocer as he made his rounds, activities which for him passed as a social life. He always dressed in a suit or sport coat and tie, even in the summer. He returned from town in time for tea with Cissy and the secretary he had hired—at Paramount he had gotten used to working with a secretary and found he needed one again, now that he had begun using a dictating machine to write and required someone to do the transcription each day. The teatimes were formal affairs, organized by Cissy with her old-fashioned sense of decorum. After tea, Cissy would suggest a drink, and Ray would bring in a bottle of sherry and pour a glass each for Cissy and his secretary, though never for himself. They would sit in the living room, before the big picture window with its view of the ocean, a view so extraordinary that Ray once wrote, "A radio writer came down here to see me once and he sat down in front of this window and cried because it was so beautiful. But we live here, and the hell with it." The truth was he disliked looking at the sea: "Too much water," he said, "too many drowned men."

He bought Cissy a Steinway grand piano and installed it in one corner of the living room and in the evenings she often played for him after dinner while he smoked his pipe. She went to bed early. They slept in separate rooms, as they'd been doing for years— Cissy in the master bedroom, which had its own bath, and Ray in his study, at the end of the long hallway, on a single bed, because they had turned the second bedroom into a space where his secretary could work. Once Cissy had gone to bed, he stayed up late, reading and dictating letters, which his secretary typed up for him in the morning. He'd always been a prolific letter writer but, with the help of the dictating machine, he became even more so, often writing to people he barely knew or had never even met— like Charles Morton, the editor of the *Atlantic Monthly*, for whom Ray began to write essays, or Hamish Hamilton, his English publisher, with whom he regularly corresponded. He got letters from fans and strangers and these, too, he answered. His letters from this period have a looseness and brilliance, a conversational quality that ranges widely across subjects, which came, in part, from being dictated. He was talking to himself in the night, in an empty room, as if holding a one-sided conversation. He needed to talk, and the letters were born of that need. As much as he disliked Hollywood, he also missed it. He felt mired, bogged down in the slough of the rich, with absolutely nothing to stimulate him except that which he found between the covers of books.

By mid-1948, he was desperate to find ways to amuse himself, and the effort to do so involved reading. He always read more than one book at a time. He would start something, and even if he liked it he often put it to one side and started another book, and then another. "Bad habit," he conceded, but "in that way when I feel dull and depressed which is too often I know I have something to read late at night when I do most of it and not that horrid blank feeling of not having anybody to talk to or listen to."

It must have been wearing, the late nights and insomnia, the worries over Cissy's rapidly declining health, the secretary arriving each morning to begin work on the screenplay whether he felt ready to work or not. Soon, his own health was breaking down. There were constant domestic problems, difficulties finding housekeepers and cooks. Cissy was chronically ill with a variety of ailments. They both suffered from flu and colds. Ray had recurring bouts of shingles. "I seem to be crumbling slowly," he wrote to a friend and listed his ailments: bronchitis, neuritis, sore throats, and skin allergies, including a rash that spread over his chest and neck and was so painful he took morphine to cope with it. "The news from here is rotten," he wrote. "Nervous, tired, discouraged, sick of the chauffeur-and-Cadillac atmosphere, bored to hell with the endless struggle to get help, disgusted with my lack of prescience in not seeing that this kind of life is unsuited to my temperament."

He needed the stimulation of a larger city—"I just go slack without that stimulation," he said. He wanted to make a trip to London, to take Cissy back to the place of his youth, and he began making inquiries, writing letters to his English publisher about hotels and visa requirements, but neither of them was fit to travel. Still he did not give up on the idea of such a trip. He missed England. It was easy for him to romanticize it, given his unhappiness in La Jolla. It represented everything he felt he hadn't found in America—manners and traditions, people who had a kind of quiet good breeding, as well as a reading public and critics who appreciated him as a literary writer and not just a hack who wrote mysteries. They continued to dream and plan for a trip to England, but nothing more came of it.

Ray had trouble finishing the *Playback* script, and the studio was less than enthused about the screenplay he delivered. He was good at dialogue, but even he admitted that his weakness was construction—the working out of plot and order of scenes—a deficiency that someone like Wilder could compensate for, but Ray had written *Playback* alone, without an experienced partner to help him. In any case the project was shelved by the studio, in part because Universal was suffering from financial difficulties and the expense of filming in Vancouver was prohibitive.

In the fall of 1948, he turned his attention back to *The Little Sister*, the story of a girl from the Midwest, Orfamay Quest, who comes to Los Angeles in search of her missing brother who has disappeared in the city. It's a dark book with a lot of nasty characters—dope-peddling doctors and women who lie and cheat and murder, drunks, rich junkies and addicts of all kinds, a beautiful tragic actress, as well as agents and Hollywood hype men, and (yet another) nymphomaniac named Dolores Gonzales who keeps trying to get Marlowe into bed. Set against the background of the film industry, it's as close as Ray ever came to writing a Hollywood novel. A kind of world-weary feeling pervades the book, especially the scene where Marlowe takes a drive over Cahuenga Pass and into the San Fernando Valley, the same drive Ray used to make with Warren Lloyd and The Optimists thirty years earlier, past Sherman Oaks and Encino, all the way to Camarillo and the Pacific coast, with the sour, bitter thoughts filling Marlowe's head—the "You're not human tonight, Marlowe" passage referred to earlier. Later Ray would write that this scene was an attempt to find out whether purely through the tone of the description I could render a state of mind. But the novel reflects Ray's mood as much as anything else, his deep disgruntlement with the state of his own life. He was depressed by the restlessness in himself, the emptiness of his world, the lack of human communication, and the indifference and ugliness of the modern world. He had seen a change in America, a transformation of the landscape, how a passion for novelty had taken hold at the expense of quality.

It was always harder for him to face the world sober. In *The Little Sister*, Marlowe discusses addiction with a fly-by-night dope-dispensing doctor named Lagardie: "Drunks," Marlowe says,

rich junkies of whom there are far more than people think, over-stimulated people who have driven themselves beyond the possibility of relaxing. Insomniacs—all the neurotic types that can't take it cold. Have to have their little pills and little shots in the arm. Have to have help over the humps. It gets to be all humps after a while.

Addicts, the doctor replies, do get cured sometimes, but Marlowe isn't having any of that.

> They can be deprived of their drug. Eventually, after great suffering, they can do without it. That is not curing them my friend. That is not removing the nervous or emotional flaw which made them become addicts. It is making them dull negative people who sit in the sun and twirl their thumbs and die of sheer boredom and inanition.

The doctor goes on:

> A hopeless alcoholic. You probably know how they are. They drink and drink and don't eat. And little by little the vitamin deficiency brings on the symptoms of delirium. There is only one thing to do for them . . . needles and more needles . . . I practice among dirty little people in a dirty little town.

It was the "needles" that had sustained Ray in the past, during his binge drinking while he completed *The Blue Dahlia*, and it would be needles that would sustain him again in the future when over and over he descended into his desperate periods of alcoholism.

The Little Sister was published in 1949. Ray seems to have been unsure about the worth of what he had written. "I rather think this will be my last Marlowe story," he told his English publisher, "and I'm not even yet sure that it's fit to print."

The novel, Ray's first in six years, received a mixed reaction, with American critics (as usual) responding more harshly than their English counterparts. One American critic, writing in *The New York Times*, attacked the book for "its scathing hatred of the human race." But on the other side of the Atlantic, *The Little Sister* was seen differently: it described an alluring world, more formless, more dangerous, more free and exciting—and also more depressing—than found in England, a *modern* world, in other words, which seemed perfectly credible as a description of what went on out there in California, the crazy cutting-edge place that would eventually end up exporting its free-form, violent, consumer-driven, personality-obsessed, and image-conscious culture to the rest of the globe. English critics and readers felt that the novel was inspired not by a hatred of the human race but a genuine concern for it. What Ray was doing was bringing news of the future to those for whom that future had not yet arrived, portraying a society in which drugs and addiction and the threat of casual, unstoppable violence was a daily reality. He offered a sense of the balefulness of hidden conspiracies, how the corrupt and powerful worked behind the scenes, undermining civilized behavior, and in that sense his California was ominous, portending what lay in store for not only America but the rest of the world. In England they got this, and in France they got it, too: his books were read by intellectuals and by serious writers, such as W. H. Auden and Somerset Maugham and Albert Camus, J. B. Priestley, and Edith Sitwell. "Chandler," Auden wrote, "is interested in serious studies of a criminal milieu—The Great Wrong Place," as he put it. It wasn't simply a question of solving a mystery, or a puzzle, but understanding the malaise the work conveyed to the reader.

"To read him is like cutting into an over-ripe melon," J. B. Priestley wrote, "and discovering that it has a rare astringent flavour. He reduces the bright California scene to an empty despair, dead bottles and a heap of cigarette butts under the meaningless neon lights . . . and suggests . . . the failure of a life that is somehow short of a dimension, with everybody either wistfully wondering what is wrong or taking savage shortcuts to nowhere."

Savage shortcuts to nowhere
A life short of a dimension
The Great Wrong Place

These are wonderful phrases. Marlowe's life was certainly short of a dimension—foremost of which was a sense of family and of belonging to anyone or any place. Yet Priestly wasn't really talking about Marlowe so much as the culture in which he found himself, that rather gelatinous, amorphous landscape of L.A., which to many people lacks, at the very least, one dimension if not more. "Real cities have something else," Marlowe says to Dolores Gonzales in *The Little Sister*, "some bony structure under the muck. Los Angeles has Hollywood—and hates it. It ought to consider itself damned lucky. Without Hollywood it would be a mail-order city. Everything in the catalogue you could get better somewhere else."

"You are bitter tonight, Amigo," Dolores replies.

He was. And so was his creator.

I wanted to visit the La Jolla house again. It had been many years since I'd made that first trip to see it. I was hoping that whoever owned the house now might be willing to let me look inside, perhaps even allow me to take some photographs. And so on a warm summer morning, I left L.A. and took the freeway down to La Jolla, arriving in the early afternoon. Nothing about the house seemed changed since the last time I'd seen it. The house had neither been painted nor remodeled, and compared to the other houses on the street it appeared ridiculously small, or rather sweetly modest, depending on how you looked at it. It was the only one-story house in sight. Over the years, all the other houses in the neighborhood had been enlarged, with spacious rooms and second levels added. The Chandler house was an anomaly, an original 1940s ranch house in an area where real estate values had skyrocketed. I learned that the locals now called this street "Camino de la Costa Plenty."

I parked near the little set of steps leading down to the beach and walked around to the front of the house, trying to appear inconspicuous so as not to alarm the neighbors, all of whom had signs on their premises announcing that private security agents protected their premises. After a while I tried the front gate and finding it unlocked, I climbed the front steps and knocked on the big white front door. I found myself thinking about how the Chandlers had hated drop-in visitors. Once, when Jonathan Latimer attempted to return a book he'd borrowed unannounced, Cissy had answered the door, opening it just a crack, and then quickly taken the book from him and retreated.

No one answered the door when I knocked. I noticed a package had been left on the doorstep and made a note of the name. Then I went back down to the street and walked around to the back of the house, which was protected by a fence, and there on the fence I saw a piece of paper nailed to the wood: NOTICE OF APPLICATION FOR PERMIT TO REMODEL.

The application was simply a form, stating a permit to remodel had been requested from the city's building department. The owner's name wasn't listed, but the name of the building inspector was, along with a phone number, and I wrote these down before I left.

During the hour-and-a-half drive back to L.A., I thought about the house—would it really be destroyed, or only moderately changed? I thought I had gotten used to the idea that in California houses were constantly being razed and remodeled, and the look of whole neighborhoods often changed, but this was different. This was Cissy and Ray's *home*, the only house they'd ever owned. The house that Cissy had loved, the place where she'd live until she died and where Ray had written his books. Somehow it had managed to survive over half a century without being significantly altered, and now all that was about to change.

The next week, I called the office of the building inspector in La Jolla, and he was quite happy to give me the name of the owner of the house, a man named Kevin. When I spoke to Kevin, it wasn't quite clear whether he was the owner or a developer speculating in real estate, but in any case he was friendly and open and willing to talk with me about my interest in Raymond Chandler. He knew that Chandler had once owned the house; the man who'd sold it to him had mentioned this. Kevin was renting the house now to a family who'd leased it on a short-term basis. The permit to remodel had already been approved, and the renters knew that within a few months the house would be torn apart and they would have to leave. He said he planned to keep the "footprint" of the house but add a second story, enlarging it to the size of its neighbors.

I asked him if I might come down and look at the house inside, and he said that would be fine, he'd just need to notify the renters I'd be coming. We agreed on a date to meet, and the next week I drove down again to La Jolla. This time I took a friend with me, the Dutch photographer Monica Nouwens, and she brought her video camera along, so we could at least document the house before it was remodeled.

Kevin met us out front. He was an affable and friendly man in his forties who looked more like a surfer than a wealthy contractor. We followed him up the front steps and he unlocked the big white front door and there suddenly I was, in Cissy and Ray's house, the large living room on the right, with the big picture window at one end. Straight ahead, sliding glass doors opened onto a sheltered courtyard, paved with flagstones and bordered by a terrace and little fountain. Off to the left a long hallway led to the bedrooms and study. On the right, I could see a formal dining room and the door that led to the kitchen and adjoining maid's room. Inside it felt somehow even smaller than it appeared from the outside.

Kevin introduced us to the couple who were renting the house, attractive and well-dressed people who announced they were heading off for lunch, but their daughter, who was in her room watching TV, would be around in case we had any questions. Kevin also had to leave but encouraged us to stay in the house as long as we wanted.

When they had gone, Monica and I began exploring the house, videotaping each room. We started in the living room. The renters had left on a gigantic television monitor that displayed a picture which didn't move—an image of a forest—and from which came the sound of horribly banal music, playing continuously, in an ever-repeating loop. Ironically the TV had been positioned so it

blocked part of the view from the big window—the fake view of
nature partially obscuring the real one. There was almost no furniture in the room—a few chairs and a low table. It felt like the
family who lived here were camping out, knowing as they did that
they would soon have to move. And yet as we walked toward the
hallway I noticed dozens of family pictures hanging on the walls
and filling every shelf of the built-in bookcase, as if they'd lived
there for years. There were wedding pictures and graduation pictures, pictures of children and parents and grandparents, seemingly every permutation of the family snapshot and studio
portrait. How at odds this seemed with Cissy and Ray's own life
where family and children had played no part.

The door to the master bedroom was locked—obviously the
renters had decided to protect their valuables against wandering
strangers—so we couldn't enter Cissy's room. Farther on down the
hall we found the second bedroom, where the secretary had
worked. And beyond that was Ray's study, a small room where a
teenage girl was sprawled on a bed watching a TV so large it took
up the better part of a whole wall.

She invited us in to look around. This of course was the room I
most wanted to see, the study in which Ray had worked. I had seen
photographs taken of him in this room. I could recognize the windows, the place where his desk had sat, facing a view of the interior patio. The girl on the bed snapped her gum lazily as we
walked around, becoming self-conscious whenever the video
camera was pointed in her direction. She said she had never
heard of Raymond Chandler. In fact, she said, she didn't really
much like to read. She was more interested in movies and video
games.

I tried to imagine this room as it had once been, and it wasn't
hard. The bookcases were still there, and the original curving set
of built-in drawers that took up one corner near the entryway. Ray
slept here, I thought. Wrote here. Sat in a wingback chair, reading
late into the night. He entertained his few visitors in this study.
Kept his books organized on these shelves. Someone who visited

him once and sat with him in this study said that there wasn't a book in his collection that Ray hadn't read and couldn't discuss at length.

While Monica continued videotaping I went outside and sat on the patio for a while. The garden was dying from neglect. The fountain no longer ran. The whole place had the feeling of being in transition. I wanted to feel Ray and Cissy here, and maybe because I wanted to so much, I could. I sensed them everywhere, and I felt that for all their troubles this house had been their shelter and refuge. But it had also trapped Ray. He had been lonely here. But then he'd been lonely everywhere.

Once Somerset Maugham visited the Chandlers here. At the time Maugham was living in the south of France, but he'd come to California where he was staying with his good friend, the director George Cukor. Maugham deeply admired Chandler's work, and the feeling was mutual. (Ray had once written to Hamish Hamilton, "Incidentally if I knew Maugham, which I fear I never shall, I should ask him for an inscribed copy of *Ashenden*. I've never asked a writer for such an inscribed copy.") Knowing how much Maugham admired Chandler, George Cukor planned to bring the two men together as a surprise for Maugham. Cukor arranged for a drive down to La Jolla, in his chauffeur-driven limousine, promising Maugham lunch at La Valencia Hotel. Secretly Cukor had already contacted Ray about surprising Maugham at lunch, and toward the end of their meal at the hotel, Cukor saw Chandler come into the courtyard and brought him to the table and introduced the two men.

The moment was later described by Maugham biographer Wilmon Menard: "Maugham's head jerked up . . . and for a few moments he stared, speechless. Standing beside Cukor was a rather solidly built man of medium height, wearing horn-rimmed glasses, with an unlit pipe in hand, attired in a fashionable tweed jacket and gray flannel trousers." Maugham felt tongue-tied for a few moments. Then Ray reached down for a handshake with his white-gloved hand, explaining that "the gauntlets are to protect a skin allergy on my hands, and it's not a dread social disease that's contagious."

Although he had seen previously published photos of Chandler on book jackets and in newspapers, Maugham was surprised by Ray's appearance. He did not look like a hard-boiled writer. He estimated Ray's age to be in the late forties (actually he was fifty-nine at the time) and found him to be "a most distinguished person, indeed, who could have been either an Oxford professor or a poet, certainly more British than American."

He also seemed "ill at ease," and several minutes later Ray explained that his wife was not too well, and he didn't want to leave her alone in the house for too long. He invited Cukor and Maugham to return to the house with him, and they followed him back to Camino de la Costa in the limousine.

As Ray opened the front door, he bowed slightly to his guests and said laconically, "The house that *The Big Sleep* and *The Lady in the Lake* movies built," and then led the way down the curving hallway to his study, calling out cheerily as he passed Cissy's closed bedroom door, "Cissy, I'm back!"

As the men settled down to talk in the study, Maugham complimented Ray on his comfortable house, with its view of the sea and feeling of tranquillity, and Ray replied rather gloomily that yes, La Jolla was a lovely spot and he should feel fortunate living in such a place, but that he was really a gypsy at heart, accustomed to a more nomadic lifestyle. "I seem to require an ever-changing scene and new people . . . I'm constantly seeking new places to stimulate me . . . anyway my wife and I lead a rather reclusive life here, as we have elsewhere, chiefly to escape boredom."

At that point Cissy tapped on the door, and Ray introduced her. Maugham later recorded his impression of Cissy:

She was a delicately attractive woman, who, even with her bleached blonde hair and rather frivolous gown, appeared to

be considerably older than Mr. Chandler. In her yellow, somewhat loose-fitting costume-party dress she could have fittingly
stepped right out of a ballroom scene in F. Scott Fitzgerald's
The Great Gatsby. In her younger years, when he wooed her out
of an unhappy marriage, she must have been breathtakingly
beautiful. Even now, with the effects of her progressive illness,
her brilliant, expressive eyes were quite remarkable. She carried herself with a sort of theatrical dignity.

Cissy was happy to meet George Cukor, whose films she
admired, and she insisted on giving him a tour of the house and
the developing landscape—they had only recently moved in, she
explained, so there was still much to be done. They left Maugham
and Chandler alone in the study to talk and, with Cukor gently
supporting Cissy by one elbow, walked out onto the patio. Once
they were gone Ray told Maugham that Cissy had once been a
model in New York City and that when she came to live in Los
Angeles she had aspirations for the stage and screen. He jokingly
added that he hoped she wouldn't badger Cukor for a minor part
in one of his movies.

Through the window of his study, he could see Cissy slowly leading Cukor along the inclined edge of the rock garden. At one point,
she suddenly stopped and pressed a hand tightly to her breast,
and Maugham noticed Chandler wince in reaction. "I must tell
you privately that my Cissy is very ill with fibrosis," Ray said.
Maugham had earlier heard Cissy's attacks of lung-racking coughing coming from the bedroom, and as a doctor, he sensed her condition might be serious, a perception which Ray soon confirmed.

In Wilmon Menard's account of the moment, Chandler's shoulders slumped, he sighed and explained that Cissy's heart was
being progressively burdened due to the fact she wasn't getting
enough oxygen to her lungs. He said, " 'Her struggles for breath
are tearing her to pieces, her suffering is killing me. I love Cissy
dearly. I don't really think I could carry on too well if she were
taken from me.' "

Taki wandered into the room at that point and Maugham made

the mistake of trying to pet the cat, which took a swipe at him. Like other visitors to the house who reported nasty encounters with Taki, Maugham felt the old cat—yowling and ill-tempered— had become as antisocial as the Chandlers themselves and did not take kindly to strangers. She finally jumped into Ray's lap and settled down now and then flicking a wicked yellow-eyed glance in Maugham's direction.

Chandler and Maugham settled into a discussion of the mystery novel, while Cissy and Cukor slowly continued their tour outside. In a touching twist, Maugham later reported that while he and Chandler had been inside discussing Cissy's illness, Cissy had been outside, confiding her own concerns about her husband to Cukor. She was worried, she said, about what Ray would do if anything happened to her.

Later they all gathered in the living room. The sun was beginning to set over the Pacific. Ray persuaded Cissy to play the piano for their guests, and she sat at the keyboard, in her frilly yellow party dress, and played a little Chopin. Then Chandler, in a high mood, suddenly became the entertainer and started regaling his guests with stories of Hollywood. As Maugham later wrote:

> I suppose it was his talent as a writer, his rather unique and acute power of observation, sharpened by the genre of the detective story, that had polished such a mimicry. He had an endless inventory of anecdotes of his studio encounters with producers, writers, actors, actresses . . . I was shortly doubled up with laughter . . . helplessly captivated by his rare altering of facial expressions, movements, and vocal changes. If Mr. Chandler had not decided to become a writer, he easily could have made a decent living as an entertainer.

When Cukor and Maugham finally departed, Ray and Cissy walked with them to the waiting limousine, Ray holding Taki in his arms. Taki even allowed Cukor to give him a small pat goodbye.

In 1949, three years after buying their house on Camino de la Costa, they put it on the market in an attempt to sell it. Ray refers to this fact in passing in letters from the time. The truth was he was deeply unhappy, badly depressed over the state of his life. He had become that thing he'd once described—a zombie with a heartbeat—a nondrinking alcoholic, stalled in a landscape where all roads seemed to lead nowhere. In fact he most likely was drinking again but keeping it hidden. Around this time he wrote a story called "A Couple of Writers." It is not a mystery story but Ray's most concentrated attempt to write literary fiction.

"A Couple of Writers" tells the story of Hank and Marion Bruton, two burnt-out writers who have been married for many years. They live with their cat in the country—"hell and gone from everywhere." Hank is a novelist, Marion a playwright ("I'm the Dorothy

Parker type—without the wit," she tells Hank when they first meet), and both are struggling with their work. The story opens early one morning: they've had an argument the night before, and as Hank fixes coffee and then takes his morning swim in the river, he tries to recall what happened. Hank is a secret drinker: he keeps a jug of whiskey in the garage, buried beneath some burlap sacks, though of course Marion knows all about his drinking. He was drunk the night before, and he vaguely remembers criticizing Marion's play, but he justifies this because he doesn't see any point in being dishonest. The play is lousy. When he returns from his swim, he finds Marion packing. She's leaving him. Was I that bad? he asks timidly, referring to his behavior the previous evening. No worse than usual, she tells him, and thanks him for not saying "again."

While Marion packs, Hank goes to the garage and hits the whiskey bottle, and when he returns he finds her in the living room, suitcase ready, trying to decide if there's anything else she should take. She eyes the manuscript of Hank's unfinished novel and says,

"Most especially I don't want that . . . you hang on to that. When you get the book finished they can put a picture of that elegant specimen of Neanderthal Chippendale on the dust cover, instead of your photograph. Because by that time you won't take a very good photograph. Unless they could photograph your breath. They'd have a real rich presence if they could do that."

"I could stop drinking whiskey," Hank said slowly through a puff of smoke.

She looked at him with a taut smile. "Oh sure. And then what? You're not a man. You're just a physically perfect specimen of an alcoholic eunuch. You're a zombie in top condition. You're a dead man with an absolutely normal blood pressure."

"You ought to write that down," Hank said.

"Don't worry. I will."

Hank tries to tell her what's wrong with her play, that actors don't talk to an audience anymore, and he repeats that her play "stinks." She says no one could write a play in such boring surroundings, stuck off in the woods as they are, "disturbed by nothing louder than the steady gurgle of a whiskey bottle." He reminds her that she had done a good bit of drinking herself in the past, including the time she passed out and he had to put her to bed. She tells him he used to have

"wit and imagination and a sort of buccaneering gaiety. But I didn't have to watch you drift into a stupor and lie awake in the night listening to you snoring the house down ... and the worst of it is ... you're not even irritable in the morning. You don't wake up with glassy eyes and a head like a barrel. You just smile and go right on from where you left off. Which marks you as the everlasting natural born sot, born to the fumes of alcohol, living in them as the salamander lives in fire."

Her voice then sharpens toward hysteria:

"Don't you know what happens to men like you? Some fine day they fly into little pieces as though a shell had hit them. For years and years there's practically no sign of deterioration at all. They get drunk every night and every morning they start to drink again. They feel wonderful. It doesn't do a thing to them. And then comes that day when everything happens all at once that ought with a normal person to happen slowly, over the months and years, reasonable steps in reasonable time. One minute you're looking at a healthy man and then next you're looking at a shriveled up horror that reeks of whiskey. Do you expect me to wait for that?"

What Marion says means nothing to Hank. He grinds his cigarette out and goes to get the car out of the garage, hitting the bottle again before he takes her to the train station. En route he notices her unattractive hat, the cigarette clamped hard between her lips "like a pair of pliers holding a bolt." At the station she tells him bitterly, "In a year I'll have forgotten you ever existed . . . it's a little sad. But how much of a woman's life does a man like you expect to drain away?"

"Take it easy," he said. "You'll put it all in a book someday."

"I don't even know where to go," she sobbed.

But go she does. And after he has watched the train pull away, Hank returns to the house, gets the whiskey jug, and takes it inside to his worktable. He reads the top page of his manuscript and feels disgusted: "Pastiche," he said drearily. "Everything I write sounds like something a real writer threw away." He begins pouring drinks and thinking about his life and the various woes of being a writer, and ironically, in the next passage, Chandler foresees what in the future will become common occurrences—writers' conferences, held in bucolic locations:

I'm not even in love with her, he thought. Nor she with me. There's no tragedy, no real sorrow, just a flat emptiness. The emptiness of a writer who can't think of anything to write, and that's a pretty awful painful emptiness, but for some reason it never even approaches tragedy. Jesus, we're the most useless people in the world. There must be a hell of a lot of us, too, all lonely, all empty, all poor, all gritted with small mean worries that have no dignity. All trying like men caught in a bog to get some firm ground under our feet and knowing all the time it doesn't make a damn bit of difference whether we do or not. We ought to have a convention somewhere, some place like Aspen, Colorado, some place where the air is very clear and sharp and stimulating and we can bounce our little derived intelligences against one another's hard little minds. Maybe for just a little while we'd feel as if we really had talent. All the world's would-be writers, the guys and girls that have education and will and desire and hope and nothing else. They know all there is to know about how it's done, except they can't do it. They've studied hard and imitated the hell out of everybody that ever rang the bell.

What a fine bunch of nothing we would be, he thought. We'd hone each other razor sharp. The air would crackle with the snapping of our dreams. But the trouble is, it couldn't last. When the convention is over and we'd have to go back home and sit in front of the damn piece of metal that puts words down on the paper. Yeah, we sit there waiting—like a guy waiting in the death house.

Dusk falls. And as Hank, now quite drunk, sits watching the changing light, he hears the sound of a truck in the driveway: it's old Simpson, the taciturn neighbor who runs an ersatz taxi business, and he's bringing Marion home. She's decided not to leave him after all. "I couldn't think of one goddamned place to go," she tells Hank. "It all seemed so pointless . . . so completely utterly without any meaning at all. No high spots, no low spots, just a lot of stale emotion."

He puts an arm around her and they begin joking how Hemingway would have known where to go. Hank thinks about how he wants to be kind, but he knows "that nothing they had said in the past or would say now or in the future really meant anything. It was all echoes." Marion wonders what is going to happen to them. She means, what is going to happen to his novel, her play?

Something turned over in his stomach because he knew the answer and Marion knew the answer and there was absolutely no sense in pretending it was an unsolved problem. The problem was never how to get something you knew you couldn't have. It was how to stop behaving as if it was just around the corner waiting for you to find it . . . there, actual, real. It wasn't there and it never would be. So why did you go on pretending it was?

Again he tells her her play stinks, and so does his novel. She slaps him and runs upstairs. Later, after a visit to the garage for another pull from the bottle, he goes to her in order to make up, but she can smell the liquor on his breath. He explains he was just drinking a toast—a "salute to a broken heart." She apologizes for slapping him, and he tells her it's all right, he might have done it himself if he thought about it. Then he simply turns on his heel and walks away. The story ends with him heading once more for the garage, "his shoes mushing on the gravel, on his endless pre-destined journey back to the jug under the pile of sacks."

Ray sent the story to his agent in New York, along with a note explaining that the story was based on some failed writers he'd known in the 1930s. "I've known a number of these not-quite writers. No doubt you have also." One of these writers, he said, had a wife who also wrote, and to hear them "discussing and ana-lyzing stories was a revelation in how much it is possible to know about technique without being able to use any." These not-quite writers, he said, are very tragic people and the more intelligent they are, the more tragic: "If you have enough talent, you can get by after a fashion without guts; and if you have enough guts, you can also get by, after a fashion without talent. But you certainly can't get by without either. These not-quite writers are very tragic people and the more intelligent they are, the more tragic, because the step they can't take seems to them such a very small step, which in fact it is. And every successful or fairly successful writer knows, or should know, by what a narrow margin he himself was able to take that step. But if you can't take it, you can't. That's all there is to it."

Ray wanted his agent to believe the story was not about himself, but the traces of his own life in the story are too clear to be missed. Like Hank, he, too, was unhappy with his writing at that moment in his life. (Of the recently published *The Little Sister*, Ray said that it was the only novel he had ever written that he actively disliked.) And like Hank and Marion, he and Cissy lived near a body of water, had a cat, and felt isolated. Hank, like Ray, loves to swim; he's been in the army and used to know a lot of men who are now dead. Hank also suffers from pains in his legs, frets over how photo-graphs might portray him, and most tellingly, never suffers from hangovers, a fact that was often mentioned in connection with Ray. But Hank most resembles Ray in his resignation; this was the moment at which Ray was realizing he would never become a "literary writer," never fulfill all those "foolish" plans, as Cissy had called them. Hank's toast, his "salute to a broken heart," was really Ray's way of acknowledging his own disappointments. *The problem was never how to get something you knew you couldn't have. It was how to stop behaving as if it was just around the corner waiting for you to find it . . . it wasn't there and it never would be. So why did you go on pretending it was?*

"A Couple of Writers" is a tired and jaded story, filled with bitterness and bickering, and much of the dialogue sounds very much like what Cissy might have said to Ray during a fight over his drinking. Cissy was not Marion—not in any literal sense—but the sentiment in the story, the world-weariness one senses in Marion, her frustration with Hank's self-destructive behavior, certainly feels real, as does the idea that Marion, like Cissy, can't really escape because there's nowhere to go. *How much of a woman's life does a man like you expect to drain away?* is a question Cissy might have asked of Ray.

The story is only marginally about a broken writer, or two burnt-out writers, as Ray claimed. It's really about a broken marriage, and a writer who is secretly drinking and causing his wife to despair, and it affords a window onto Cissy and Ray's life in 1950, when she was eighty, and he was sixty-two and very likely drinking again, perhaps stashing a bottle in the garage or some other part of the house. It's about conversations that have become "echoes" of earlier dialogues, and about emotions that have become "stale." It's about a woman preparing to leave her husband (in Cissy's case through death) and a worried and depressed man trying to drown those worries in alcohol. The dual pall of age and fear had descended at this point in Ray's life, and the real source of his anxiety came from the thought of losing Cissy. This was now not a distant possibility but the inevitable outcome of her serious illness, growing closer every day.

I made one last pass through the house, looking in every room, except of course Cissy's locked bedroom. I stood in the small bathroom off the extra bedroom and peered into the tile shower and wondered if this was the bathroom where Ray had attempted to commit suicide in the shower stall, firing those two bullets from a pistol just a few months after Cissy's death. Or was it the other bathroom, the one adjoining Cissy's bedroom?

I took one last look in his study. The girl was still engrossed in her TV and seemed barely aware of my presence in the room. For a long time I stood at the spot where Ray's desk had been and stared out the window at the view he would have seen: patio, birds, plants, rock wall, pepper trees, kitchen door.

I looked one last time in the kitchen. It appeared completely antiseptic, devoid of any human activity. Every surface was white and clean except for the area around a large hard frozen brick of hamburger sitting on the counter and slowly thawing. A little pool of blood-tinged water had oozed out onto the formica and lay puddled around the meat.

I went into the living room and stood before the big window for a while, looking at the sea. How restless it was. Like Cissy and Ray, constantly moving. The house had sheltered them for a while. The house had trapped him. It was a haunted space, filled with a sense of loneliness and suffering. The house came along too late for Cissy. It lasted too long for Ray. Yet it held them together for eight years, until only one of them was left.

Over the next few months I returned to the house again and again. As it began to change, I shot more photographs of it, as if trying to hold on to the last vestiges of the old rooms and the lives that had been lived in them. By then the renters had moved out. The house was empty, except for the piles of trash left behind. I was able to go into Cissy's room, the room that had been locked before. There wasn't much to see. It had a dark, cool feeling and a shut-up smell, like an invalid's room. There was only one window, which faced the street and was covered with a heavy blind. Bushes grew up against the window and blocked out most of the light. I could see where the bed would have gone, how she would have faced the doorway. I imagined her in bed, consumed by a racking cough, unable to catch her breath, sedated by the drugs that helped ease the pain. I saw her consumed by boredom. I saw her reading books. One Christmas he gave her a set of Henry James as a gift. They both loved James—"my beloved James," as Ray called him. Another time he wrote to a bookstore: "My wife wants Peter Cheyney's 'Dark Duet,'" and specified that the condition of the book was to be "fine only."

Dark Duet. It could have been the title for their own final years together.

Did he love Cissy, did he hate Cissy, or was he just wed to her, as Hank was to Marion, forever? Cissy was the only thing standing between him and alcoholic dementia—his debt to her was great. But imagine owing your life to a woman who kept you sane but also kept you from indulging the thing you loved most: booze. Would you love her? Would you hate her? Or would you love-hate her? Like the albatross mother whom you loved, whom you also had to nurse until she died a slow death. Two women, both invalids at the end of their lives, who look to no one but you to care for them and whom you could never leave even if you wanted to. Do you love them? Do you hate them? Do you love-hate them? Or do you just make a fantasy world and a man named Marlowe and live with him there for much of the time, looking for that one male friend you never had? It's a place to go, anyway. A place to hide out and be your best self, away from all the needy good women. There you can meet real female foes, and sex sirens, blond bombshells, ladies who can't get enough, and you can be the one to tell them to go get lost. You can have the bon mot for every occasion. You can be the ladykiller, the guy all the girls come on to. You can play them along with a little repartee and then you can set them straight and let them know you don't come cheaply, you might not come at all, because you have your morals, you have your code.

This is your fantasy world you can enter at will, by picking up your pen, and when you leave it you can still be Gallibeoth the Chivalrous, because that is the name she christened you with. You are a knight. Funny how the identity she assigned you, you gave over to Marlowe. So who really made Marlowe?—you or her? Or were you, as Natasha Spender suggested, so codependent on each other and your respective fantasies that each was the other's "enabler"?

The last time I visited the house, holes had begun appearing in the floor here and there: Kevin cutting through the wood to check the state of the foundation. A huge crater had appeared in the kitchen floor where a pipe burst and water began seeping out. It was as if the heart of the domicile had begun caving in, falling away, breaches opening underfoot, the skeleton exposed. Although a few local people petitioned the La Jolla Historical Society in an

effort to save Chandler's house, its fate had already been decided. But Kevin offered a few concessions: he wanted to do what he could, he said, to honor Chandler's memory. He agreed to save as much of his study as possible—the built-in drawers and bookcases, the shelving and original windows. Perhaps he could even preserve the front door to the house. But shelving and a door do not a house make, although the idea of saving the door amused me. Ray once said that the only part of a house in California you couldn't put your foot through was the front door. I found it ironic that it might end up being the most enduring part of his own house. It was clear to me, however, on that last visit I made to Camino de la Costa Plenty, that all trace, all feeling of Cissy and Ray, was about to be permanently effaced from that house, and why not, given his own lack of sentimentality about the place?

I lingered a while longer in the house during that last visit. I sat in the corners of rooms amid debris and gaping holes. I reconstructed movements. Remembered stories. Envisioned scenes. I held on, in other words, not only to what I knew, to all the stories I had read that had come out of this place and all the images those stories conjured up but also to what I had imagined, all the moments that had arisen out of the facts of his life and been enlarged by my own imagination. Ray wouldn't have much cared what happened to this house. He couldn't leave it fast enough after Cissy died. He sprang from it like an animal released from a trap.

He might, however, have been amused by one final detail. The house had been completely stripped of all belongings, any personal touches, except for one thing: the renters had left behind one of their family photographs on the dining room wall, a picture of a couple, a beautiful blond woman and a handsome dark man, who stared out from the wreckage of the room. Who knew why they'd had chosen to leave this photograph behind—perhaps it was a mistake, or maybe an intentional castoff—but in any case there they were, the blond woman, the handsome man, nailed to the wall like the last remaining witnesses.

Ten

During all the time they were married, throughout their peripatetic years, the Chandlers never left California. Though they had moved almost constantly, they never managed even to cross the state line, except for day trips to Tijuana. But in the early 1950s, after twenty-eight years of marriage and in spite of the fact Cissy was ill and Ray suffering from a variety of ailments, they decided to make their long-awaited trip to England.

They kept putting off the departure date, however, and in the meantime they took shorter trips. They drove out to Palm Springs in the Oldsmobile and stayed in their favorite motel, Harlowe Haven. The dry desert climate helped to ease Ray's recurring bronchitis and Cissy's chronic cough. Ray could swim in the pool while Cissy sat in the shade and read. They had always liked the desert: life was easy there, or as easy as it ever got for them. They also went up to San Francisco for a few days. They stayed in the Clift Hotel. Like Nabokov, Ray always liked hotel living; one gets the feeling that if he could have lived in hotels all the time he would have been a happy man. For thirty-two years, even before their marriage, they'd been taking vacations in San Francisco. Ray enjoyed the anarchic spirit of that city, what he called its "go to hell attitude." They had all the time in the world now to enjoy their vacations, the trips out to the desert, the spectacular drives up the coast.

They also continued to visit Erle Stanley Gardner at his ranch in Temecula, occasionally spending the night so Cissy could gaze through Gardner's telescope. That was a vacation they could manage, an overnight at the ranch, and the drive back home the next day in the Olds.

Of all the trips they made at this time, however, none stands out as being as odd and out of character as their visit to a posh Santa Barbara dude ranch in September 1951. One wonders what they were thinking, booking that kind of a vacation. Neither was capable of being active any longer—nor did they have any interest in horses, except maybe Whirlaway, Ray's little amuel. A week at a dude ranch was the sort of vacation Ray had once accused rich Hollywood people of taking. But maybe he liked the notion of mingling with that crowd again. Or perhaps they just liked the idea that amid the encroaching boredom they might have a stimulating new experience among the rich horsy set.

The dude ranch was called Alisal, which as Ray explained in a letter to Hamish Hamilton, means a grove of sycamores in Spanish. The setting was lovely, but the trip was less than a success. His account of their stay also reflected his abiding interest in fashion:

We found the place both very amusing and intensely boring, expensive, badly run but nicely laid out with the usual swimming pool, tennis courts, etc. The kind of place where the people in the office wear riding boots, where the lady guests appear for breakfast in levis riveted with copper, for lunch in jodhpurs with gaudy shirts and scarfs and in the evening either in cocktail gowns or in more jodhpurs and more gaudy shirts and scarfs. The ideal scarf seems to be very narrow, not much wider than a boot lace, and run through a ring in front and then hangs down one side of the shirt. I didn't ask why; I didn't get to know anybody well enough. The men also wear gaudy shirts, which they change constantly for other patterns, all except the real horsemen who wear rather heavy wool or nylon and wool shirts with long sleeves, yoked in the back, the kind of thing that can only be bought in a horsy town. I imagine the place is lots of fun for the right sort of people, the kind who go riding in the morning, swimming or tennising in the afternoon, then have two or three drinks at the bar, and by the time they arrive for dinner are able to be quite enthusiastic over the rather inferior and much too greasy cooking. For us who were rather tired and out of sorts and consequently much too finicky, the place was a trial. But it was fun to see a whole army of quail strolling unconcernedly past the bungalows in the evening and to see birds which look like jackdaws, which we never see anywhere else . . . while I was there, I read three of the Hornblower novels by C. S. Forester . . . appallingly dull to my mind.

The letter is revealing of their state of mind—tired, out of sorts, much too finicky, mired in boring books. They must have made an odd couple in such a setting, two aged introverts, dressed in their old-fashioned clothes, wanting nothing more than to be left to themselves, and yet there's a feeling in his letter that Ray would actually have liked to be the sort of person he described for whom dude ranch life was perfect. Such pleasures—riding, tennis, cocktails, socializing—could only be taken vicariously now. Their main "sport" was people watching. Just noting what everyone showed up in for meals was enough to keep them amused.

By then Ray had started another novel: he'd written about fifty thousand words of what would become *The Long Goodbye*. He hoped to finish the book by the next year, but he was having difficulty with the writing, and just a month after returning from the dude ranch he wrote to Hamish Hamilton, complaining about his lack of progress on the book and detailing the difficulties of their life:

The old zest is not there. I am worn down by worry over my wife . . . we have a big house, rather hard to take care of, and the help situation is damn near hopeless. For months after we lost our last cook, Cissy wore herself out trying to get someone, to endure what we got, to give up and start again. We cannot live here without help. Cissy can do very very little, she has lost a lot of ground in the last two years. She is a superb cook herself and we are both pretty much overfastidious, but we can't help it. I have thought that the sensible thing might be to get a small house and do for ourselves, but I am afraid she is no longer capable even of that. When I get into work I am already tired and dispirited. I wake in the night with dreadful thoughts. Cissy has a constant cough which can only be kept down by drugs and the drugs destroy her vitality . . . I am afraid it is chronic and may get worse instead of better. She has no strength and being of a buoyant disposition and a hard fighter, she fights herself to the point of exhaustion. I dread, and I am sure she does, although we try not to talk about it, a slow decline into invalidism. And what happens then I frankly do not know. There are people who enjoy being invalids, being unable to do anything, but not she. She hates hospitals, she hates nurses, and she does not greatly love doctors. In bad moods, which are not too infrequent, I feel the icy touch of despair. It is no mood in which to produce writing with any lift and vitality . . . we still hope for "Europe in the Spring," but is it more than hope now?

In 1950, he had hired a full-time secretary named Juanita Messick and turned the second bedroom into an office for her. As the domestic situation deteriorated he came to rely heavily on Mrs. Messick for all kinds of assistance. She fit well into the household, and Ray seems to have not only liked but trusted her, occasionally even confiding his troubles to her. With Cissy almost continuously ill, Ray found himself in need of all the help he could get: because his shy personality often prompted him to behave in a manner viewed as rude or sarcastic, the help often chose to leave rather than put up with him. He'd spent so much time alone that he found it difficult to treat cooks or housekeepers in any sort of natural way. His criticism could be unnecessarily caustic: he would wait, for instance, until the gardener had planted shade plants in full sun to berate him for his foolishness rather than diplomatically mentioning the error as he saw it taking place. "He is nervous and jittery," one visitor to the house noted, "and walks with a loping, disjointed walk. He is ill at ease talking to strangers and rarely looks at the person he is addressing." During the eight years he and Cissy lived in La Jolla he claimed they had gone through more than fifty cooks and housekeepers, until finally they simply gave up and, as Cissy weakened, Ray took over most of the domestic chores himself.

In a memo to Mrs. Messick he explained the new regimen and also mentioned his newfound interest in cooking:

> It looks to me as if until my wife gets better, I'm going to have to do most of the cooking. I'm a pretty good short order cook. I can cook steaks, chops and vegetables far better than the restaurants can . . . and I rather like the idea of learning to be a little more of an accomplished cook, though I prefer to stop short of the elaborate stage. But it's a grind and there's no doubt about that.

He rose every morning at eight. It took him two hours, he said, to make two breakfasts—Cissy's was often delivered to her in bed on a tray—and then tidy up. From ten a.m. to one p.m. he tried to write, working on *The Long Goodbye* in his study. Then he went to town to market and run errands. By three thirty or four p.m. he had to be back for "the damned tea," as he put it, and by five he was in the kitchen, doing the prep work for dinner. After dinner and the cleanup he felt exhausted, and he lamented not having someone to at least come by in the morning to make breakfast and tidy up from the night before. In his memo to Mrs. Messick, he repeated what he'd told Hamish Hamilton about Cissy's condition:

> I've got to face the fact that Cissy hasn't got any stamina . . . she's never going to get back to where she once was. And I

dare say she knows it, although we don't talk about it . . . so I guess it's up to this tired character as long as he holds out. Of course things are not so hard when you get into a routine. You learn not to waste motion and not to do unnecessary things and not to walk your legs off.

He told Mrs. Messick that for the time at least they were going to suspend the afternoon tea, not only because it often now interfered with Cissy's naps but because it was just too much effort to keep it going.

In May 1952, Ray completed a first draft of *The Long Goodbye*, which had the working title "Summer in Idle Valley." Just six months earlier he'd written to his agent in New York, Carl Brandt, to say he was having a tough time with the book. He'd finished a draft, he said, but he was going to have to do it over again because "I just didn't know where I was going and when I got there I saw that I had come to the wrong place. That's the hell of being the kind of writer who cannot plan anything, but has to make it up as he goes along and then try to make sense out of it." Six months later he had managed to complete the revision, and he seemed to feel quite confident of what he'd accomplished.

When he sent the manuscript to his agents in New York, the reaction was mixed. Both Carl Brandt and Bernice Baumgarten felt the book had problems, foremost of which was their feeling that Marlowe had become "Christ-like" and a sentimentalist. Their letter to Ray upset him deeply, and he fired off a telegram asking that they return the manuscript to him immediately. Later he followed up with a chilly letter to them:

It may be that I am no good anymore. God knows I've had enough worry to drive me off the beam. Being old-fashioned enough to be deeply in love with my wife after twenty-eight years of marriage I feel the possibility that I have let emotion enter my life in a manner not suitable to the marts of commerce, as the cliché has it. Of course there is also the possibility—faint as it is, I admit—that you could be a little wrong. Curiously enough I seem to have far fewer doubts about this story than I had about *The Little Sister*.

Baumgarten realized that she had offended him with her hastily composed letter and wrote to apologize, and Ray, without entirely absolving her, further explained the difficulties he was having revising the book.

My kind of writing demands a certain amount of dash and high spirits—the word is gusto, a quality lacking in modern writing—and you could not know the bitter struggle I have had the past year even to achieve enough cheerfulness to live on, much less put into a book. So let's face it: I didn't get it into the book. I didn't have it to give.

It seems extraordinary, given his weariness and her fragile health, that just a few months later, in early September of 1952, Ray and Cissy found the energy to make the trip to England.

Flying was out of the question—Cissy would not even consider taking an airplane, nor would she let Ray fly—and so instead they booked passage on the *Guyana*, a Swedish merchant ship leaving from Los Angeles and bound for Southampton via the Panama Canal. Neither one of them knew anything about traveling, and an immense amount of work went into the planning, some of it entirely unnecessary. Fearing, for instance, that there might still be wartime shortages in England, even seven years after the war's end, Ray, who was openly drinking again, had a case of Scotch and gin shipped to the Connaught Hotel, where they had booked a room. As he would discover, there was no scarcity of liquor at the Connaught, and the hotel staff must have found it amusing to see twenty-four bottles of hard liquor arrive for their guests' three-week stay.

For many years Ray had longed to return to England—certainly since 1939, when he laid out his plans for the future that Cissy had typed in his notebook. He had not been back in thirty-four years, not since just after the war. Now he was returning not as a young man but as a famous older novelist whose work had been much admired in England. He had no idea, really, the enthusiasm with which his visit would be greeted.

He could not have made the trip without Cissy, and no doubt she knew this and agreed to go with him—in spite of her frail condition—as a kind of gift to him, because in fact she knew something that he still very likely did not, and that was exactly how old she really was. She was now eighty-two. He may have at this time thought her to be, at most, in her mid-seventies. Only she (and her sister Lavinia) knew the truth. And certainly she understood that if they did not go then, regardless of her poor health, there would be no second chance for them.

On August 20, 1954, they boarded the *Guyana* for the three-week voyage. From the very beginning there were difficulties. They had packed the wrong clothes, bringing only tweeds and woolen coats and sweaters for what they imagined might be a cool September in London. Ray had been overly worried about Cissy's catching cold and had not taken into consideration it would be terribly hot on the passage through the Panama Canal and the stops at ports in the Caribbean islands. On the ship, they suffered in their heavy clothes, and with nothing lighter to wear, they were confined to their cabin, where there was at least air-conditioning. Ray tried not to drink on the voyage, Cissy attempted to appear well, and both efforts took their toll. By the time they arrived in Southampton, after three weeks on the ship, they were exhausted from the journey. Roger Machell, an editor who worked for Hamish Hamilton, met them at the boat and delivered them to the Connaught, but by then Cissy was so weakened that she couldn't leave her bed for ten days. They intended to stay several weeks in England, if all went well, but it was a shaky start to their sojourn, with Cissy unable to leave the room. Ray had hoped that the trip might somehow infuse her with new energy, but once he saw that the opposite was happening, his own nerves began to fray, and he developed a condition called angioneurotic edema, which caused his face and hands to swell.

In London, everyone wanted to meet him, even the other guests at the hotel. His publisher had planned a welcome party shortly after their arrival, but Ray begged off, saying he didn't want to leave Cissy alone in the hotel. He was also embarrassed by his swollen condition. The whole situation became increasingly complex. He had imagined showing Cissy the London of his youth, touring the countryside in a Rolls-Royce, enjoying his status as a celebrated author ("In England I am an author. In the U.S.A. just a mystery writer. Can't tell you why.") Instead, he grew more worried over Cissy's health. He would leave her for only an hour or two at a time, to visit a nearby bookstore or give an interview with one of the many reporters who wished to speak with him. One article, published in *The Sunday Times* under the headline "The Unconventional Mr. Chandler Comes to Town," reported, "His smile is younger than his face, and only the young at heart could wear such a necktie." To cope with the stress, Ray began drinking more heavily, which only exacerbated his physical problems.

When Cissy was finally well enough to leave the hotel, she fell getting into a taxi and bruised her leg. The injury caused her a great deal of pain and made it even more difficult to get around. But she wasn't a whiner. She did her best not to complain and continued to venture out with Ray on modest excursions. Hamilton invited them to another dinner party he'd organized in honor of Ray, but over the phone he made a casual reference to the fact Ray might want to wear a dinner jacket without realizing how this would upset him, because Ray hadn't brought a dinner jacket. Hamilton, understanding his mistake, quickly agreed that the evening should be informal. Still, both Cissy and Ray began worrying about what to wear. Being totally inexperienced travelers, they realized they had brought the wrong clothes to London. Cissy in particular felt she didn't have the right dress—nothing suitably dressy for the kind of dinners they were being asked to—and on the day of Hamilton's party they spent hours, in spite of her injured leg and enfeebled condition, wandering through shops on Bond Street, trying to find just the right frock. In the end, nothing seemed right, and an hour before the dinner was to begin, Ray called Hamilton to say they wouldn't be able to make it. In an attempt to save the evening, Hamilton suggested Ray might come alone, but this only upset Ray further. His nerves were already shot. The day had depleted them both. And he felt it was outrageous that Hamilton could even suggest he leave his wife for the evening. In the end, the dinner took place without them.

It wasn't the only time during their London stay that Ray became upset when he felt that not enough attention was being paid to Cissy. It annoyed him that people did not show the same interest in her that they did in him. They both felt a little out of place at the upscale Connaught with its sophisticated clientele. The bar was too cold for them, the prices far too high. They found the food inferior, as they did everywhere. They worried constantly over their health, and their clothes; in spite of the fact they had brought ten suitcases with them, they seemed not to have anything to wear. These wardrobe concerns became very troubling and drained their energy, mostly because they had so little to begin with. Ray needed a pair of warmer socks, for instance, and spent the better part of one whole day looking for just the right pair without ever finding them. For so many years they had led very private, reclusive lives, and they were simply overwhelmed by the unpredictable demands of even a modest social life, let alone being thrust into the public eye and feted as celebrities in a large, bustling city.

The invitations continued to arrive. J. B. Priestley organized a lunch at his flat to celebrate the Chandlers' visit. He later recalled that he had gotten entirely the wrong impression of Cissy during the lunch, simply because he had not known how old she really was. "She seemed to be a rather affected woman in her early sixties, quite pleasant and good conversation and so on, whereas of course as I learned afterwards, long afterwards, she was in point of fact at that time about eighty, and so a very gallant eighty indeed."

One senses what a game woman Cissy was, how gallantly, as Priestley put it, she always attempted to rise to the occasion. One of the most moving descriptions of her during the London visit comes from Dilys Powell, the film critic for *The Sunday Times*, who with her husband, *Times* literary editor Leonard Russell, were great fans of Ray's writing. They knew almost nothing of Cissy, except the little they had heard about her through Hamish Hamilton. Having emerged from the austerities of the war years, Powell and her husband had, by 1952, begun entertaining again, and they were anxious to meet Chandler and introduce him to their writer friends, and so an invitation was sent to his hotel, a dinner was organized, and again Ray's response included inquiries about the appropriate dress—would it be black tie or white? He was relieved to learn the dinner would be informal, and so he accepted.

Dilys Powell later recalled that evening in her essay "Ray and Cissy":

What we expected of the Chandlers I don't know, but I can still see their arrival at our house: Raymond stocky, middle-aged in glasses—I have the impression of the colour brown; just as with Cissy I associate a pale, almost extinct canary colour.

At first Raymond seemed a little on the defensive, Powell said, as if slightly suspicious of the rather high-hatted company in which he found himself (other guests included Val Gielgud, the cartoonist Nick Bentley, and Campbell Dixon, a film critic), but Powell felt it was more likely he was defensive on behalf of Cissy, who was sitting next to Leonard at the other end of the table. Like Priestley, Dilys Powell was also initially unaware of Cissy's advanced age.

I have been quoted as saying that she was older than her husband. So she was, but I was speaking out of hindsight. I didn't that evening notice her age, and it was only when our guests had left and Leonard commented that I thought about it. At dinner I now and then looked to see how she was getting on. Conversation flowed round her: about California, the cops, Raymond's work. She appeared to be taking a modest part in it; and leaning amiably towards Leonard, she smiled and listened.

At the end of the dinner, feeling it was time to leave the men to their drinks, Powell tried to catch Cissy's eye in order to signal the women would be gathering in the next room, and Ray, amused by this arcane ritual, jumped up and cried, "Cissy! Cissy, look at this! An old English custom," and began clapping, as if delighted.

A few days later, Powell and her husband were invited to have drinks with the Chandlers in the bar of the Connaught—"just a couple of pink gins," as Ray put it.

Neither Raymond nor Cissy looked entirely at ease in the hotel, chic haunt of eminent transatlantic visitors. But we were friends. He didn't need, now, to defend Cissy, only to watch over her. Looking at her then, I could see the creases in the pale face. But she still managed to be a pretty woman. The features small, neat, regular, the faded hair fluffy, dressed, as it must have been dressed when he first knew her, in the fashion of the 1920s—a vestigial feminine charm still lingered. The manner was gentle, sweet; she still smiled, still leaned to listen, watchfully took her drink. What did she talk about? Nothing: one heard only the exchanges of polite society. But I thought I detected in her something propitiatory—propitiatory for her age, her physical frailty, the gradual extinction of her energy.

I was struck by the word *propitiatory:* to win or regain the favor of by doing something that pleases. Coming from the Latin, propitious, favorable—or gracious. Dilys Powell's description of Cissy, with its multitude of details and intelligent insight, was a revelation to me, and I felt she had understood something very important about Cissy and disclosed the key, perhaps, to her personality—i.e., the propitiatory quality Powell had sensed in her, the singular attribute Cissy carried with her throughout her life—this desire to please others, to do the favorable thing, especially for her husband, and this was not a cloying desire but a gracious and understated one. It was part of what endeared her to Ray and what kept him devoted to her. She was not a shrew, a taker, a whiner, a woman who nagged or complained or went on about what she wanted, though I knew that she did have wit and it could bite, and that she could (and did) speak her mind and wasn't at all afraid of a fight when a fight was needed, and as Ray put it, "would wade right in." But she also attempted to make it easy for those around her. As Dilys Powell pointed out, such a quality can seem all the more affecting coming from a woman of advanced age and diminishing energy. But perhaps this is the very definition of graciousness: to be able to think of others, even as your own needs increase.

They managed to stay the entire three weeks in England and even enjoy parts of their stay. Just bad luck, Ray would say later, that Cissy hurt herself. They had had some of their best times with the editor Roger Machell, who put them at ease with his innately charming manner and sense of humor: he had taken them on drives and given them tours of the city, including the bombed-out East End, fixed great pitchers of martinis for them, told them funny stories, and then finally seen them off in Southampton on October 20, as they boarded the *Mauretania* for the return voyage to New York, and in their minds he would always be one of the great highlights of their London visit. They had also taken a great liking to Leonard Russell and Dilys Powell, so much so that later Ray, in a letter, suggested that Cissy had cared a bit too much, perhaps, for Leonard, while he had been just a little too effusive in his response to Dilys, but more than causing any serious disagreement between them, their responses seem to have amused them.

They were not amused by the voyage home on the *Mauretania*, however—"It wasn't a ship at all," Ray later complained, "it was just a damned floating hotel." The entire voyage was difficult for them, and by the time they reached New York, they felt exhausted. You can see the tiredness written on their faces in the photograph of the two of them taken by customs officials on their arrival in New York.

This is the only photograph I know of showing the two of them together—the one I found in the file at the Bodleian Library that had so affected me that I left the reading room for a while and took a short walk in order to calm myself before coming back to really look at it. It shows them at the end of their lives—or at the end of hers, anyway. You can still see her beauty in this picture. How attractive she still is.

Yes, one senses their exhaustion and the difficulty of the journey they have just made—you see this especially on Ray's face (but by then he had begun scowling for the camera, so this for him was not an unusual look). You can also see their fragility and dependence on one another. But one senses also her solidity, her sense of humor, her stylishness, her inner and outer *beauty*, really. And you can also see something else in the way she looks at the camera, as if to please it. The propitiatory quality is clearly there. Looking at this photograph at the Bodleian, my first thought had been what an attractive woman she was, in every sense of the word. I found an openness in her look and good humor, a sweetness I had always imagined might be there—evidence of that "buoyant personality" Ray had spoken of. The picture was powerful, a moving portrait of the two of them, and I felt it spoke volumes about their relationship. Here was the photograph I had longed to find, showing Cissy at the age of eighty-two.

They stayed for several days in New York, in an attempt to recover from the ocean voyage before facing the transcontinental train trip back to California. They were in no mood to enjoy the city, however. They disliked their hotel, and New York itself upset them. It seemed "a dirty, lawless, rude, hard-boiled place," Ray said, one which "made even Los Angeles seem fairly civilized." It had none of London's civility, and all of America's hustler mentality. "I have never been in any place that gave me such an acute feeling that no one had the time or inclination for even a modicum of good manners unless there was a quick buck in it for him."

The train trip to California was, as it turned out, another arduous leg of their journey that took over three days. Cissy's injured ankle got worse on the train. Ray blamed the doorman at the Connaught for the accident, faulting him for not taking the trouble to get the taxi close enough to the curb. The strap on Cissy's delicate shoe had slipped as she attempted to step into the cab. The bruise was more serious than they had first thought. Her ankle should have been bandaged immediately, but not until they were on the ship was it attended to. A large vein had been ruptured, and slowly the subcutaneous hemorrhaging became more evident. On the train trip across country, she developed an infection in the wound, which Ray felt came from the harsh towels that had been provided and which had not been thoroughly rinsed of detergent.

By the time they reached La Jolla, they had been away from home for almost two months. Cissy's sister, Vinnie, had been staying in the house and was anxious to get back to her own life, but Ray persuaded her to stay on and help them out for a while, since they were both badly drained by the trip.

Ray wrote to Hamilton, thanking him for all he had done to try to make their stay in London a pleasant one. Hamilton had indicated he felt Ray snubbed him, refusing to come to the dinner, failing to appear for interviews, and generally using Cissy as an excuse for not keeping appointments, and Ray wanted to assure him he did appreciate his efforts and was sorry for any inconvenience: it was true certain things about their stay had been annoying, he said, but in retrospect even these things didn't seem so bad. He concluded his letter to Hamilton by telling him he thought the trip had done Cissy a lot of good. "She had bad luck, but psychologically she was buoyed up no end."

Whatever benefit Cissy might have gained from the trip psychologically, physically it had been devastating. A few weeks after their return she entered the hospital. Ray expressed his worry in a letter to Leonard Russell, written in December 1952. A sad and world-weary tone invades his words:

> My wife has been very ill. She is back from the hospital but still very frail and still in bed. Mostly on that account we have decided to forget all about Christmas this year, cards included. So may I now wish you and Dilys Powell whatever in this sad world remains of peace and happiness, such as red sunsets, the smell of roses after a summer rain, soft carpets in quiet rooms, firelight, and old friends.

Both in London and on the voyage home Cissy and Ray had begun drinking together again in a way they had not for years. In the bar of the *Mauretania* they had discovered the gimlet, a drink they liked very much, and he later claimed that through this discovery he had finally learned how to become a controlled drinker (not true, unfortunately). Once back in La Jolla, he and Cissy continued the ritual of having a gimlet every night. Just one. And always together. Though after she went to bed at her usual early hour, who knows how many more he felt free to consume?

Ray had put aside the manuscript of *The Long Goodbye* in July 1952 in order to focus all his energy on arranging the trip to London, but now, at the beginning of 1953, he went back to work on revising the book.

It has been said that the main theme of *The Long Goodbye* is friendship and the need for love. Marlowe is certainly a more sentimental character in this novel, especially in his feelings for Terry Lennox, the war veteran he discovers stone drunk in a Rolls-Royce Silver Wraith at the book's opening, and whom he rescues, then befriends, and eventually helps to escape to Mexico after Lennox's wife is discovered murdered. This male friendship is a driving force in the plot, as is Marlowe's involvement with Roger Wade, the alcoholic writer. It is also the novel in which Marlowe has his most erotically charged encounters with women—he becomes "as erotic as a stallion" over Roger Wade's wife, a cool, beautiful blonde ("the blond icicle," as someone says of her) who offers herself naked to Marlowe one night while her husband is passed out in the next room. He also spends the night with Linda Loring (his first sleepover with a woman in six books), daughter of an extremely wealthy man, who is married to a prudish doctor she is in the midst of divorcing. Linda will reappear at the end of Ray's final novel, *Playback*, where she proposes marriage to him, and in the few pages of his unfinished novel, *Poodle Springs*, they appear as a married couple. Both in the mind of the author and in his fiction, she will be Marlowe's unresolved story, the one Ray was trying to work out at the time of his death.

In *The Long Goodbye*, however, Linda Loring is simply the dark-haired, beautiful woman with whom Marlowe bonds one night over drinks in Victor's bar—the same bar where he used to meet Terry Lennox. This is after Terry has disappeared and both Linda and Marlowe are each interested in his whereabouts. Very tellingly, when Marlowe first sees Linda, she is sitting at the bar alone, drinking a gimlet—the same drink that he and Terry used to share before Terry disappeared. He sits down at the bar and studies her: "She had that fine-drawn intense look that is sometimes neurotic, sometimes sex-hungry, and sometimes just the result of drastic dieting." When he orders a gimlet himself, Linda turns and, by way of an icebreaker, says to him, "So few people drink them around here." The barkeep mentions how he had bought a bottle of Rose's lime juice just so he could make a proper gimlet for Marlowe and his friend Terry, but then they stopped coming around after Terry disappeared, and the bottle of Rose's had sat unopened until Linda appeared that evening and requested a gimlet. It's a beautifully modulated scene, and one loaded with significance: when Marlowe shares a gimlet with Linda, he is transferring some of the male camaraderie he's shared with Terry to a woman. "The woman in black watched me," he says. "Then she lifted her own glass towards me. We both drank. Then I knew hers was the same drink."

The gimlet takes on an uncommon importance—like a knight's drink of friendship, cementing allegiance, creating a deep bond between first Marlowe and Terry, and then between Marlowe and Linda, who like so many of Chandler's women possesses male attributes. Marlowe finds her attractive, but when he tells the barkeep to bring their next round of gimlets to a private booth, it doesn't seem to matter much to him if she joins him or rejects him: "She might or might not blow me down. I didn't particularly care. Once in a while in this much too sex-conscious country a man and a woman can meet and talk without dragging bedrooms into it. This could be it, or she could just think I was on the make. If so, the hell with her." She chooses to join him. But by then Marlowe has already made his own ambivalence clear.

Terry and Linda are the two people in the story Marlowe cares most about, although one could argue he cares much more about Terry and is therefore more disappointed in the end by Terry's eventual betrayal. The gimlet signifies the holy grail of friendship—Gallibeotì's very own drink, which he had recently discovered on the *Mauretania* and was imbibing every night in the house on Camino de la Costa as he was revising the book, and through this grail he connects the male and female halves of his psyche and, quite possibly, his erotic desires.

For much of 1953, Ray worked on revising *The Long Goodbye* as Cissy lay in her room, slowly, ineluctably, and very painfully growing weaker by the day. Later he would say that she died not by inches, but half inches.

By August he had decided he could no longer afford a secretary and wrote to Juanita Messick, thanking her for her past help and informing her that sadly they were going to have to part company. He bemoaned the fact that certain things, under the circumstances, would have to be neglected, but what did that matter now anyway?

I am a worn, tired man. I have lost my appetite and I have lost so much weight that I've had to punch two fresh holes in my belt. My clothes don't fit me any more. I'm depressed often and sleep badly. I have a sick wife who is not getting any better. I hope she will, and above all I hope that by the spring of this next year she will be well enough to go away somewhere for a long time. I'd like to go to Europe for a year. The cost of living in this country is so outrageous that when you begin to get old and have a little money saved up, it seems ridiculous not to go somewhere where life is a little cheaper. We have no binding ties. I have found out that in my need nobody helps me. I'm not complaining. Nobody has that obligation.

Mrs. Messick must have understood his desperation: only a very desperate man, out of touch with reality, would contemplate moving to a foreign country with a dying wife and somehow imagine they could start over. But that's what Ray had always done when he faced any difficulties: his solution to any problem was to just pack up and move. *Go geographic.* The illusion he could outrun his problems, solve everything by just getting away, and start over somewhere new was a powerful one for Ray.

Mrs. Messick must have chosen to stay on and help Ray under a new more flexible arrangement, because in his next note to her, written just a few days later, he lays out a different schedule for her, more open-ended: in this note Ray takes up the subject of Cissy's delicate feelings about her limitations and suggests how they might be dealt with:

There is another thing you are probably aware of, although I am a little reluctant to mention it, and that is that my wife is not able to do what she did only a few years ago. When we came down here in 1946, sometimes she did all the housework, or almost all of it . . . she cooked the meals; she did the marketing; she dealt with painters and people of that sort; and she liked doing it. And I know that secretly she feels a bit depressed that she can't do it now, and I wouldn't even talk to her about it. Won't mention it to her. But the fact is, she can't. For instance, she would say to me, "Will you forget about the gardener. I'll get a gardener and handle him and attend to him. Just put it out of your mind." Then she'd get busy on the telephone and wear herself out talking to various people and finally get a gardener and he'd come and she'd follow around with him and spend a lot of time with him. And I could see it was tiring herself too much. And then I'd gradually edge in and take over, and I wouldn't like it. I mean I wouldn't like to have to do it. I'm a man who takes very little lightly.

He went on to suggest that Mrs. Messick tread very lightly with Cissy's feelings. He understood being a secretary "in a home" was often an awkward position because it wasn't only the man's home but the wife's, too, and a secretary might be confused as to what things she should take on, what is "rightfully her business."

So I should suggest to you that if the thought occurs to you, "Well I could do that if he'd let me or he wants me to," or "I could do that for Mrs. Chandler, if she wants me to." Then I suggest that you say so right off, and that you ask my wife if she wouldn't like you to do so and so. But never hint to her that you don't think she's able to do it. And if you see me starting to do something which you know is going to end in my getting mad at somebody, why not come right out and say, "You'd better leave me to do that. I think I can handle it. And if I can't I'll tell you." Or something to that effect. You can be even blunter. You don't have to be so damned polite.

Ray was attempting to navigate an impossibly difficult time, and his letter is full of revealing details about his relationship with Cissy, his protectiveness and concern, his wish to spare her any embarrassment or humiliation, and also their inability to discuss her condition frankly (a situation reflected in two book titles Cissy had once proposed to him: *Between Two Liars* and *Places Where We Aren't Going Back*). It also suggests his ability to take a hard look at himself and assess his own limitations. In another part of the letter he admits he has a "pugnacious temperament" and that he's often blunt and offensive, irritated by plumbers, electricians, painters—"all the types that you have to have to do things for you."

What is clear from these notes is how much of the day-to-day work of taking care of the household had fallen to Cissy over the years and how unfit Ray was to take over such chores. Perhaps part of the reason he'd never wanted to own a house was to avoid the feeling of being tied down by such responsibilities. Not only did he take no pleasure in being a householder, he found it took time from his writing. He and Cissy were now playing a kind of game: neither was able to face the fact she was dying. There was still talk of selling the house. Maybe moving to France. Possibly her even getting better. Instead, she got steadily worse.

·　　·　　·

The Long Goodbye is certainly Ray's most poignant novel, the one in which he invests Marlowe with the greatest emotional range, and this seems fitting given Ray's own heightened state of feeling as he was writing the book. At times, he becomes the philosopher and has characters muse on everything from the emptiness of American consumer society to the prevalence of homosexuals in the arts. In this book, as Natasha Spender pointed out, Ray divided his own psyche between the three leading male characters: Terry Lennox, the battle-scarred ex-soldier and man of pride; Roger Wade, the successful middle-aged, alcoholic and eccentric writer; and Philip Marlowe, who represented Ray's ideal self. All three characters are drinkers. In Natasha's view, "Roger Wade [was] his 'bad self,' Philip Marlowe his 'good self' and Terry Lennox his anxious one." In certain passages, one can hear Ray's voice like a cry from the void that had begun to open up around him. One passage, in particular, stands out, written, no doubt, as he sat up drinking alone one night. It comes from the suicide note written by Roger Wade, which Marlowe finds crumpled in the trash can:

> The moon's four days off the full and there's a square patch of moonlight on the wall and it's looking at me like a big blind milky eye, a wall eye. Joke. Goddamned silly simile. Writers. Everything has to be like something else. My head is as fluffy as whipped cream but not as sweet. More similes. I could vomit just thinking about the lousy racket. I could vomit anyway. I probably will. Don't push me. Give me time. The worms in my solar plexus crawl and crawl and crawl. I would be better off in bed but there would be a dark animal underneath the bed and the dark animal would crawl around rustling and hump himself and bump the underside of the bed, then I would let out a yell that wouldn't make any sound except to me. A dream yell, a yell in a nightmare. There is nothing to be afraid of and I am not afraid because there is nothing to be afraid of, but just the same I was lying like that once in bed

and the dark animal was doing it to me, bumping himself against the underside of the bed, and I had an orgasm. That disgusted me more than any other of the nasty things I have done.

There is nothing to be afraid of and I am not afraid because there is nothing to be afraid of . . .

In truth there was everything to be afraid of, and Ray *was* afraid. The passage stands out because it is utterly unlike anything he had written before or would ever write again. A raw expression of his own anguish—from a writer who can't resist a simile and is sick of the lousy racket.

"I'm a spoiled writer who doesn't believe anymore," Roger Wade tells Marlowe in an earlier scene where they discuss writers and books. "I have a beautiful home, a beautiful wife, and a beautiful sales record. But really all I want is to get drunk and forget."

The Long Goodbye was published in England in at the end of 1953 to largely favorable reviews, including one by Leonard Russell in *The Sunday Times*. It came out nine months later in the States. During the time in between Ray didn't think much about writing or the way the novel would be received: his full-time job became caring for Cissy.

Neil Morgan, the young journalist who worked for the *San Diego Tribune*, had become one of Ray's closest friends. Many times Ray had mentioned to Morgan that he would like him to meet Cissy, but even though Morgan had visited the house on a number of occasions over the years, he had never even glimpsed her, until one night when he was visiting, and Ray escorted Cissy from her bedroom to meet Morgan and play the piano for him. Morgan recalled the meeting later in a conversation with Tom Hiney:

I had a great sense of magnolias, old lace, and the chivalry of maybe the American South echoed for me there, he was escorting her as you would take a child. She was dying of fibrosis of the lungs, a long tedious death, I think probably often under heavy sedation. But that evening she was dressed in silk and came out and took her place at the bench of the concert piano, that Steinway, and played two or three Chopin waltzes. It was a recital, it was a presentation and Chandler hovered over her and finally said, "That's enough, dear" and helped her up and took her back to her bedroom. He cooked her meals, he served her meals, he didn't trust anybody else to take care of Cissy. That was his driving life force.

In the quiet house of the sick, and in the dull hours he spent alone there, television became his main distraction, a way of passing the time. He stayed up late and watched *The Jack Benny Show* and *Fireside Theater.* He watched *Arthur Godfrey and His Friends* and *The Ray Milland Show, Dragnet,* and *The Saturday Night Fights,* and *You Bet Your Life* and *The Gillette Cavalcade of Sports.* He watched *I've Got a Secret* and *Topper.* He did not watch Red Buttons or Gene Autry or *The Adventures of Rin Tin Tin* or *The Adventures of Ozzie and Harriet* or *Life with Father* because he did not like these shows, but he never missed the *Pabst Blue Ribbon Bouts* or *Great Moments in Sports.* He thought television was great for sports. He loved watching TV because he felt less lonely. The new medium of television both fascinated and repelled him. It was "perfect," he said, what people had been looking for all their lives, demanding no concentration or engagement, like "watching the bubbles in the primeval ooze . . . you don't miss your brain because you don't need it. Your heart and liver and lungs continue to function normally. Apart from that, all is peace and quiet. You are in the poor man's nirvana." All his days and nights now resembled one another, in the quiet house of the sick.

In the fall Cissy grew critically ill. Up to that point she had still been able to get up for at least a small part of each day and eat her dinner sitting at the table, but now she could no longer do that. Late in October, in a last-ditch effort to try something new, they changed doctors. The new doctor started her on cortisone, which he had used with some success on other fibrosis patients. But the drug affected Cissy badly: it addled her memory and made her very uncomfortable. He started her on another drug, ACTH, which Ray administered daily by hypodermic needle. This didn't help either. She sank lower and lower. On November 30 she developed pneumonia and was taken to the hospital by ambulance, but the next morning she was on the phone to Ray, pleading that she be released from the hospital and taken home immediately. Ray persuaded her to stay one more day and then brought her home against the advice of the doctors.

By the next morning she was again struggling for breath and asking to be taken back to the hospital. Again, she was admitted. The doctor wished now only to make Cissy as comfortable and free from pain as possible. He told Ray she would have to spend whatever life she had left in a sanitarium. But again Cissy demanded to be taken home, and Ray complied. As she was now so ill and weak she could not be left alone, he hired nursing care round the clock, but Cissy grew worse, gasping for air and coughing violently. Ray understood the end had come:

By December 7th I realized she was dying. In the middle of the night she suddenly appeared in my room in her pajamas looking like a ghost, having evaded the nurse somehow. We got her back in bed and she tried it once more, but this time the nurse was watching. At three A.M. on the morning of December 8th her temperature was so low that the nurse got frightened and called the doctor, and once more the ambulance came and took her off to the hospital. She couldn't sleep and I knew it took a lot of stuff to put her under, so I would take her sleeping pills and she would tie them in the corner of her handkerchief so that she could swallow them surreptitiously when the nurse was out of the room. She was in an oxygen tent all the time, but she kept pulling it away so she could hold my hand. She was quite vague in her mind about some things, but almost too desperately clear about others.

Once she asked me where we lived, what town we lived in, and then asked me to describe the house. She didn't seem to know what it looked like. Then she would turn her head away and when I was no longer in her line of vision, she seemed to forget all about me. Whenever I went to see her she would reach her handkerchief out under the edge of the oxygen tent for me to give her the sleeping pills. I began to be worried about this and confessed to the doctor and he said she was getting much stronger medicine than any sleeping pills. On the 11th when I went to see her I had none and she reached out under the edge with the handkerchief, and when I had nothing to give her she turned her head away and said, "Is this the way you wanted it?"

These were very likely the last words she ever spoke to him.
Is this the way you wanted it?
Later that day the doctor called and told Ray he should come to the hospital: it might be the last chance to see her. When he arrived he found the doctor injecting Cissy with Demerol, which he found ironic since it was the same drug he'd written about in *The Long Goodbye*. She no longer seemed to recognize him or even know he was there. At noon the next day, December 12, a nurse summoned him to the hospital again, saying Cissy was very low.

When I got there they had taken the oxygen tent away and she was lying with her eyes half open. I think she was already dead. Another doctor had his stethoscope over her heart and was listening. After a while he stepped back and nodded. I closed her eyes and kissed her and went away.

Of course in a sense I had said goodbye to her long ago. In fact, many times during the past two years in the middle of the night I had realized that it was only a question of time until I lost her. But that is not the same thing as having it happen. Saying goodbye to your loved one in your mind is not the same thing as closing her eyes and knowing they will never open again. But I was glad that she died. To think of this proud, fear-less bird caged in a room in some rotten sanitarium for the rest of her days was such an unbearable thought that I could hardly face it at all.

A death certificate was made out for Pearl Eugenia Chandler. Amazingly, even in death Cissy had somehow managed to alter her age. She was eighty-four at the time she died: on the death certifi-cate, her age is listed as sixty-eight.

Ray didn't really break down until after her funeral, in part because he felt obligated to help hold her sister Vinnie together, and partly because he had begun drinking heavily to cloak his pain. The funeral was held in St. James Episcopal Church in La Jolla, which neither Cissy nor Ray had ever attended. Ray had the chapel covered with hundreds of flowers. Juanita Messick helped him organize a simple service at which only the minister spoke. Ray turned up drunk at the funeral—perhaps the only way he could get there at all. There were only seven other mourners pres-ent. He did not accompany the body to the Cypress Grove Mau-soleum in San Diego, where Cissy's body was cremated and eventually interred.

"I am sleeping in her room," he wrote to Hamish Hamilton, three weeks after her death:

I thought I couldn't face that, and then I thought that if the room were empty it would just be haunted, and every time I went past the door I would have the horrors, and that the only thing was for me to come in here and fill it up with my junk and make it look the kind of mess I'm used to living in. It was the right decision. Her clothes are all around me, but they are in closets or hidden away in drawers. I have a couple of old friends staying with me, and they are patient and kind beyond any expectation. But the horrors are all mine just the same. For thirty years, ten months and four days, she was the light of my life, my whole ambition. Anything else I did was just the fire for her to warm her hands at. That is all there is to say.

Within a few months he had sold the house on Camino de la Costa, although he did not leave the house right away. He spent a couple of months there before the escrow closed. He wrote to Hamish Hamilton,

> I try not to think too much about Cissy. Late at night when people have gone to bed and the house is still and it is difficult to read I hear light steps rustling on the carpet and I see a gentle smile hovering at the edge of the lamplight and I hear a voice calling me by a pet name. Then I go out to the pantry and mix a stiff brandy and soda and try to think of something else.

Gradually he sold most of the furniture, including the Steinway piano, and the rest he put in storage. After the movers had taken most of the furnishings away, he stayed on in the house. The friends he'd spoken of (really a former accountant and his wife) who had been staying with him left. He was alone now on the frozen star. Like the last man, he said, on a dead world.

As the reality of Cissy's death sank in he began drinking more and more, isolating himself in the largely empty house. He read poetry, though the emotions it brought up often seemed unbearable. On January 15, just over a month after her death, he wrote an untitled poem for her:

> *There is a moment after death when the face is beautiful*
> *When the soft tired eyes are closed and the pain is over,*
> *And the long, long innocence of her comes gently in*
> *For a moment more in quiet to hover.*
>
> *But there are always the letters.*

There is a moment after death, yet hardly a moment
When the bright clothes hang in the scented closet
And the lost dream fades and slowly fades
When the silver bottles and the glass, and the empty mirror,
And the three long hairs in a brush and folded kerchief
And the fresh made bed and the fresh plump pillows
On which no head will lie
Are all that is left of the long wild dream.

But there are always the letters.

I hold them in my hand, tied with a green ribbon
Neatly and firmly by the soft, strong fingers of love,
The letters will not die.
They will wait and wait for the stranger to come and read
them.
He will come slowly out of the mists of time and change.
He will come slowly, diffidently, down the years,
He will cut the ribbon and spread the letters apart,
And carefully carefully read them page by page.

After the long, long innocence of love will come softly in
Like a butterfly through the open window in summer,
For a moment in quiet to hover.
But the stranger will never know. The dream will be over.
The stranger will be I.

The letters will not die.

I had never stopped longing to see those letters, in which the *long, long innocence of love* might have been revealed, just as I'd never stopped wondering why he chose to destroy them, effectively killing them off and with them any true picture we might ever have gotten of her. What do we really have of her without them?

One note, written in her hand: *Dear Raymio, you'll have fun looking at this later and seeing what useless dreams you had. Or perhaps it will not be fun.*

A few photographs of her at various stages in her life.

Some of her writing on Ray's childhood pictures.

An account of the imaginary adventures of Alfred, Ray's childhood doll.

A love note to him, addressed to Gallibeoth, which once accompanied a birthday present.

One of his poems, hand-copied in her turquoise ink and addressed to him.

Her recipe box, crammed with handwritten cards and magazine clippings.

Her list of amuels, also carefully written out in turquoise ink.

A few recollections from the people who (very) briefly met her.

And his stories, of course, about her great wit and charm and their perfect marriage, some of which we can believe and some of which we cannot.

"Cissy came from Ohio and that is nearly all we know about her," Patricia Highsmith once wrote in an essay about Ray, "A Galahad in L.A." "She barely seems alive and yet she existed, and indeed was Chandler's anchor, his shrine of worship, his raison d'etre."

He thought so much about her at the end of his life, and even her painful end took on a kind of hallowed beauty in retrospect:

I watched my wife die by half-inches and I wrote my best book in the agony of that knowledge, and yet I wrote it. I don't know how. I used to shut myself up in my study and think myself into another world. It usually took an hour, at least. And then I went to work. But I always listened. And late at night I would lie on the eight-foot couch reading because I knew that around midnight she would come quietly in and that she would want a cup of tea, but would never ask for it. I always had to talk her into it. But I had to be there, since if I had been asleep, she wouldn't have wakened me, and wouldn't have had her tea.

Do you think I regret any of this? I'm proud of it. It was the supreme time of my life.

She was the beat of my heart for thirty years, he said.

She was the music heard faintly at the edge of sound.

Everything I have ever done was just a fire for her to warm her hands at.

He never felt he had written a book worthy of dedicating to her, so he dedicated his books to no one. Except the last book, published three years after her death: he dedicated *Playback* to Jean and Helga, the two women who were most important to him at the time.

In the end he effaced her by burning her letters. Why he did this we'll never know. Perhaps he simply couldn't bear to share her with anyone. Or perhaps he could not tolerate the possibility of any version of his marriage finding its way into the public consciousness except his own.

Two months after Cissy's death, Ray attempted suicide, by taking a gun into the bathroom of the house on Camino de la Costa and firing it twice. He had called the captain of the La Jolla Police Department to warn him of what he was about to do before he did it. It was the action not of a man who really wanted to die, but one who wished to be rescued. It's interesting to note how much his own suicide attempt resembled the one he had described in *The Long Goodbye*.

The difference was he wasn't successful, whereas his character Roger Wade was. He was consigned to living a few more years—very painful, chaotic, and sad years—without the woman who had kept him together for such a long time.

When former neighbors from Santa Monica, with whom he and Cissy must once have had a falling-out, wrote to Ray expressing their sadness on reading of his suicide attempt in the *L.A. Times*, he wrote them a scathing letter, asking why they had bothered writing now: "Cissy never forgave you for it," he said, referring to the unnamed incident, "and had she been able to she always planned to go to Santa Monica and see you and have it out with you."

She was never afraid of a good fight, he said, she always marched right in . . .

When I think of Cissy, I see a gentle feistiness, and hear her high-brow accent, and the rather Blanche DuBois image of her arises—the frilly dresses, the fading beauty, the perfumed languor—but what I really think of are the words written by Dilys Powell, recalling the encounter with her on that ill-fated trip to London, which suggest that not only did Cissy provide Ray with his entry into his world of fable, as Powell put it, but also that Ray provided Cissy with a persona that has endured, as if the two of them were each other's creations, and the marriage itself was a myth, encased forever now in what Ray once called a beautiful crystal casket.

"Looking back now," Powell wrote,

I realize that, leaving aside the brilliant literary gifts which first seduced me, I like Raymond best in his relationship with Cissy, that smiling, propitiatory figure whom he guarded and defended. And created: she lives on in his image of her, the adored creature to be consulted, encouraged, constantly and proudly displayed. Marlowe was his fantasy image of himself, tough and daring in a world without Cissy. In a world with Cissy he showed another kind of gallantry; he shielded her. And he needed her. Without her he had lost not only his accustomed place in the everyday world but the entry to his own world of fable; the decay of his working years after her death is proof of that. Whatever his errancies, she was the stable point in the life of reality.

We met him many more times than we met her. But I can no longer summon up his image. It is Cissy whom I see: the fading eyes in the drained face, the look—I know now what it was—of appeal.

Eleven

Ray lived a little over four years after Cissy's death. Without Cissy and the domicile that had grounded him for so long, he became unmoored—some might say unhinged. After he sold the house on Camino de la Costa, he took a suite at the Hotel del Charro, closer to the La Jolla village center, and once again returned to a nomadic existence. He began making plans to go to England. He had friends in London, people who cared about him and valued his work. And it was, after all, the place of his youth.

In April 1955, just a month after his unsuccessful suicide attempt, he booked passage on the *Mauretania,* the same ship he and Cissy had taken on their return trip from England. He was a lonely man, setting out to sea, with no firm plans for the future. On the ship he met an intelligent and attractive American woman named Jessica Tyndale, a senior executive in the English banking firm of Guinness Mahon, and they struck up a friendship that would last for the remainder of Ray's life. From now on all his relationships with women would be friendships, no matter how much he wished otherwise: his increasingly excessive drinking had most certainly rendered him impotent, though his romantic impulses, as one would expect, were completely undeterred. In London, he was once again greeted as a celebrity. The recent publication of *The Long Goodbye* had only increased his fame. Through Jessica Tyndale he met Helga Greene, whose father was chairman of the Guinness Mahon Bank. Helga had been previously married to Hugh Greene, director general of the BBC and brother of the novelist Graham Greene. As a lifelong lover of books, she had recently started her own literary agency. Initially Helga and Ray did not hit it off: he found her cool and aloof, but later she would become not only his agent but his most trusted and devoted friend.

In London he stayed once again in the Connaught Hotel and began spending money freely. He also began drinking heavily. He gave interviews in which he talked less about literary matters than about the recent death of his beloved wife and his own suicide attempt, about which he seemed to feel no embarrassment or shame. He saw old friends and made new ones. For a while he enjoyed all the attention that flowed his way—the parties given in his honor, the nightly dinners at expensive West End restaurants. But as his drinking worsened he often grew despondent and would again threaten to kill himself.

It was then that he met Natasha Spender, a rising concert pianist in her thirties, who organized her women friends into the female rescue brigade, devoted to keeping him company. For a while it seemed to work: Ray enjoyed the dinners and lunches and, being his courtly self, he sent the women flowers and expensive jewelry, which they often discreetly returned to the jeweler. He was so emotionally needy that he fell in love with practically every woman he met, especially if he believed that she was in any way vulnerable and needed rescuing. The irony was of course that it was he who needed help.

A month into his stay at the Connaught, he was asked to leave the hotel, owing to drunken behavior. He moved to the Ritz Hotel. His drinking worsened: he entered a frenetic stage in which erotic fantasies played a part. He began writing little pornographic sketches, which he sent off to friends—Dilys Powell remembered receiving a few of them and finding them mildly embarrassing and of no literary value. Alcohol had always stimulated his libido, and now that he was alone again he became rather preoccupied with erotic subjects. He began fabricating sexual encounters, which he would report to friends—tales of lovely blond women met in hotel elevators who invited him to their rooms and then seduced him. He became unpredictable in various other ways, concocting dramatic stories of all sorts. He sometimes failed to appear at dinner parties or else arrived late and often drunk and then offered up fantastic excuses, tales of being accosted by thugs en route from whom he had only barely managed to escape.

He spent money wildly and freely. He opened accounts at Harrods and other chic haunts and dined out every evening at expensive restaurants like Boulestin's. He was hardly ever seen without an attractive woman, often a member of the rescue brigade. After years of living modestly with Cissy, he was now hemorrhaging money, and he didn't care. He told one interviewer that this was what money was for, for taking beautiful women to dinner and showering them with gifts, and many women were happy to dine with the famous author Raymond Chandler and take his largesse. Sometimes the results were embarrassing: once he wrote a check to a woman he'd dined with that he later canceled. It turned out she needed money to start a business (or so she said), but Ray, realizing his mistake the next morning, stopped payment. In return she wrote him a scathing letter, accusing him of damaging her reputation with her bank and suggesting he was nothing but a bore: "I do feel sorry for you. Nothing can be more pathetic than the way they call you Raymond (The Big Sleep) Chandler." Even as he courted women, he still spoke incessantly of Cissy, of his perfect marriage and his devotion to her. As Ian Fleming put it,

> Since the death of his wife, he was lost without women and, in the few years I knew him, he was never without some good-looking companion to mother him and try and curb his drinking. These were affectionate and warm-hearted relationships and probably nothing more. Though I do know this, I suspect that each woman was, in the end, rather glad to get away from the ghost of the other woman who always walked at his side.

In death, Cissy became even more enshrined, just as the marriage became ever more perfect in retrospect. He was asked, during this time, by a newspaper interviewer, if he would consider marrying again. Perhaps, he said, but only a woman in her thirties. He told reporters that in all the years of his marriage he had never once been unfaithful to his wife. Not once, he said, had he even been tempted to look at another woman.

He began writing erotic poetry, and aside from these poems, and the mildly pornographic sketches he was composing, he wrote almost nothing else except the occasional letter to a friend. He started a correspondence with a fan in San Francisco named Louise Loughner who had written to tell him how much she admired his work, and through the letters he fell in love with her and they began making plans to meet. Yet for all this activity, his address book soon began to look strangely empty: there had many dates penciled in during his first few weeks in London, but soon, day after day, week after week, the pages were left blank.

He was asked to leave the Ritz Hotel, because of his drinking and also because he'd broken the hotel's rules forbidding women visiting him in his room, though the woman in question was Helga Greene, who arrived on an errand of mercy, in order to check on him as he had failed to appear for an interview. Helga helped to find him a flat at 116 Eaton Square, very near where she lived, with the hope she might be better able to keep an eye on him. But there was nothing she could do about his drinking. To a friend he admitted not having drawn a sober breath since arriving in England.

There were good times at Eaton Square. He liked the company of Helga Greene, who often visited him at the end of the working day, arriving late for a drink and departing well after midnight. But alone in a flat by himself, without the communal life of a hotel to distract him, he grew increasingly bored and unhappy. Cissy had been the only thing that had stood between him and alcoholic self-destruction; now she was gone, and no one else was up to the job.

He began to turn more and more to Natasha Spender for comfort and companionship. In their own way each had experienced an unconventional marriage—Ray to a much older woman, Natasha to a man who had previously lived his life as a homosexual. Ray began imagining that Natasha, like all the women he'd ever cared about, needed rescuing. He became convinced that her husband, Stephen, didn't treat her properly, even though she was clearly happy with Spender and by then had two small children with him. Ray began telling friends he and Natasha were having an affair, which deeply annoyed Natasha. Nevertheless she stood by him as a friend because she understood that his drinking was out of control: he was losing touch with reality and indulging the wildest fantasies.

And then suddenly, perhaps realizing the gravity of his situation, Ray stopped drinking. He did it on his own, through an act of will and determination, just as he had done at previous times in his life, most notably after being fired from Dabney Oil. Without drink, however, he felt dead. He grew morose. His mind became slack, and he lost the feeling of exuberance he so valued. He didn't miss drinking physically, he said, but he did miss it mentally and spiritually.

Sober, he entered that flat landscape he'd once spoken of, where all roads appeared equally uninteresting and seemed to lead nowhere.

To lift his spirits, Natasha organized a trip to Italy for just the two of them. They went to Lake Garda, where the Spender family often vacationed and stayed in a hotel. The trip wasn't much fun for either of them. Without drink Ray could summon no enthusiasm for the sightseeing outings that Natasha organized in an effort to entertain him. I simply refused to look, he said later, as if proud of his recalcitrance. For Natasha it was like traveling with a zombie: each day Ray went through the motions of life without registering the slightest indication of any real pleasure.

In October 1956 his visa expired, and he was forced to leave England, after nearly six months abroad. Still sober, he returned to America. He said that without drink the voyage home was hell.

He returned to La Jolla and rented rooms once again in the Hotel del Charro. Hotel life was less lonely than apartment living, more compatible with his nomadism and his interest in people watching. According to visa regulations he was barred from returning to England for twelve months, but when Natasha wrote to say she was having surgery on December 12—which unbeknownst to her was the anniversary of Cissy's death, just a year earlier—Ray panicked and decided to return to London to be with her, fearing the worst. In truth Natasha faced only a routine operation about which neither she nor her family were much concerned. But that didn't matter. Ray's rescue instincts had become fully engaged.

By the time he returned to London, he had begun drinking again. He arrived in a state of high anxiety. In order to relax her and help prepare her for surgery, Ray suggested to Natasha that he treat her to a vacation in Tunisia. Without realizing that Ray was once again teetering on the edge of another alcohol-induced breakdown, she agreed to go.

The trip was a difficult one, with Ray drinking constantly, often locking himself in his hotel room and failing to appear for meals. Natasha soon realized that the situation was out of hand. A bitterness had crept in: "He spoke almost incessantly of Cissy, but his previous moods of lyricism and resignation gave way to far more complex emotions concerning his whole past life, and he would often become submerged in retrospective anger and despair." It was all Natasha could do to cope with Ray in his deeply anxious state. She was not equipped to deal with someone in this extreme alcoholic condition: he needed the sort of help that only a trained professional could give.

Back in London, while Natasha underwent surgery, Ray moved into the Spender house in the St. John's Wood area of London, and Stephen Spencer cared for him as best he could. Ray was shadowed in silent grumpiness. Often Spender stayed up part of the night talking with Ray, helping him through his darkest hours. Just before Christmas, Ray entered a London hospital to dry out. Upon his release he moved into the Ritz and resumed drinking.

He decided that he should begin living more economically, that he could no longer afford long stays at expensive hotels like the Ritz. In January 1956, Natasha found him a flat near the Spenders' house, at 40 Carlton Hill. It was a quiet residential neighborhood, too quiet, as it turned out, for Ray's tastes. He felt the flat was beastly, but the real problem was that he was bored stiff, stuck off in a suburban area populated by families and married couples. He felt trapped by the long English winter. His health was poor, although he knew the real cause of his problems wasn't really physical: "All that is really wrong with me," he wrote, "is I have no home, and no one to care for in a home, if I did have one."

He suffered deliriums. Natasha was often summoned in the middle of the night by a frantic Ray, and she, in turn, would call the doctor to sedate him. He entered another clinic in the spring. He came out and began drinking again.

In May he returned to America: having overstayed his visa, he was now in trouble with the immigration and tax authorities. In New York he checked into the Grosvenor Hotel. A few days later, he went to see his friends in Old Chatham again. He fell down some stairs in their house one night and was taken by ambulance to a New York hospital where he was given a sixteen-hour blood transfusion. He was severely malnourished and suffering from what he described as "total mental, physical and emotional exhaustion masked by my drinking enough whisky to keep me on my feet." By the fifth day in the hospital, after receiving constant treatment and nourishment, he awoke and felt a sense of peacefulness overcome him. "I felt happy, absolutely happy, for the first time since my wife died. All the rest had been play-acting." He wrote to Helga Greene, "It was as though some Authority had looked down on me and decided: 'This man has had enough, endured enough, failed enough, but always loved too much. He is not going to have any more trouble. He is not even going to have to fight.' A strange, almost mystical experience and not at all in my line."

If only it were true that he was spared more trouble. But it was not to be. He returned to La Jolla and rented an apartment at 6925 Neptune Place, just a block or two from the beach, but he continued to feel bored and homesick for London. The worst thing, he said, was eating alone, going out to restaurants by himself. He attended a few parties but found the La Jolla crowd as banal as ever: "I am already sick to death of skins like burnt oranges and smiles like gashes. I am sick of people who never put a glass down ... Alas, not all my country is hopelessly vulgar, but this part of it certainly is."

He began drinking again. He decided to fly to San Francisco in July to finally meet his fan Louise Loughner. He stayed a month at the Clift Hotel. In the beginning, they seemed to have gotten along well: he wrote to his English solicitor saying that he was thinking of marrying her and wished to change his will in her favor. But soon things fell apart. His drinking got so bad he had to return to Southern California and check into a clinic in Pasadena for a while. He saw Louise a few times after he got out, but the relationship had soured: "I can't stand quarrels," he wrote. "I don't quarrel myself: they say it takes two. It doesn't. I'm very sorry and very lonely, but I know the same sort of thing would happen periodically."

During his stay in the Pasadena clinic he had begun talking with a psychiatrist, one of the few shrinks he'd ever met whom he didn't ridicule: he felt the doctor understood him in a way few others had. "You think you are depressed," the psychiatrist told him, "but you are quite wrong . . . all that's the matter with you is loneliness. You simply cannot and must not live alone. If you do, inevitably you will drink, and that will make you sick." The doctor's words touched him deeply, because of course they were true. "I hadn't expected anything so penetrating," Ray said. As soon as he left the clinic, however, he went back to living alone in the house on Neptune Place, and he also started drinking once more. He could not quit alcohol for any length of time. The problem was there was no one to help him, no woman by his side to ease his loneliness and help him control his addiction. Cissy was gone.

He began writing again, thanks to the support and encouragement of Helga Greene, who was now his sole literary agent. Helga had a wonderful way of making him believe he could actually finish another book. She was still in London, running her literary agency there, but he spoke to her regularly by phone and found her encouragement heartening. He began work on *Playback*, adapting the original screenplay he'd written earlier into a novel set in a town very much like La Jolla, called Esmeralda. It would be the only book he ever wrote while drunk.

In December 1956 he learned that Natasha Spender was coming to America for a concert tour and he wrote to her, insisting that she meet him in Arizona where, he promised, she could have a restful time with him in the warm winter climate of the Southwest before she set off on her nationwide tour. Natasha agreed, believing that Ray, recently released from the Pasadena clinic, was in good shape. Instead she was met at the Phoenix airport by an inebriated Ray who nearly crashed the car as he attempted to drive away from the airport. He had arranged accommodations for the night in nearby Chandler, Arizona, no doubt as a little joke, and it was here they spent the first night of what would become for Natasha a very strained and trying vacation. By the time they parted, a few weeks later, following a weekend spent in Palm Springs with Christopher Isherwood, Don Bachardy, and Natasha's friend Dr. Evelyn Hooker (whose husband had died suddenly of a heart attack just the week before), Ray's relationship with Natasha had been seriously damaged, in part because of his behavior toward Evelyn Hooker. His drinking was one thing, Natasha said, but his complete self-absorption and the insensitivity he showed toward Evelyn and her recent loss were really inexcusable.

He returned to La Jolla. For a while he dated a woman with the interesting name of Fay Crooks, and he even proposed to her, but she ended up marrying another man. As he continued to work on his novel *Playback*, he felt he needed a secretary again and he placed an ad in the newspaper, soliciting applications for the job. When a woman named Jean Fracasse responded, he hired her on the spot. An attractive, vibrant blonde, she was Australian by birth, educated in Paris and London. She had moved to La Jolla with her doctor husband, with whom she had two young children, a boy and a girl. Jean had worked in television, held a doctorate in music and, like both Cissy and Natasha, played the piano.

Soon Jean and her children had established themselves as part of the household on Neptune Place. He liked Jean's children very much, especially her daughter, Sybil, who charmed him with her intelligence and sweetness. They seem to have been the first children whose company Ray actually enjoyed. Often he watched television with them while Jean worked in another room. Sometimes the kids helped him with little chores. It was Sybil's job to cut the sheets of paper down to the half-size he used for typing. When Jean's husband sued her for divorce, not long after she had come to work for Ray, Ray became deeply involved in the proceedings. He came to Jean's rescue by hiring a divorce lawyer for her and giving her extra money. He took Jean and the children on a vacation to Palm Springs, and soon he was suggesting to friends in England that he intended to marry Jean, though Jean seems to have had little interest in remarrying.

In late 1957, Helga Greene paid Ray a visit in La Jolla: not only did she want to see him but she wanted to check on how his novel was coming along. They, too, went to Palm Springs together for ten days and had a very good time. They took walks and went dancing and dined out every night. Helga soothed him: he felt she had that quality common to certain well-bred people and all true aristocrats—a natural ability to put others at ease. *Playback* was almost finished, and later he would say it was entirely due to Helga's support and encouragement that he'd been able to write the book at all.

Over Christmas he told Helga that, in the spring, he was planning to go to Australia with Jean and the children and intended to live there for a while. First, however, he hoped to come to London. Helga thought this a good plan. Like many people who cared about Ray, she realized his best hope lay in another relationship, and she felt Jean and the children offered him a kind of ready-made family in which he could assume the role of stepfather. But things didn't work out that way.

In February 1958, he flew to London and checked into the Ritz and spent a month alone in the city. He was no longer sure he wanted to go to Australia with Jean. He was fond of her, but no longer, he said, in either a "marrying or love-making way." She was becoming "a drain," as he put it. He began asking friends in America if they knew of anywhere in Florida where he might settle her and her children. Jean had a forthright and demanding per-

sonality, plus she had expressed no real interest in marrying him, even if he had been so inclined, though she did not mind accepting his support. Australia was so far away, a completely unknown place to him. He felt he lacked the energy to make such a trip. He decided to stay in London, but he generously bought first-class tickets for Jean and her children and sent them off to Australia alone.

He moved into a flat at 8 Swan Walk in Chelsea, just across from the Chelsea Physick Garden where medicinal plants had once been raised for the Royal London Hospital. The flat was only a block from the Thames, within walking distance of Helga's house off Eaton Square. A young woman in her early twenties lived in the flat above him, a dress designer whom he developed a crush on. He wrote her charming little flirtatious letters. "Mr. Chandler is a very lonely gentleman and longing for company," began one, "I hope this can be arranged." Later he asked: "Do you really think you could become emotionally involved with a man of my age? . . . be careful. Every girl has her weak moments. Save yours for me. I know how to treat you with respect and tenderness and only you could ever decide that I could go as far as I should like to. After all I am only a man." He sent her red roses and little presents, but his real role was limited to fatherly advice. It was Helga, in fact, who provided him with as much companionship as she could, given her busy schedule. Sometimes they played darts together in nearby pubs. They went to her country house in West Clandon. They took dancing lessons in an attempt to learn the newer dances of the 1950s, which Ray found inferior to his favorite dance, the waltz. They can fool around all they like with other dances, he said, but "they must leave my waltz alone, my waltz is my own."

In an attempt to provide him with company, Helga introduced him to a friend of hers, Kay West, who lived not far from Swan Walk and who often spent afternoons with him watching sports on TV. He began to feel badly about Jean, and to ease his conscience he decided to sign over all the rights to *Playback* to her, an extravagant gesture that left him financially vulnerable. Helga immediately negotiated to buy back the rights with her own money. Ray was becoming badly confused, running through his assets rapidly. His mind and spirit were clouded by drink, and again he suffered a breakdown and ended up in a clinic near Queen's Gate in Kensington. To make matters worse, the tax authorities demanded he pay $50,000 in back taxes to the British government on earnings paid to him during an earlier stay, a situation he could find no way out of and which deeply upset him.

When *Playback* was finally released the reviews were less than glowing: at best they generated a kind of warm appreciation for Chandler's career as a whole while gently skirting the subject of the book at hand, which was unarguably inferior to his earlier novels. His resources were fast dwindling, although Helga was doing her best to protect him and help keep him afloat. His loans to Jean continued. He could not refuse a woman in need. "I seem to be the sort of idiot who will sacrifice himself for anyone in trouble," he said, "especially a woman because my wife made me tender to all women, but if I ever have the slightest suspicion that I am, even unconsciously, being used, I get very tough." He did not get tough with Jean, however. He had agreed to help her and felt honor-bound to do so. Even if he no longer had any interest in marrying her, or she him, neither could he simply cut her off. She seems to have understood this. Also, he genuinely cared for Jean and also for her children, and when it came to women, he had never taken his responsibilities toward them lightly.

In the summer of 1958, while still living at Swan Walk, Ray began plotting a new novel with the working title "Poodle Springs," a book that would open with Marlowe married to the millionaire playgirl Linda Loring, who first appeared in *The Long Goodbye* and resurfaced at the end of *Playback*. Ray was weak, physically depleted, but determined to try to write. Helga hired a live-in male nurse named Don Santry to look after him, and for a while during that summer in the flat on Swan's Walk things seemed to go better for him, until something happened to change everything.

In La Jolla, Jean's ex-husband, Dr. Fracasse, suffered a sudden heart attack and died, and immediately Jean and her children returned to the States from Australia. Ray paid for their return passage and felt compelled to join them there, and he gave up the flat on Swan's Walk. Don Santry, his male nurse, accompanied him on the trip back to America and agreed to stay with him in La Jolla for a while. Ray rented a small cottage at 824 Prospect Street from a woman named Mrs. Murray and settled in there with his nurse.

Dr. Fracasse had cut his ex-wife and children out of his will, a result no doubt of the acrimonious feeling between them in the wake of their bitter divorce, and Jean was left with no money and mounting bills. Ray once more felt compelled to step in. He gave her his car, rented a house for her and the children, and lent them some of his furniture that had been in storage in order to help them start over. By that time he had discovered that Jean was not really a suitable secretary, but nonetheless she continued to be involved in his affairs. She wanted to find work as an actress, and she also wished to write, and Ray helped her find a literary agent and place at least one article about the inequities of the divorce system in America.

Don Santry found Ray's drinking all but impossible to cope with. Ray made life hard for Don, complaining about his cooking, finding fault with almost everything that he did. In the fall Ray entered a clinic for a week's stay. He was seriously ill now, vomiting blood, suffering blackouts and delirium tremens. Writing had always been the one thing that had saved him in the past, but he was no longer able to focus on a book. Jean still turned up at the cottage most days, but she and Don Santry had a falling-out, making his position in Ray's life even more difficult, and Don decided to return to England, leaving Ray alone in the cottage.

Concerned, but unable to leave London herself, Helga instead sent Kay West to La Jolla to stay with Ray and assess the situation. The idea was that Kay would help him assemble a cookbook, based on Cissy's recipes, that Helga and Ray had begun to put together and in this way keep him occupied. It was to be called *The Idiot's Cookbook*—Ray's title—and focus on the basics of preparing simple meals. For a while the plan seemed to have worked. Initially Kay and Ray had a good time together, cooking meals, playing darts, watching TV, and working on the cookbook. Within two weeks Ray had proposed to Kay West and informed his London solicitor he was considering changing his will in her favor, making Kay his heir instead of Jean. Perhaps Jean got wind of this; in any case, relations began to sour between the two women, and the constant drinking and stress of coping with Ray and the tension with Jean became too much for Kay, who became so exhausted that she suffered an emotional breakdown and had to enter a hospital for a short stay before she felt well enough to return to London.

Kay began to feel that Jean was a part of the problems plaguing Ray. "We could all take care of Ray," she wrote to Helga, "if it weren't for the additional disturbances." What these additional disturbances were, she didn't exactly say, but she left no doubt they were engendered by Jean. "It's all very well for Jean to think she stimulates him mentally, but what's the good of that if he's going to collapse from lack of proper feeding? Not to speak of the state he'll get into without proper cleaning."

Ray spent Christmas 1958 alone, staying at the Harlowe Haven Motel in Palm Springs for several weeks. His biggest problem was his physical deterioration. But he was also worried about money. He was worried about his new book. He felt uncertainty about the future, and worst of all, his drinking was out of control. During one of his stays in a clinic the previous fall he had tried to switch from scotch to champagne, at the suggestion of his doctor, but the results had been disastrous. Of his few remaining friends, almost no one visited him now except Jean. She continued to come by the cottage almost every day, but the exact nature of their relationship was unfathomable to many. Another male nurse was hired, Leon Johnson, but he was not really equipped to deal with Ray's drinking, and no one could force him to eat. Ray became malnourished and began taking vitamin shots again to sustain him. The truth was, no one knew how to help Ray.

In February 1959, Helga Greene flew to La Jolla, even though she had recently had surgery herself and was still in a somewhat weakened condition. She had agreed to marry Ray, finally accepting a proposal he'd made months earlier. Marrying Ray had become the only chance she felt he might have at life. If she could bring him back to London and care for him there, help him to get writing again and provide him with the companionship he craved and the full-time nursing care that he needed, perhaps he might still be able to draw back from his precarious position.

In early March, having helped him pack up his cottage and send some belongings to England and put others in storage, Helga flew with Ray to New York. Before leaving La Jolla, Ray drew up a codicil to his will, naming Helga, instead of Jean, as his sole heir and literary executor. By then Jean and Helga had grown increasingly suspicious of each other—Helga because she had begun to suspect that Jean didn't have Ray's best interests at heart, Jean because she realized that the financial support she'd been receiving from Ray was in danger of drying up. There was also the question of the will. Jean knew she had been named his beneficiary in an earlier will, and what if that was to change?

In New York, Ray and Helga stayed at the Beaux Arts Hotel on East 44th Street. The weather was cold and rainy and had a bad effect on Ray, as he was already seriously weakened. Ray had agreed to address the annual meeting of the Mystery Writers of America, which had just elected him their new president. Also, Helga's father was due to be in town, and Ray had insisted on meeting him in order to ask for his daughter's hand. Helga tried to dissuade him from this meeting; she felt it was entirely unnecessary. But Ray persisted. It was a matter of honor with him, a courtesy necessitated by his old-fashioned manners, and so a dinner was arranged for just the three of them, at which Ray and Helga would announce their marriage plans.

On the day of the Mystery Writers of America meeting, a cocktail party had been organized by the group in his honor. There was some doubt as to whether Ray would have the strength to attend the event but, with Helga's assistance, and leaning heavily on his cane, he managed to appear and deliver a short speech.

He thanked the group for their kindness in honoring him. He said he felt a certain embarrassment because he knew that although he would be the titular president of the organization, someone else would certainly be doing all the work. He said he didn't know how such people found the time and energy to be a writer and serve in such a capacity. "I have, on rare occasions," he said, "got up at four or five in the morning and pounded the type-writer for ten hours straight without food, but not without whiskey. Of course I often had to throw the stuff away—I don't mean the whiskey—but it was a nice try if no cigar."

He ended his speech by saying, "I thank you all again for your great kindness to me, and I am sure you will be relieved to know that, however much love I may have inside me, I have no more words that need be said."

All that was left to do now before they departed for London was to dine with Helga's father, which they did a few nights later. Ray was nervous about meeting Mr. Guinness. The situation tapped into some of his oldest and deepest fears, which had been played out in a sublimated form in his fiction. All the wealthy old men who had appeared in his novels, from General Sternwood in *The Big Sleep* to Linda Loring's millionaire father in *The Long Goodbye* were figures Marlowe in some way was eager to please, even if he did at times denigrate them. The fatherless Chandler, the boy who had been humiliated by his rich uncle upon whom he was nevertheless dependent, was coming face to face with an immensely wealthy and powerful man who was almost exactly his own age—seventy-one—in order to ask permission to marry his daughter. H. S. H. Guinness was still vibrant and active, sure of himself, and extremely fond of his daughter. Ray was fond of her, too, but he was only a shadow of his former self, and he had to muster all the strength and courage he could to appear at the dinner that he alone had insisted on.

He did not drink the day of the dinner, wishing to be sober to meet Mr. Guinness, and this left his nerves very raw. His hands were in bad shape, he was shaky and ill, but he dressed carefully, down to his white gloves, and turned up at the restaurant with Helga on his arm, his chivalry intact, if not his health.

We'll never know exactly what happened that evening at dinner, but the meeting did not go well. When Helga's father saw the state Ray was in, he could not hide his disapproval. He made it clear he thought the marriage was a disastrous idea. Ray was shattered by this reaction. Whatever strength or resolve he had left, whatever confidence and optimism he'd managed to muster, was utterly destroyed. No doubt Mr. Guinness felt the need to speak up and express himself honestly out of an impulse to protect his daughter from entering a union in which she could find herself saddled with a very sick and self-destructive husband. He most likely couldn't have known what effect his words would have on Ray. How they would crush him. How they would cause him to retreat from all hope. Ray decided he could not go on to London with Helga. It was too cold there anyway, he said. Besides, Jean had been writing him pathetic letters, describing all the troubles she and the children were experiencing back in La Jolla, making it appear she was in dire straits and asking him to return. His mind was now unclear, his spirit broken. Depressed and despondent, Ray decided to return to California. At least it would be warm there, he said. At least he would be back in familiar surroundings.

He did not understand why he had been so snubbed by Mr. Guinness. As he later wrote to Helga,

> It seems very strange to me that your father should have turned so completely against me, when you said I behaved beautifully the night he had us to dinner. I know he thought I was a bit old—but he is a bit old himself. Someone must have told him things to my discredit for him to refuse to see me. Of course many things could be said to my discredit, but he would have no knowledge of them unless they were told him.

It did not matter to Ray that Helga did not feel bound to gain her father's approval of their marriage. She tried to point out to him that she was a woman of independence, possessed of a strong will: she had defied her father in the past and still maintained a loving relationship with him, and she was prepared to defy him again and marry Ray. But Ray had made up his mind. He was going back to California. At least until the weather changed. At least, he said, until he felt better.

He returned to the cottage on Prospect Street, which Mrs. Murray had not yet rented to anyone else. He isolated himself and began drinking heavily, largely neglected by his few friends. Less than two weeks later, on March 23, he was taken by ambulance to the La Jolla Convalescent Hospital. Two days later, terminally ill with pneumonia, he was transferred to the Scripps Clinic, where he passed away at 3:50 in the afternoon on March 26, 1959. In his briefcase, which he took with him to the hospital, were the first seventeen pages of his unfinished novel "Poodle Springs," which he had taken to carrying with him everywhere.

There was little ceremony surrounding his death. No church service. No memorials or public occasions. He died as he had lived—very privately, with few friends to note his passing. Sadly no one thought to honor his wish to be interred with his wife. Instead he was buried a little distance away, in a different cemetery. Seventeen people turned up for the graveside service, where a few brief words were spoken by a pastor Ray had never met.

To the end he remained a "split personality," a man divided between two countries, two languages, two cultures and continents. The American boy who had been taken from the sunblasted open spaces of the demotic Midwest and deposited in the clotted urban realms of class-conscious London. A boy with an American father and an American accent and American habits who was thrust into that most English of environments—the public school. The tradition-bound, moralistic world of Dulwich College dwarfed him, made him feel small. He was the day student who went home every night to his Irish-English mother, constantly harried by her financial worries and her own sense of belittlement. Did he ever become fully English? No. Did he ever really embrace America? No, though he seems, in the end, to have felt a deeper bond with the country of his birth. He was, in a certain way, like Alfred, his childhood doll who had fallen overboard and miraculously swum the Atlantic. Ray made the trip across those waters a number of times at the end of his life: in the absence of Cissy, he became a lost man looking for himself, shuttling back and forth between the east and west of his psyche. He loved England, and he hated it. He loved America, and he also hated it. As with most things, he was looking for perfection, and he never found it, not here, not there. He was forever trying to reconcile his feelings for these two places, and death caught him in the midst of one of his bitterest struggles: he had gotten as far as the Atlantic coast before turning his back on England and returning to the western shore.

Obsessed and anxious after Cissy's death, Ray became ever

more conflicted in an attempt to reconcile his frustrated sexual desires with his code-obsessed inner nature. Increasingly, the ethical view of himself became the cover behind which he could hide his unmet longings. "Thank God I can still copulate like a thirty-year-old," he wrote with touching bravura to his English solicitor in the last year of his life—only true, I'm afraid, if the thirty-year-old happened to be addicted and impotent. His life had become a series of failures and rejections where women were concerned.

With Helga, he was more honest. "I haven't had a woman since ages ago," he wrote to her in 1957. "Perhaps as the years dump their refuse on me, the time will come when I don't need one. It hasn't come yet and it makes me pretty damned nervous at times." Later, he added, "Surely you understand that the older I get, the more desperately I long for the presence of someone I love, to hold her and touch her and fondle her and that nothing else is any good at all. No number of letters, however loving, can add up to one long clinging kiss."

The long embrace. One clinging kiss. So chaste had he become at the end, this is all he longed for.

It was the time I spent in Oxford, I believe, working in the Chandler archive at the Bodleian Library, that finally brought me closest to Ray. I lived in a small room at one of the colleges, taking my breakfast each morning in the large formal dining hall, a cavernous room lined in dark oak, with pictures of former college presidents covering the walls. Great leaded windows looked out on manicured lawns and the college chapel. At one end of the dining room was a massive fireplace, never lit in the mild autumn months. It was September when I visited. The term had not yet started, and very often at breakfast I sat alone in the big room, on a hard wooden bench at one of the long tables, waited on by five or six people who in turn took my order and served up coffee and the full English breakfast of ham, bacon, toast, potatoes, fried tomatoes, baked beans, and eggs, all of which I sometimes ate in order to work all day at the library without taking a break until the place closed at seven p.m. I worked in the Modern Papers room of the Bodleian, on the first floor of the library, at the end of a long hallway, in a space that has been described by one scholar as "a severe room, not unlike a classroom," where box by box I made my way through the archive, until on my last day, in the last hour of my Oxford stay, I finished examining all eighty-two boxes of the Raymond Chandler papers.

In those boxes I found the appointment books that Ray had begun keeping when he first came to London after Cissy's death, so full of promise in the beginning months, so largely empty as time went on. I saw how the dates for his women friends' birthdays were carefully noted: *Send flowers,* he would write next to their names. Carnations for Jessie. Roses for Natasha. Lilies for Helga. Often these were the only dates filled in for weeks on end.

I found his list of London restaurants—only the best, the most expensive, for dining with his lady friends. He had personally tried all these restaurants, he wrote in the margin, and gave each one a short critique. I discovered that he had owned eighteen pairs of shoes, that he could rewire a faulty lamp, that he called his father "utter swine." I realized how deeply he had distrusted, even despised, the husbands and lovers of all the women he had ever cared for—from his father, to Julian Pascal and Dr. Fracasse—yet what a reluctant knight he was at heart, and what price he paid for his illusion of rescue.

I discovered the little gold locket his mother had worn around her neck, with the tiny picture of young Ray inside, and unearthed the photograph of her as a prim young Quaker girl destined for an unhappy life. I pored over Ray's poems to Cissy, touched by the fact that even though he was not a poet, as he well knew, he nonetheless continued to write his lovesick poems throughout his life. I copied out the list of his and Cissy's amuels, amazed by such a collection. I knew the amuels were real objects, animal figurines that they had actually possessed, because of the way they were all named and described in such detail—like Baby, the "small yellow glass rabbit," and Sasaonsum, "a very pretty green glass crocodile," and Little Three Legs, a "bone-colored china dog" with one broken leg. What ever happened to them? I wondered. In the last pages of *Lady in the Lake*, Marlowe gazes at little glass animal figures in a Santa Monica shop window—amuels, like those the author had owned.

In one box I found Cissy's divorce decree from Julian, in which she was awarded all the furniture plus a hundred dollars a month and one-half of all their Victory Bonds. I learned that Cissy's aunt, May Lewin, had lived in a house at 347 West Channel Road in Santa Monica Canyon, next door to where I had once lived. I held Cissy's death certificate where, in the box marked "usual occupation," Ray had written "At home." I also realized that it must have been he who filled in her age as sixty-eight on the certificate, complicit to the end in the fiction she had created, and which had also become so necessary for him.

At times, the experience of looking into those boxes felt rather painful, such as the moment when I came across Ray's address book and discovered 90 percent of the names had been crossed out. Other times I had a good laugh, because, after all, Ray was Ray, full of trenchant wit and dry humor, evident in nearly everything he wrote.

I realized what a kind and thoughtful man he'd been, how, during WWII, when England experienced severe shortages, he'd sent food packages to the warehousemen who worked in the shipping department of his publisher, and also to H. F. Hose, his former Classics master at Dulwich, then an elderly man. "He would always bat for the underdog," Helga said. "If at a party there was someone in a corner or a bit neglected, he would try to see that woman had a good time, whether she was beautiful or not." Voices were important to him. And lovely hands.

As the weeks wore on in Oxford, I began to feel as if I were living entirely in the past, caught up in the rhythms of the charming old city as well as Ray's long-gone world. He was my most steady, most constant companion. I kept to myself, dined alone in the evening, retired early to my room, ate my solitary breakfast, and went off to the library to join him again. Sometimes I took long walks through the cobbled streets of Oxford, past All Souls and Jesus College and the sign advertising the guided ghost tour of haunted university sites. In the evening, after a long day at the library, I often stopped at the same little pub and had a drink, always sitting at the same table in the corner of the cozy room and always aware of being an outsider, mute witness to a kind of English bonhomie I was not a part of. In time I grew used to my solitariness. But one morning when I entered the dining hall I found it full of students, all sitting at the long tables and chatting with a few professors seated among them. I learned that a seminar in physics had drawn the students to the college for a few days, and that we would be dining together for a while.

That first morning I sat across from one of the professors, shyly hoping for conversation, but after a brief, polite hello, the professor chose to ignore me, preferring to chat with his students. My own reticence prevented me from pressing small talk upon him. An English friend once said to me that in the U.K. there's an intimacy within a group where you're known and accepted; otherwise, nothing. Whereas America, by contrast, she felt to be a vast nation of strangers whose casual politeness and social interest is a way of negotiating that strangeness. Whether this is the case, I don't really know, but the professor I sat across from in the dining hall at Oxford did seem intent on making it clear to me, once he had heard my American accent, that there would be no negotiating our strangeness, no way of my entering the confines of the intimate group of which he was a visible leader.

For several days I sat at his table, largely ignored by him, until one morning, he turned to me and unexpectedly said, "And what, exactly, brings *you* to Oxford?" I told him that I was working on a book about Raymond Chandler and I had come to Oxford to consult the Chandler archive in the Bodleian Library.

"Raymond Chandler?" he exclaimed, his face suddenly brightening. "But I'm a great fan of Chandler's! I absolutely love his work. I first discovered his books as a young man and I read everything of his I could get my hands on. I still keep those books in a bookcase next to my bed and occasionally reread them."

With the mention of Chandler's name, the icy reserve of the professor melted. We had managed to negotiate the frozen terrain separating our worlds and arrived in the sunny clime of mutual affection. As it turned out, the seminar ended the next day. I never saw the physics professor again.

Still, I think of him now and then. He reminds me of how many Chandler fans there are in the world, and of their great variety, how Ray's work cuts across age and class and background, reaching into all cultures, seemingly erasing time itself as each new generation discovers his work and revives it with enthusiasm. At the end of his life, Ray understood the great appeal of his work, and he relished the idea that his books could reach so many people, including the intellectuals who had sometimes snubbed him. He once said that only he and Marilyn Monroe had managed to reach all the brows—highbrow, lowbrow, and middlebrow—an observation Billy Wilder echoed in an interview about Chandler.

"It's a peculiar thing," Wilder said, "you know, in all the forty years plus that I have been in Hollywood, when people have come up and asked questions—newspaper men, researchers, or letters from all over the place—the two people that I've been connected with whom everyone is most interested in are Marilyn Monroe and Raymond Chandler. There is some kind of fascination, as well there might be, because they were both enigmas. I knew them well—I made two pictures with Monroe and I wrote and lived on the fourth floor of Paramount for a long time with Chandler—and they were, indeed, enigmas."

"No one understands me, Mrs. Loring," Marlowe says in *The Long Goodbye*. "I'm enigmatic."

Monroe and Chandler. Marilyn and Marlowe. In a way they represent the idealized sexual poles of the American psyche: Marlowe as a kind of archetypal male—the man of honor and action, immensely attractive to women, friend to those in need, like the cowboy of American myth only he goes back much further than that, to the medieval Round Table—the American cowboy and English knight rolled into one. Monroe as a kind of lushly gorgeous female icon, her naked sexuality all the more attractive for the vulnerability and unthreatening sweetness that comes with it. It's the vulnerability we feel in these characters, and I wonder if it isn't, at least in part, that sense of vulnerability that touches our psyches so deeply and gives these figures their staying power. Poor Marlowe, you know, always getting beat up. And poor Marilyn, in her own way always getting beat up, too. In their sad goodnaturedness, we see ourselves.

"Most writers are frustrated bastards," Ray once said, "with unhappy domestic lives. I was happy for too long a time perhaps. I never really thought that I was anything more than a fire for Cissy to warm her hands at. She didn't even much like what I wrote. She never understood that to get money you have to master the world you live in, and not be too afraid to accept its standards. Most people never understand that you go through hell to get money and then you use it mostly for other people who can't take the punishment but nevertheless have needs."

What he was saying was, I did it all for Cissy, because she had needs and she couldn't take the punishment of the world. But I could. I had to protect her. And I did.

And what did Cissy do for him? Besides provide him the entry into his world of fable, by nurturing his role as her Gallibeoth? She kept him sane. She watched over him, cared for him, worried about him. That look of appeal that Dilys Powell had spoken of, the somewhat urgent expression on Cissy's face the last time she'd seen her—I felt that Cissy understood what was going to happen to Ray when she died. She knew he was alcoholic and needy—a shy, awkward, vulnerable man who could not possibly live alone.

"What a man wants and needs," he said, "and surely a woman, too, is the feeling of a loving presence in the home, the tangible and ineffable sense that a life is shared."

It's what Ray wanted anyway. It's what most of us, I think, want in the end.

The ineffable sense that a life is shared.

Cissy knew how badly things might go for him when she was gone. That was the look of appeal which Dilys Powell had noticed in her eyes the last time she saw her with Ray, in the bar of the Connaught Hotel. Do help him, she was saying. I appeal to you, take care of Ray.

Well, what the devil, as Ray might say.

Skip it, why don't you?

For Pete's sake, give it up.

I always was a man without a home.

Still am.

Raymond Chandler Addresses
in Los Angeles and Southern California

713 South Bonnie Brae, Los Angeles

Bunker Hill (downtown L.A., exact address unknown)

311 South Loma Drive, Los Angeles

1343 Westlake, Los Angeles (mid-Wilshire district)

127 South Vendome Street, Los Angeles

224 South Catalina, Redondo Beach

Huntington Beach (address unknown)

733 Stewart Street, Santa Monica

2863 Leeward Avenue, Los Angeles

700 North Gramercy Place, Los Angeles (at Melrose Boulevard)

1200 Meadowbrook Avenue, Los Angeles (mid-Wilshire district)

2315 West 12th Street, Los Angeles (mid-Wilshire district)

1104 Longwood Avenue, Los Angeles (mid-Wilshire district)

1024 South Highland Avenue, Los Angeles

4616 Greenwood Place, Los Angeles (near Vermont and Los Feliz Boulevards)

1637 Redesdale Avenue, Silverlake (Los Angeles)

Santa Barbara (address unknown)

Riverside (address unknown)

San Bernardino (address unknown)

943 Harzell, Pacific Palisades

818 West Duarte Road, Monrovia (Los Angeles suburb)

1265 Park Row, La Jolla

1155 Arcadia Street, Arcadia (Los Angeles suburb)

449 San Vicente Boulevard, Santa Monica

857 Iliff Street, Pacific Palisades

12216 Shetland Lane, Brentwood

Big Bear (various rented cabins, addresses unknown)

Idyllwild (various rented cabins, addresses unknown)

Cathedral City (adjacent to Palm Springs)

1040 Havenhurst Drive, Los Angeles

6520 Drexel Avenue, Los Angeles

6005 Camino de la Costa, La Jolla

Del Charro Motel, La Jolla

6925 Neptune Place, La Jolla

La Jollan Hotel, La Jolla

834 Prospect Street, La Jolla

Photographic Credits

Acknowledgments

My first thanks must go to Graham C. Greene, executor of the Raymond Chandler estate, for allowing me to quote from Chandler's letters and fiction and for granting permission to use photographs of the Chandlers, some of which have not been published before.

I wish also to thank my editor, Dan Frank, for his kind assistance, exceptional editorial skills, and devotion to books and writers. I owe a deep debt to Fran Bigman, editorial assistant, Pantheon Books, for her good-natured and unwavering help with many aspects of the book's production.

I am grateful to my literary agent, Joy Harris, who has, over the years of our long association, provided the support and encouragement necessary to staying the course with each new book: I thank her for her abiding friendship, advice, and support.

On the research front, I am especially grateful to Dr. Victoria Steele, Head, UCLA Charles E. Young Research Library, Department of Special Collections, who graciously accommodated my every request while I worked in the Chandler archive and became a friend in the process. The entire staff of Special Collections was so helpful. I particularly wish to thank Lucinda Newsome, Octavio Olvera, and Lilace Hatayama. Thanks as well to Stephanie Day Iverson, Curator of the Bonnie Cashin Collection at UCLA Special Collections. To the staff of the Modern Papers room, Bodleian Library, Oxford, especially Colin Harris, I wish to express my appreciation, and also to Carolyn Cole, curator of the Photography

Department at the Los Angeles Public Library, who assisted with archival images of L.A.

Lady Natasha Spender generously provided insights into, and remembrances of, Raymond Chandler, and I am grateful to her for our lengthy telephone conversations. To Don Bachardy for granting me a most amusing and informative interview I also wish to say thanks. On separate occasions, the photographer Monica Nouwens and the documentary filmmaker Terry Sanders traveled with me to La Jolla to videotape the Chandlers' house; I wish to thank them, as well as Kevin Weber, who permitted these visits.

I very much appreciate the support of the Rothermere American Institute at Oxford where I was a visiting fellow in the fall of 2005. Thanks to Marina Warner for making me aware of the Rothermere's fellowship program, and to Kathy van Praag and Paulina Kewes for enriching my stay in Oxford. Alison Crosby was my London guide, and I am grateful to her for braving a very wet day to help me track down Chandler's London residences.

I could not have written this book without the help of many friends, in particular Rae Lewis, Carolyn See, Kenneth Turan, Patty Williams, Leo Braudy, David Freeman, Timothy Steele, Vanessa Place, Richard Schickel, M. G. Lord, Tina Barney, Barbara Feldon, Anne Taylor Fleming, Karl Fleming, Robert Mundy, and Van Gordon Sauter. Thank you all for your stimulating conversation and support. Grant Rusk provided much useful information on nineteenth-century photography, and Todd Thorn assisted me with mapping Chandler residences. Anthony Hernandez not only photographed the La Jolla house for me but also provided the kind of affectionate encouragement every writer needs.

Ruth Leys, Isobel Armstrong, and Judith Grossman were my excellent advisors on all things English: their insights were invaluable. I also wish to thank Michael Fried, whose invitation to come to Johns Hopkins University as a visiting writer provided the perfect environment for completing this book.

Finally, I owe a deep debt of gratitude to the late Frank McShane, author of the 1976 biography *The Life of Raymond Chandler*, whose original research into Chandler's life provided such valuable information. I also wish to thank Tom Hiney for his fine 1997 biography *Raymond Chandler:* his perceptive work added to my understanding of the writer and his marriage. Last of all, I acknowledge a personal debt to the late Helga Greene, whom I never met but whom I came to deeply admire in the process of writing this book. Chandler could not have had a more intelligent and responsible person to care for his legacy and reputation. In this regard, he was a fortunate man.

Index

343

ALSO BY JUDITH FREEMAN

A DESERT OF PURE FEELING

Twenty-five years after she lost him, Lucy Patterson has encountered Dr. Carlos Cabrera, the man who saved her son's life and wrenched her own life onto a violent new trajectory. Now Lucy has sought refuge in an isolated motel outside Las Vegas, hoping to make sense of the past that has finally caught up with her. But in the next room the present is calling, in the person of a young woman—a single mother, stripper, and prostitute—who is as needy and troubled as Lucy herself once was. What ensues—between these two women and between Lucy and the ghosts of her former life—makes A Desert of Pure Feeling as wise as it is poignant, a powerful exploration of what it means to be a lover, a mother, an artist, and a friend.

Fiction/978-0-679-75271-4

RED WATER

In 1857, at a place called Mountain Meadows in southern Utah, a band of Mormons and Indians massacred 120 emigrants. Twenty years later, the slaughter was blamed on one man named John D. Lee, previously a member of Brigham Young's inner circle. Red Water imagines Lee's extraordinary frontier life through the eyes of three of his nineteen wives. Emma is a vigorous and capable Englishwoman who loves her husband unconditionally. Ann, a bride at thirteen years old, is an independent adventurer. Rachel is exceedingly devout and married Lee to be with her sister, his first wife. These spirited women describe their struggle to survive Utah's punishing landscape and the poisonous rivalries within their polygamous family, led by magnetic, industrious, and considerate husband, who was also unafraid of using his faith to justify desire and ambition.

Fiction/978-0-385-72069-4

VINTAGE AND ANCHOR BOOKS
Available at your local bookstore, or visit
www.randomhouse.com